# FOREIGN
# LANGUAGE
# EDUCATION

# OTHER RECENT VOLUMES IN THE
# SAGE FOCUS EDITIONS

# FOREIGN LANGUAGE EDUCATION
## Issues and Strategies

### Edited by
### Amado M. Padilla
### Halford H. Fairchild
### Concepción M. Valadez

**SAGE** PUBLICATIONS
*The International Professional Publishers*
Newbury Park   London   New Delhi

*For information address:*

SAGE Publications, Inc.
2111 West Hillcrest Drive
Newbury Park, California 91320

SAGE Publications Ltd.
28 Banner Street
London EC1Y 8QE
England

SAGE Publications India Pvt. Ltd.
M-32 Market
Greater Kailash I
New Delhi 110 048 India

Printed in the United States of America

Library of Congress Cataloging-in-Publication Data
Main entry under title:

Foreign language education : issues and strategies / edited by Amado
    Padilla, Halford H. Fairchild, Concepcion M. Valdez.
        p.    cm. — (Sage focus editions ; v.   113)
    Includes bibliographical references.
    ISBN 0-8039-3640-0 — ISBN 0-8039-3641-9 (pbk.)
    1.   Languages, Modern—Study and teaching (Elementary)—United
States.    I.   Padilla, Amado M.    II.   Fairchild, Halford, H.
III.   Valdez, Concepcion M.
LB1580.U5F67    1990
372.6'5044—dc20                                                    89-27827
                                                                        CIP

**FIRST PRINTING, 1990**

Sage Production Editor: Diane S. Foster

372.65
F714
1990

# Contents

# Preface

The authors of the various chapters in this volume and in its accompanying volume were all associated in one way or another with the Center for Language Education and Research (CLEAR) at the University of California at Los Angeles at the time this project was planned. All the authors were committed to assisting in the development of a language-competent American society—that is, a society in which all residents of the United States have a realistic opportunity to develop the highest possible degree of proficiency in understanding, speaking, reading, and writing English, whether it is their mother tongue or a second language. Simultaneously, a language-competent American society includes opportunities for English-speaking individuals to develop an ability to understand, speak, read, and write a second (foreign) language while those who are not native speakers of English should have an opportunity to develop proficiency in their mother tongue.

It was our belief that the development of a language-competent society should be accorded our highest educational priority. We felt that researchers and practitioners who work within the domain of educational linguistics could play an active role in achieving a language-competent society.

Throughout the world today, there are many more bilingual individuals than there are monolingual; and there are many more children who are educated via a second language than are educated exclusively via their mother tongue. Thus, in most of the world, bilingualism and innovative approaches to education involving the utilization of more than one language constitute the status quo—a way of life, a natural experience. The phenomenon of bilingualism in most countries is not problematic, and achieving competency in more than one language is not particularly onerous or burdensome. Nor is participation in bilingual education programs or other innovative language education programs particularly novel or different.

As educators, we have much to teach others concerning the choice and sequencing of languages for purposes of initial literacy training and for basic instruction. Even more important, we have much to learn from other nations concerning the successful implementation of bilingual education in public schools.

In these days of increasing global interdependence, all American residents will benefit—personally and socially—if the largest possible number of residents can speak, read, write, and understand at least one language in addition to English. Language is an important thread that runs, albeit too often without recognition, through a variety of issues fundamental to national development and to public policy. Educational practice can be improved and social equity can be facilitated by applying knowledge gleaned from research conducted within the domain of the language sciences.

Innovative instructional programs can and should be designed to encourage the development of second-language skills for as broad a spectrum of school-age students as possible. Despite more than a decade of federal and state involvement, there continues to be much confusion and disagreement concerning the nature and goals of our programs for second-language learning.

Although the approach selected to facilitate the development of bilingual skills may vary depending upon local circumstances, it should be possible to offer an appropriate language education program for all students. We must make a societal commitment to encourage innovative language education programs, and we should make a professional commitment to offer our insights and our professional expertise to articulate appropriate educational goals for our children, to help design and implement responsive pedagogical programs, and to document and evaluate their relative efficacy. We should be able to document the course, causes, and correlates of second-language learning and to communicate the findings about the personal and societal benefits of bilingualism to others.

If members of our profession are to assume strong leadership roles, we should be able to assist in the development of a language-competent American society. It is this set of interrelated beliefs that have worked to unite our efforts to describe work conducted during the course of four years that was directed at understanding ways in which linguistic majority and linguistic minority students could achieve competence in two languages.

*Amado M. Padilla*
*Halford H. Fairchild*
*Concepción M. Valadez*

# PART I

# Political and Historical Perspectives

*Foreign language education has undergone a number of dramatic changes in the United States. Its history, and concomitant political agendas, are reviewed in Part I.*

G. Richard Tucker, in "Second-Language Education: Issues and Perspectives" (Chapter 1), notes a critical shortage of "language-competent" residents in the United States. An exceedingly small number of Americans engage in any meaningful foreign language education, and fewer still demonstrate oral or aural proficiency. Associated with this foreign language incompetence, schools and universities are left without adequate materials, curricula, or instructional staff.

Using an international perspective, Tucker notes that bilingualism and multilingualism are worldwide norms. Indeed, so-called less developed countries are far advanced with respect to foreign language instruction. As a result, Tucker identifies a number of policy needs that underscore the positive benefits of foreign language education, including cognitive and intellectual benefits as well as benefits in the international trade arena.

11

Tucker also notes the projections for a changing American demography that indicate an increasing linguistic diversity within the continental United States. In sum, Tucker suggests that the native English majority in the United States must redress five concerns: (a) the lack of foreign language education programs, particularly those that are geared to produce true communicative proficiency; (b) the lack of an "articulation" of interdisciplinary collaboration in different foreign language programs (e.g., from elementary school through college); (c) the failure to fully develop teaching methods and curricula that produce foreign language competence; (d) the confusion resulting from mistaking language as an educational *end*, versus a *means* to an end; and (e) the failure to accept language minority students as role models of the target foreign language.

Lynn Thompson, Donna Christian, Charles W. Stansfield, and Nancy Rhodes, in "Foreign Language Instruction in the United States" (Chapter 2), provide a thorough historical chronology of foreign language education in the United States. Their major premise is that foreign language education programming reflected, and was affected by, broader social and political events in the society and the world at large.

Thompson, Christian, Stansfield, and Rhodes identify changing foreign language needs as a result of European immigration during the nineteenth and early twentieth centuries and underscore important changes mandated by the world wars. The authors also trace how foreign language teaching methodologies evolved to the current emphasis on communicative competence and proficiency in reading, writing, speaking, and listening. These changes, then, were reflected in the changing guidelines by ACTFL for evaluating foreign language competence (also see Stansfield & Kenyon, this volume, in this connection).

Thompson, Christian, Stansfield, and Rhodes conclude with a future-oriented perspective that sees an increasing emphasis on communicative proficiency, practical applicability, immersion models, and content/language integration. They note, however, a need to increase the priority given to foreign language education by the American public, educators, and policymakers.

# 1

# Second-Language Education

## Issues and Perspectives

G. RICHARD TUCKER

The United States is today faced with a critical shortage of "language-competent" residents. Popular attention to this looming crisis was aroused by publication of the report of the President's Commission on Foreign Language and International Studies (1979). That report focused on the exceedingly small number of students who had studied foreign languages during the compulsory period of American education (see also Chapter 2 of this volume) and, more important, on the even smaller number that had achieved any degree of demonstrable proficiency in the target language.

Nevertheless, that report did point out that more than 75% of the American residents who were sampled in a specially conducted public opinion poll wished that they had enjoyed the opportunity to study foreign languages in school and that these same respondents (more than 80%) would urge their children to do so. However, not much improvement followed, and in spring 1984 a report by Lambert (1984) decried even more sharply the lack of trained specialists, appropriate pedagogical materials, adequate assessment devices, and teaching programs—particularly for the so-called less commonly taught languages (operationally defined in the United States as all languages other than English, French, German, Italian, Portuguese, and Spanish). During the reauthorization of the Higher Education Act in 1986, Senator Paul Simon (see Padilla, 1990) introduced a successful amendment directing the secretary of education to conduct a study on the feasibility of establishing a national foundation to promote the teaching of foreign languages and international studies. Secretary Bennett, however, declined to conduct the study.


## DEVELOPING A LANGUAGE-COMPETENT SOCIETY


Despite the continuing scarcity of language training programs and the generally low level of foreign language proficiency of most American residents, many American educators, administrators, and parents are beginning to recognize the desirability and the necessity of developing a "language-competent" American society (Tucker, 1984). Many individuals now believe that non-English mother tongue speakers should be provided an opportunity to understand, speak, read, and write English while at the same time developing a comparable ability in their own mother tongues. Similarly, English speakers should be encouraged to develop a comparable proficiency to the maximum degree possible in some language other than English. In a "language-competent" society, all individuals should have an opportunity within the public education system to develop the highest possible degree of bilingual proficiency. Is this a realistic or attainable goal? What is the situation in other countries?


## AN INTERNATIONAL PERSPECTIVE


To place this matter in broad perspective, it is interesting to note that there are many more bilingual individuals in the world today than there are monolingual, and that, in addition, many more children throughout the world have been and continue to be educated in a second or later-acquired language than are educated exclusively in their mother tongue. Thus, in many parts of the world, bilingualism and innovative approaches to education involving the utilization of more than one language constitute the status quo.

The phenomenon of bilingualism in many parts of the world is not problematic, and bilingual education programs in many parts of the world are not even particularly innovative or novel. In many ways, the so-called developing countries have made much greater progress in dealing with questions concerning the choice and sequencing of languages for purposes of initial literacy training and basic instruction. They have also made more progress in the implementation of educational programs to facilitate personal and societal bilingualism than have the so-called industrial countries (see Clyne, 1988; Gonzalez & Sibayan, 1988; Paulston, 1988). For example, the recently promulgated Constitution of the Philippines—together with an implementing Executive Order from the Secretary of Education, Culture and Sports (1987)—calls for the development of a bilingual citizenry: "The aspiration of the Filipino nation is to have its citizens possess skills in both languages equal to their functions and duties in Philippine society and equal to the needs of the country in the community of nations." As Campbell and Lindholm (1987) note, the perception of language competence as an indigenous natural and national resource is not widely shared in the United States.

POLICY NEEDS

Almost a decade ago, Lambert and Tucker (1981) prepared a position paper for the National Council for Educational Research discussing ways in which the then National Institute of Education should stimulate innovative language learning and teaching. We claimed that there were few aspects of our educational system that were in as much need of a fundamental review and reorientation as the domain of foreign or second-language teaching. We argued that more, not fewer, Americans needed to develop genuine competency in English and *at least* one other language. This argument was based upon three basic tenets:

(1) Bilingualism has important positive cognitive benefits for individuals in terms of creativity, cognitive flexibility, and social tolerance; and it serves to expand occupational options.

(2) The changing demography of the American school system suggests a need to teach English more effectively to non-English-speaking immigrants and refugees who are arriving in increasingly large numbers.

(3) As our nation becomes increasingly dependent upon foreign trade, and as international and political events exert more influence upon us, a largely monolingual population will be a greater and greater handicap to our national growth and development.

In developing policy with respect to the role of language(s) for literacy training and for basic education, we distinguished four types of students who bring different needs and resources to the classroom: students who have no or limited English proficiency (LEP); students who are, at the time of school entrance, "balanced bilinguals"; those who are English-dominant but come from some other ethnic background (e.g., Spanish ethnic origin but English mother tongue); and monolingual English-speaking students. Each of these groups brings different needs and resources to the classroom, each of them calls for a different strategy tailored to their particular situation, but for each the goals should be similar—bilingual language competence. This, in fact, has been a major concern of CLEAR's work.


## THE CHANGING AMERICAN DEMOGRAPHY


How are individuals to achieve this goal? The limited-English-proficient (LEP) student population includes minority children—some of whom are immigrants or refugees to the United States and others who are U.S.-born—who are dominant in their home language with varying degrees of ability in English ranging from limited to none at all. This group is growing exceedingly rapidly and a majority of the participants in school systems in many of our large urban metropolitan areas will be LEP students by the next decade (see Padilla, 1990). This group has, to date, been the central focus of much discussion of federal- and state-funded bilingual education in the United States (see Ovando & Collier, 1985; Ramirez, 1985) and of considerable interest to CLEAR (Malakoff & Hakuta, 1990; Padilla, 1990).

The balanced bilingual population comprises both minority and majority students who are able to function effectively in two languages. Unfortunately, there are no known national estimates of the numbers of these students. There is, however, one fascinating monograph (Grosjean, 1982) that deals, at least in part, with the concerns of such individuals, including those bilingual in English and American Sign Language. Several other general treatments (Hakuta, 1986; Hamers & Blanc, 1984) examine the cognitive, social, and personal correlates and consequences of individual bilinguality. Some students may have previously been in the LEP category but have now attained a level of proficiency equal to that of their home languages. The language majority students may have acquired a second language in their home and thereby enter school as balanced bilinguals. The challenge for members of this group is to sustain their skills in both languages—a nontrivial concern, as recent work in language attrition has revealed (Lambert & Freed, 1982).

The third group, English-dominant language minority students, consists of those students who have never fully acquired the language of their parents or who have not maintained their first language. This group comprises, for example, students of Hispanic, Korean, or Ukrainian ethnic origin who have English as their mother tongue. Some have come to the United States relatively recently, whereas the families of others have been here for many generations. Although there are no accurate statistics on the size of this population, it is estimated to be the largest of the first three categories, with the widest range of heterogeneity in terms of heritage language proficiency. CLEAR has been interested in the rejuvenation of language skills by Korean Americans (see Campbell & Lindholm, 1987) as a prototypical demonstration of practical steps that can be taken to restore bilingual language proficiency for a major minority group.

The fourth group, the native English majority monolingual, clearly comprises the largest number of individuals and is the one most frequently overlooked for language training. For this group of students, there are at least five major categories of problems that serve to prevent their attaining bilingual language competence: (a) the complete lack of foreign language programs in many elementary or secondary schools; (b) the lack of "articulation" or fit between the various levels of existing programs; (c) prevailing methods or approaches and assessment procedures that reward mastery of grammatical forms rather than development of communicative proficiency; (d) a philosophy that emphasizes the study of foreign language as an end in itself rather than the means for acquiring other new knowledge; and (e) the widespread tendency to avoid using language minority youngsters as peer group models or tutors for individuals studying *their* language. How do we provide the best possible language training for such students?

PROGRAM EFFECTIVENESS

What do the data suggest generally about the effectiveness of foreign language training? Students who participate in foreign language experience (FLEX) programs typically do so for mere exposure to the language and to obtain information about the peoples and cultures they are studying. Often, the teacher is introduced to the target language at the same time as the students. The intention, in this regard, is merely to "experience" the flavor of the language and to learn a little bit about the people and the culture. Students do not generally develop any measurable degree of proficiency by participation in FLEX programs.

Unfortunately, for other programs, very little is known about their effectiveness, particularly those at the elementary and secondary levels. What appears obvious is that, as a nation, we seem to promote the decline of non-English language competence in newcomer populations at the same time that we encourage, albeit very poorly, the development of such competencies among English speakers. The current system of delivering foreign language education (a) seems reasonably exclusively focused on developing lower levels of proficiency; (b) provides an opportunity for students to study too few and often the wrong languages in terms of national need; (c) measures competency often in terms of time or length of study rather than in proficiency achieved; (d) pays virtually no attention to the retention or reinforcement of language proficiency once acquired; and (e) seems to encourage approaches in which the teaching of language becomes an object in itself rather than a tool to learn other content material. Thus it might be argued that there is a national need to reexamine our entire system of delivering foreign language instruction.

## INSTRUCTIONAL OPTIONS

What options are typically available and how well do they work? It is possible to divide the delivery of foreign language instruction into four major types: FLEX programs; "typical" foreign language in the elementary school (FLES) programs; foreign language immersion programs; and two-way, interlocking, or developmental bilingual programs. The evaluation of various types of existing foreign language education programs, together with the development, implementation, and evaluation of innovative programs comprising—for example, content-based language instruction and two-way bilingual education—have constituted an important part of CLEAR's agenda and are well represented in this volume and its companion volume, Padilla, Fairchild, and Valadez (1990). In addition to these volumes, reviews by Rhodes (1983), Schinke-Llano (1985), Allen and

Swain (1984), Genesee (1987), and Van Els and Oud-de-Glas (1984) provide useful overviews.

What about the approximately 22% of American students who study foreign languages at the elementary school level, mainly in FLES (foreign language in the elementary school) programs? Do they achieve demonstrable proficiency in the foreign language? Again, for the most part, the answer remains that they achieve only minimal proficiency in the language. In most, but not all, programs, the language is studied as an end in itself. There is very little attempt to integrate the teaching of the foreign language and the teaching of content material (but see Spanos & Crandall, 1990). The outcome is clearly different, however, for children who participate in foreign language immersion programs (see Campbell, Gray, Rhodes, & Snow, 1985; Lindholm, 1990) and for those who participate in two-way or interlocking bilingual programs (see Lindholm & Fairchild, 1990; Lindholm & Padilla, Chapter 9, and Rhodes, Crandall & Christian, Chapter 8, this volume).

CONCLUSION

A major thrust of CLEAR's activity during the past three years has been to foster two types of integration: first, that which has involved the development of models, methods, and techniques for integrating language and content instruction for both language majority and language minority individuals, and, second, activities to develop, implement, and evaluate programs that seek to bring language majority and language minority students together within the same classroom to provide opportunities for maximal bilingual language development and subject matter mastery. These latter activities have typically involved content-based language instruction (or language-sensitive content instruction), peer group modeling, and cooperative learning within supportive environments.

What is the national mood concerning our attempts to foster the development of bilingual language competence? Since 1981, 32 new federal programs have been enacted that contain some specific provision to encourage the development of foreign language competence, for example, legislation to promote language-competent (American) embassies, the Japanese technical literature program, the English literacy grants program, the inclusion of "critical" foreign languages in the Education for Economic

Security Act, and the new international programs within the Omnibus Trade Bill. A majority of the programs that support foreign language education not only have been "authorized" but have also received appropriations. Federal funding for foreign language study, although still not adequate, has doubled since 1980. Funding for compensatory education, bilingual education, and magnet schools has increased more rapidly than inflationary pressures. Foreign language training has also increased significantly within the areas of defense and intelligence. Various groups and organizations have convened symposia, national forums, and policy discussions to survey and to urge an enhancement of foreign language teaching, most notably, the National Governors Association, the Southern Governors Conference, and the Council of Chief State School Officers.

Quite clearly, the pendulum is swinging from the apathy of the mid-1970s to a sharper awareness of the importance of developing bilingual competence. The identification, evaluation, and encouragement of programs to encourage innovative foreign language education will become a higher social priority during the 1990s than it has been during the past several decades.

REFERENCES

Allen, P., & Swain, M. (1984). *Language issues and educational policies: Exploring Canada's multilingual resources* (ELT Documents 119). Oxford: Pergamon.

Campbell, R. N., Gray, T. C., Rhodes, N. C., & Snow, M. A. (1985). Foreign language learning in the elementary schools: A comparison of three language programs. *Modern Language Journal, 69*, 44–54.

Campbell, R. N., & Lindholm, K. J. (1987). *Conservation of language resources* (Clear Educational Report No. 6). Los Angeles: University of California, Center for Language Education and Research.

Clyne, M. (1988). Bilingual education: What can we learn from the past? *Australian Journal of Education, 32*, 95–114.

Genesee, F. (1987). *Learning through two languages: Studies of immersion and bilingual education.* Cambridge, MA: Newbury House.

Gonzalez, A., & Sibayan, B. P. (Eds.). (1988). *Evaluating bilingual education in the Philippines (1974–1985).* Manila: Linguistic Society of the Philippines.

Grosjean, F. (1982). *Life with two languages: An introduction to bilingualism.* Cambridge, MA: Harvard University Press.

Hakuta, K. (1986). *Mirror of language: The debate on bilingualism.* New York: Basic Books.

Hamers, J. F., & Blanc, M. (1984). *Bilingualité et bilingiusme.* Bruxelles: Solédi-Liege.

Lambert, R. D. (1984). *Beyond growth: The next stage in language and area studies.* Washington, DC: Association of American Universities.

Lambert, R. D., & Freed, B. F. (Eds.). (1982). *The loss of language skills.* Rowley, MA: Newbury House.

Lambert, R. D., & Tucker, G. R. (1981). *The role of NIE in stimulating innovative language learning and teaching.* Paper prepared for discussion by the National Council for Educational Research, National Institute of Education, Washington, DC.

Lindholm, K. J. (1990). Bilingual immersion education: Criteria for program development. In A. M. Padilla, H. H. Fairchild, & C. M. Valadez (Eds.), *Bilingual education: Issues and strategies.* Newbury Park, CA: Sage.

Lindholm, K. J., & Fairchild, H. H. (1990). Evaluation of an elementary school bilingual immersion program. In A. M. Padilla, H. H. Fairchild, & C. M. Valadez (Eds.), *Bilingual education: Issues and strategies.* Newbury Park, CA: Sage.

Malakoff, M., & Hakuta, K. (1990). History of language minority education in the United States. In A. M. Padilla, H. H. Fairchild, & C. M. Valadez (Eds.), *Bilingual education: Issues and strategies.* Newbury Park, CA: Sage.

Ovando, C. J., & Collier, V. P. (1985). *Bilingual and ESL classrooms: Teaching in multicultural contexts.* New York: McGraw-Hill.

Padilla, A. M. (1990). Bilingual education: Issues and perspectives. In A. M. Padilla, H. H. Fairchild, & C. M. Valadez (Eds.), *Bilingual education: Issues and strategies.* Newbury Park, CA: Sage.

Padilla, A. M., Fairchild, H. H., & Valadez, C. M. (Eds.). (1990). *Bilingual education: Issues and strategies.* Newbury Park, CA: Sage.

Paulston, C. B. (Ed.). (1988). *International handbook of bilingualism and bilingual education.* New York: Greenwood.

President's Commission on Foreign Language and International Studies. (1979). *Strength through wisdom: A critique of U.S. capability.* Washington, DC: Government Printing Office.

Ramirez, A. G. (1985). *Bilingualism through schooling: Cross-cultural education for minority and majority students.* Albany: State University of New York Press.

Rhodes, N. C. (1983). *Foreign language in the elementary school: A practical guide.* Washington, DC: Center for Applied Linguistics.

Schinke-Llano, L. (1985). *Foreign language in the elementary school: State of the art.* Orlando, FL: Harcourt Brace Jovanovich.

Spanos, G., & Crandall, J. (1990). Language and problem solving: Some examples from math and science. In A. M. Padilla, H. H. Fairchild, & C. M. Valadez (Eds.), *Bilingual education: Issues and strategies.* Newbury Park, CA: Sage.

Tucker, G. R. (1984). Toward the development of a language-competent American society. *International Journal of the Sociology of Language, 45,* 153–160.

Van Els, T., & Oud-de-Glas, M. (Eds.). (1984). *Research into foreign language needs: Proceedings of an international seminar held at Berg en Dal, the Netherlands.* Augsburg: Universitat Augsburg.

# 2

# Foreign Language Instruction in the United States

LYNN THOMPSON
DONNA CHRISTIAN
CHARLES W. STANSFIELD
NANCY RHODES

Foreign language instruction in the United States has been molded by forces both internal and external to the field. Knowledge of other languages has been prized, ignored, or deemed suspect, depending on international events and national attitudes. As a result, foreign language instruction has been subjected to the positive and negative effects of national and international change.

The demands for language instruction have also affected the goals and methods of language instruction. These influences have combined, with developments in education and linguistics, to bring about changes in language teaching methods. In order to understand the current situation, it is useful to trace the development of foreign language instruction in the United States as it reflects both the impact of national and international events on public attitudes and the evolution of thought in linguistics and related fields.

## PRE-WORLD WAR II

Prior to the mid-nineteenth century, foreign language study in the United States was almost totally confined to the study of classical languages (Latin and Greek). The methodology of choice was Grammar-Translation, which focused on developing reading and writing abilities through extensive memorizing and grammar rules, analysis of written language forms, and practice in translation. The era of immigration (1840–1910) saw the introduction of modern foreign languages (particularly German and French) to public and private school curricula, but the Grammar-Translation method remained the most common method used in the United States through the 1940s. The study of Latin and Greek was predominant through the late nineteenth century, and even following the advent of modern foreign language study no modern foreign language overtook Latin until after World War II. In 1934, 16% of all secondary school students were enrolled in Latin, 11% in French, 2% in German, and 6% in Spanish (Grittner, 1969).

The desire to maintain some sense of cultural and linguistic identity within the American "melting pot" led to the creation of ethnic bilingual schools. The contributions of German Americans were particularly noteworthy during this time. As early as 1840, English-German bilingual schools were organized in a number of cities, including Baltimore, Cincinnati, Cleveland, Indianapolis, Milwaukee, and St. Louis. By 1889, for example, Baltimore had seven public English-German schools, enrolling over 7,000 students. These schools continued in operation until 1917, when German was removed from the schools (Katsareas, 1987).

The goals of language study during this period led to certain methodological innovations as well. The ability to translate written material would not suffice as a goal in a society where new citizens wished to see listening and speaking skills in their native languages passed on to their children. Further, the use of other languages as the medium of instruction in schools forced a change in how languages were taught. In bilingual schools, the "Parallel Method" was widely practiced. Through it, content in subjects such as math was taught to students, first in one language, then in another (Katsareas, 1987).

In the latter years of the nineteenth century, educators began to recognize the desirability of developing speaking proficiency in a foreign language as opposed to reading comprehension and knowledge of grammar. Researchers looked at how children learn languages and attempted to fashion teaching techniques based on those principles. The efforts of advocates of the "Reform Movement" led to support for natural methods of language teaching (Richards & Rodgers, 1986). The Direct Method placed emphasis on listening and speaking skill development, that is, usable fluency in the foreign language (Stern, 1983). According to this approach, students learn language best by using it in real-life communicative contexts. Grammar was taught only inductively, and translation played little or no role. A number of commercial language schools emerged during this era in an effort to implement this new approach to language teaching. The best known of them was founded in New York City by Maximilian Berlitz, a Polish-born immigrant to the United States. To this day, the Berlitz schools continue to rely on the Direct Method of language teaching.

The influence of the field of linguistics became apparent during the Reform Movement. Linguists such as Sweet (1899) argued for teaching methods that were based on the scientific study of language and language learning. The emerging view among linguists that spoken language was primary coincided with the goals of some communication-oriented members of the language teaching field. This period of convergence of interests marks, according to Richards and Rodgers (1986, p. 6), the "beginnings of the discipline of applied linguistics—that branch of language study concerned with the scientific study of second and foreign language teaching and learning."

Although the Direct Method achieved some success in Europe and in commercial language schools in the United States, it was not widely adopted in public education in this country for a number of reasons. First, teachers found it very difficult to implement, because it required a high level of language proficiency, and the actual instruction was very demanding on the teacher.

Second, World War I aroused great antipathy in the American public toward foreign languages, which were viewed as symbols of foreign threats to the nation. Foreign language instruction was not only deemphasized, it was actually banned in some cases. For example, in 1919 the Nebraska legislature made it a criminal act to instruct a student below the ninth-grade level in a language other than English. This law, like a number of similar ones in other midwestern states, was aimed at preventing the use of German. The law was challenged by a parochial school teacher, after he was found guilty of breaking the law by teaching a 10-year-old student from a book of Bible stories written in German. Although the Nebraska Supreme Court upheld the constitutionality of the law, the U.S. Supreme Court, in the 1923 review of *Meyer v. Nebraska* (Lyons, 1988), ruled it unconstitutional. In reaction to the events surrounding World War I, American policymakers turned from the international to the national arena, and foreign language study came to be viewed as irrelevant except for its contribution to the development of mental discipline.

Finally, the recommendations of a major study known as the Coleman Report (Coleman, 1929) turned the focus of language instruction firmly away from speaking. Based on the conclusions of research on the success of various methods of language teaching, Coleman recommended that reading fluency should be the sole goal of modern language study. This goal was considered to be more reasonable, given the limited time available to secondary and college-level students for language study and the limited oral language skills of teachers.

Despite the intense discussion of language instruction prevalent from the late nineteenth century on, the Grammar-Translation method continued to predominate until World War II. However, the debate was extremely significant for the development of modern foreign language teaching. It contributed, for example, to the establishment in 1883 of the Modern Language Association of America along with other professional associations of foreign language teachers. These associations later served as vehicles for methodological change (Stern, 1983).

## WORLD WAR II TO THE PRESENT

### The Influence of World War II

American involvement in World War II drastically altered attitudes toward language study. Instead of mistrusting those with skills in other languages, the U.S. government, especially the Department of Defense, realized that these skills were essential to the war effort, and language training took on new importance. The limitations of the Grammar-Translation method became glaringly evident in view of the very practical communication needs of the military.

Theoretical linguists, who at the time were interested in structural linguistics, were given major roles in helping the nation meet its new language learning needs. They were asked to describe lesser known languages, and they devised course materials, based on descriptive linguistics, to help students learn to communicate in new languages. Wartime language programs represented a major shift away from traditional language teaching: Classes were intensive and oriented toward equipping military personnel, as quickly as possible, with sufficient listening and speaking ability to "survive." Although students did not always attain the desired level of fluency, a considerable degree of success was achieved, and the manner in which students were instructed had a profound impact on post-World War II language teaching.

About the same time, linguists began to teach English as a foreign language, as growing numbers of foreign students came to the United States for university study. In most cases, they needed to learn English first, and English language institutes were established at American universities (the first in 1939 at the University of Michigan) to teach English to foreign students. Linguists began to apply the principles of structural linguistics to language pedagogy, with a resultant emphasis on the need for students to be drilled on the basic structures (pronunciation and grammar) of the language to be learned. The use of contrastive analysis to predict areas of potential interference for the language learner became a cornerstone of the new approach to teaching English.

Charles Fries, director of the University of Michigan's English Language Institute, laid the foundation for the Structural Approach in his 1945 book *Teaching and Learning English as a Foreign Language*. Fries and his colleagues set the course for the teaching of all languages in the United States at that time (Richards & Rodgers, 1986).

## The Audio-Lingual Method in the Postwar Era

The growing importance of the United States as a world power during and after World War II ensured that foreign language instruction would improve and become more widespread (Met, 1988; Stern, 1983). During the postwar period, the recognition of several languages as world languages (by such international organizations as the United Nations and UNESCO), immigration, and increased international travel, trade, and scientific and cultural exchange underscored the importance of foreign language study. Enrollments in linguistics courses, and interest in the discipline by psychologists and sociologists, increased substantially (Stern, 1983).

Emerging theories of learning and behavior from these fields, along with developments in science and technology, were applied to the task of improving language instruction. The Structural Approach (from structural linguistics) merged with behavioral principles to produce an approach to teaching that emphasized the primacy of listening and speaking skills, along with drills and exercises to develop proper speech habits. This approach was commonly called the audio-lingual method (ALM). ALM emphasized the use of practice (repetition, substitution, and transformation) to teach language, utilizing the language laboratory for the many hours of practice required. Classroom techniques reflected the belief that language learning is a process of habit formation so that the target language's structures must be taught and practiced (in sequence) until they became automatic. The primary goal was the development of speaking skills.

With the launching of Sputnik in 1957 came an additional impetus to promote foreign language study. The U.S. government became committed to narrowing the perceived educational gap with the Soviet Union. As a result, federal spending for the improvement of educational programs in math, science, and foreign languages increased dramatically. Three years after the launching of Sputnik, modern foreign language enrollments had risen impressively—from 1958 to 1960 there was a 65% increase in the number of high school students enrolled in foreign language classes.

The preferred mode of instruction was the audio-lingual method with the accompanying language laboratory. Federal dollars helped bring ALM to the attention of the foreign language teacher through the installation of language laboratories and through the development of audio-lingual curricula. One set of materials, developed with federal support by the Glastonbury Connecticut Public Schools, was later published by a major textbook publisher, Harcourt, Brace & World (1967), under the title *Audio-Lingual Materials.*

With support from the federal government, from 1957 to 1961, the number of secondary schools with language laboratories increased from 100 to 2,500, and by 1967 it increased to over 8,000 (Galloway, 1983). However, the outpouring of dollars and energy did not produce students with actual, usable language skills. Both the government and, in turn, the public, had quickly adopted a method that was based on inconclusive research (Galloway, 1983). Instead of fluent speakers, ALM was producing "parrots" who could mimic phrases in a foreign language but who had neither receptive nor productive foreign language skills (Met, 1988).

As ALM was being instituted in secondary schools across the country, foreign language in the elementary school (FLES) programs began to emerge. FLES programs faced multiple problems from the start, including overly ambitious goals, lack of articulation (sequencing) with secondary school foreign language programs, lack of foreign language teachers trained to impart instruction at the elementary school level, lack of support from local educational administrators, and, ultimately, lack of visible results. It is not surprising that many FLES programs disappeared almost as rapidly as they emerged. There were also articulation problems at the secondary level because less than 20% of secondary schools offered a three-year sequence (Galloway, 1983).

Partly in reaction to the audio-lingual method, which was based on the development of speech habits, a cognitive-code theory was developed (Carroll, 1966). This theory emphasized the importance to the learning process of understanding the structure of the language. The difference between the cognitive-code theory and ALM can be illustrated by the way each made use of contrastive analysis. When English and the target language were contrasted, points of difference were identified by teachers in both camps as likely areas of difficulty. A teacher using the audio-lingual method would use that information to prepare pattern drills designed to prevent the development of incorrect language habits. On the other hand, a teacher making use of the cognitive-code theory would carefully explain to the student the difference between the native language and the target language.

While the cognitive-code theory emphasized the development of oral language skills, as did ALM, it did not succeed in producing large numbers of successful language learners. In addition, the theory was viewed by some as a form of heresy and, because of this, the theory had little or no impact on most foreign language teachers.

## The Move Toward Communication and Proficiency

Apart from the failure of the audio-lingual method, in the late 1960s and early 1970s there were other problems that affected foreign languages in the schools. Americans experienced a period of disillusionment. The Vietnam war, racial tensions, and political assassinations led to increasing dissatisfaction. Teachers and administrators scrambled to make curricula "relevant" in the face of increased student and parent demands, deteriorating schools, and decreased funds. Due to the consolidation of school districts and the tremendous increase in population due to the baby boom, classes were now overcrowded. The increased cost of meeting the educational needs of students was not matched by increased public support. A 1973 Gallup Poll showed that parents were disillusioned with schools (Galloway, 1983).

Between 1970 and 1974, modern foreign language enrollments in the United States fell from 26% to 23% of the total secondary school population. Almost 400,000 students dropped modern language classes: This meant a loss of 15,000 language classes or 3,000 full-time language teachers (Galloway, 1983). Because of the demand for "relevance" in the curriculum, the decline of the classics was even more precipitous. Between 1962 and 1976, public school enrollment in Latin plummeted 80%, from 750,000 to 150,000 (LaFleur, 1987).

Out of this disillusionment, however, came a renewed impetus to make language learning relevant and effective. The importance of creating a supportive classroom environment (as opposed to the critical environment that typified the audio-lingual method) in order to facilitate language learning was recognized, and students were encouraged to express their own thoughts and use their knowledge of the foreign language creatively. Foreign language teachers moved from a concentration on form to an emphasis on communication, resisting the urge to correct and allowing the student to hesitate or be silent (see, for example, Savignon, 1972). Again, developments in linguistics, sociology, and psychology led to new ideas about language teaching based on current understandings of the nature of language and of learning processes. New methods, such as Community Language Learning, the Silent Way, the Natural Approach, and Total Physical Response were proposed, creating a period of eclecticism in foreign language teaching. However, all these methods took into account the need to support the student and encourage the development of communicative language skills. The goals of language study shifted from knowledge of a language's structure or vocabulary to the ability to use language that is appropriate to the communicative context (Oller, 1979).

This orientation toward functional language instruction has been labeled the "communicative," or "proficiency-oriented," approach. The term *communicative* has its origins in ideas that developed in the 1970s, largely due to the results of a study by Savignon (1972). The term *proficiency*, however, has its roots in government training objectives and developments in testing. As previously mentioned, during World War II, government training schools did much to influence the orientation of language learning in the public sector by stressing the development of listening and speaking skills over reading and translation skills. Within government training programs themselves, this orientation toward survival skills prevailed, and a procedure, the Oral Proficiency Interview, was developed to measure student attainment of language skills. Language skill attainment was seen in terms of degrees of proficiency—adequate functional language skills to perform specified language tasks effectively when called upon to do so, such as in a foreign country or in a situation requiring bilingual interpretation.

As methodologies for the teaching of foreign languages increasingly reflected the above orientation, foreign language instructors once again looked to government training programs as models. Thus the meaning of "proficiency" shifted from reference to a type of assessment to a more general reference to the ability to communicate effectively in a language. In this instructional sense, the proficiency orientation contrasts with some earlier methods, such as Grammar-Translation, which focused on the learning of grammar and vocabulary as an intellectual exercise.

Events external to the foreign language field intervened, once more, in the late 1970s to give this orientation impetus. Economic pressures and an increasing deficit trade balance brought the importance of foreign language study once again to the forefront. In 1978, a presidential commission was formed to study the nation's resources in foreign language and international studies. The commission's report was highly critical of international education in the United States. The following passage is typical of the report's findings:

> Americans' scandalous incompetence in foreign languages also explains our dangerously inadequate understanding of world affairs. Our schools graduate a large majority of students whose knowledge and vision stops at the American shoreline, whose approach to international affairs is provincial, and whose heads have been filled with astonishing misinformation. (President's Commission on Foreign Languages and International Studies, 1979)

Although not as significant as Sputnik, the president's commission report did influence foreign language education in the United States. Significant efforts were made to reorient thinking about the goals of language study, including attempts to reach a consensus on what foreign language instruction goals should be and on how progress or lack of progress in attaining those goals might be measured. In addition, the report led to efforts by federal agencies and private organizations to inform educators, administrators, and the public about the need for foreign languages and international studies. Professional associations for foreign language teachers also began to assist teachers in improving their language instruction by offering training in teaching and testing for functional language skills.

Simultaneous with efforts to reorient and train teachers have been attempts to establish common criteria for the assessment of language proficiency as well as for the organization of materials and curricula. The precedent for use of testing procedures similar to those of the government training schools was set in 1967 by John Carroll when French, German, and Spanish undergraduate language majors were administered the Foreign Service Institute Oral Proficiency Interview. The interview was part of a battery of tests used to determine the level of proficiency attained by language majors. Descriptions of language proficiency at different levels of ability were developed by the American Council for the Teaching of Foreign Languages (ACTFL) through funding from the Center for International Education of the U.S. Department of Education. These language skill-level descriptions, commonly known as the ACTFL Guidelines, were developed cooperatively by college-level foreign language educators and federal agencies involved in language training.

Such cooperation evolved from increasing contacts between foreign language organizations and government language training agencies through the Inter-Agency Language Roundtable. Other factors have contributed to it, however, including research (such as that of Carroll) representing an intersection of interests, the increasingly similar goals of both the government and the public in light of a perceived decline in America's competitive edge in business, and the lobbying of some individuals and organizations to establish national or international standards for determining language proficiency (Levy, 1985).

## The National Survey of Foreign Language Instruction

What have been the effects of these trends and activities on foreign language teaching in the second half of the 1980s? In 1987, the Center for Language Education and Research (CLEAR) sought to document the status of foreign language instruction in the United States by conducting a national survey of elementary and secondary schools (Oxford & Rhodes, 1988). Questionnaires were sent to 1,416 elementary schools and 1,349 secondary schools, constituting a stratified random sample of approximately 5% of the public and private schools in the United States. The questionnaire sought information on such topics as amount and kind of foreign language instruction offered, the background and training of foreign language teachers, methods of articulation, and the major problems encountered by foreign language programs.

Key findings showed, not surprisingly, that secondary schools greatly outdistance elementary schools in teaching foreign languages. Approximately 87% of the responding secondary schools, in contrast to 22% of the responding elementary schools, reported teaching foreign languages.

However, of the schools offering language instruction, the majority reported that fewer than half their students were enrolled in foreign language courses.

The most popular languages taught were the same in elementary and secondary schools—Spanish, French, German, and Latin. The proportion of schools offering other major world languages, such as Russian, Chinese, Japanese, and Arabic, was minuscule, involving only 3% of the responding schools that teach languages. Finally, over 90% of the elementary and secondary schools offering language programs provided only nonintensive classes.

The following facts about language teachers emerged from the survey: 44% of the elementary schools and 63% of the secondary schools had no foreign language teachers who were native speakers of the languages being taught. About half of the elementary schools and nearly a third of the secondary schools said their foreign language teachers had received no in-service training during the previous 12 months. Finally, about half of the elementary schools said that none of their foreign language teachers were appropriately certified for elementary foreign language teaching.

The most common problem facing foreign language programs is a shortage of funding. This problem was cited by more than half of the responding elementary and secondary schools. Three additional problems—shortage of teachers, lack of high-quality materials, and difficulties in articulation—were also frequently cited. With regard to articulation, one-third of the elementary schools reported that students who began the study of a foreign language in elementary school had to start the sequence over in secondary school because there were no special classes for those who had been enrolled in a FLES program.

Other serious problems cited by schools included lack of an established elementary school foreign language curriculum, inadequate testing and counseling, unrealistic public expectations, and lack of time for foreign language instruction.

It is evident from these results that national attention needs to be focused on developing more rigorous foreign language programs, with instruction beginning in the early grades and continuing through high school until fluency is reached. In order to develop strong language programs at all grade levels, with commonly agreed-upon proficiency goals, energies need to be focused on (a) improving and expanding teacher training opportunities; (b) planning more effective articulation between elementary and secondary schools; (c) initiating innovative programs (especially at the elementary level); (d) developing age-appropriate materials; and (e) increasing the teaching of major world languages that are not commonly taught (Oxford & Rhodes, 1988).

## CURRENT TRENDS AND ON TO THE FUTURE

The intense efforts being made to familiarize teachers with communicative teaching and the ACTFL Guidelines have resulted in increased acceptance among language teachers of teaching for functional proficiency. However, acceptance of this orientation does not mean that foreign language teaching practices have changed. A few hours or days of in-service training in communicative language teaching cannot change the classroom as long as curricula, text, tests, and training are still oriented toward academic achievement rather than oral proficiency. The 1980s have seen much effort to create uniformity of objectives, texts, and teaching styles.

Although a great deal of work remains to be done, three encouraging and significant trends can already be identified in foreign language education in the United States. These trends are the development of proficiency-based language teaching, the increase in elementary school programs, and the teaching of a wider variety of languages. Both of the first two trends reflect the general orientation toward mastery of communication skills (by providing proficiency-oriented instruction and by beginning that instruction as early as possible). The expansion in the number of different languages being taught emerges from a growing awareness that, in order to participate effectively in the world community, the United States must strengthen its capacity to communicate in the world's languages.

Within the scope of foreign language programs, three programmatic trends can be identified: integrating language and content, immersion (total/partial), and two-way immersion. The integration of language and content instruction helps students achieve both foreign language and academic objectives by combining language development and content objectives during instruction. A prime example of the integration of language and content, language immersion programs teach the regular curriculum through the foreign language for the entire school day (total immersion) or half the day (partial immersion). Immersion programs have spread throughout the United States to 62 schools in 17 states. A variation of this standard immersion program designed for English-speaking children is an innovative two-way model that includes both native English speakers and native speakers of the target language. The goal of two-way immersion programs is for both groups of students to learn both English and the target language. Because the classes include native speakers of both languages, this model has the added advantage of students being able to use their fellow classmates as language resources.


## CONCLUSION


Through a century and a half of growing pains, the foreign language profession in the United States has learned much about what constitutes sound foreign language teaching practice. No doubt, future years will see increasing use of technologies, including computer-assisted instruction and interactive video, which are becoming standard equipment in more and more schools. Changing teaching methods and establishing national proficiency-based standards will be more difficult to accomplish. Although language organizations are supporting such efforts, developing foreign language proficiency may never be a priority of more than a handful of our elementary and secondary schools. Surveys indicate that administrators see only a weak relationship between foreign language goals and the goals of the total school curriculum. Administrators cite the difficulty of providing funding for a program that only a small percentage of students want. They also believe that the goal of producing fluent speakers requires more instructional time, which would detract from the teaching of basic skills (Galloway, 1983).

It seems appropriate, then, to end this overview on a mixed note. The trends within foreign language education are encouraging. The concern for developing real proficiency and the interest in a wider range of languages within the language education community could contribute to significant increases in the language competence of the United States. The influence of emerging technologies could further enhance instruction. However, at the same time, the wider society and the schools may not be placing a high priority on the development of language abilities. Without substantial support from all quarters, it is questionable whether the foreign language skills of students in the United States in the next quarter century will advance significantly beyond their current level.

## REFERENCES

Carroll, J. B. (1966). The contributions of psychological theory and educational research to the teaching of foreign languages. In A. Valdman (Ed.), *Trends in language teaching* (pp. 93–106). New York: McGraw-Hill.

Coleman, A. (1929). *The teaching of modern foreign languages in the United States.* New York: Macmillan.

Fries, C. C. (1945). *The teaching and learning of English as a foreign language.* Ann Arbor: University of Michigan Press.

Galloway, V. (1983). Foreign language in the schools: Through the looking glass. *Modern Language Journal, 67*(4), 342–355.

Grittner, F. M. (1969). *Teaching foreign languages.* New York: Harper & Row.

Harcourt, Brace & World, Inc. (1967). *Audio-lingual materials.* New York: Author.

Katsareas, D. (1987). *Research in the history of bilingualism: The public and private English-German schools of the city of Baltimore, 1834–1904.* Unpublished manuscript.

LaFleur, R. A. (1987). *The teaching of Latin in American schools: A profession in crisis.* Atlanta: Scholars.

Levy, S. (1985). *Introduction, proficiency, curriculum, articulation: The ties that bind.* Middlebury, VT: Northeast Conference on the Teaching of Foreign Languages, Inc.

Lyons, J. (1988). Language and loyalty. *EPIC Events, 1*(2), 5–7.

Met, M. (1988). Tomorrow's emphasis in foreign language: Proficiency. In R. S. Brandt (Ed.), *Content of the curriculum: 1988 ASCD Yearbook.* Alexandria: Association for Supervision and Curriculum Development.

Oller, J. W., Jr. (1979). *Language tests at school.* London: Longman.

Oxford, R. L., & Rhodes, N. C. (1988). US foreign language instruction: Assessing needs and creating an action plan. *ERIC/CLL News Bulletin, 11*(2), 1, 6–7.

President's Commission on Foreign Languages and International Studies. (1979). *Strength through wisdom: A critique of U.S. capability.* Washington, DC: Government Printing Office.

Richards, J., & Rodgers, T. (1986). *Approaches and methods in language teaching: A description and analysis.* Cambridge: Cambridge University Press.

Savignon, S. (1972). *Communicative competence: An experiment in foreign language teaching.* Philadelphia: Center for Curriculum Development.

Stern, H. H. (1983). *Fundamental concepts of language teaching.* Oxford: Oxford University Press.

Sweet, H. (1899). *The practical study of languages.* London: Dent.

# PART II

# Research Perspectives in Immersion and Foreign Language Education

*Part II provides an overview of a number of research perspectives in language education. Topics include language and cognition, second-language learning strategies, assessment, and the development of proficiency guidelines, particularly for the "less commonly taught languages."*

Amado M. Padilla and Hyekyung Sung, in "Information Processing and Foreign Language Learning" (Chapter 3), provide a nontechnical review of the way in which cognitive psychology and information processing can be applied to second/foreign language acquisition and instruction. Key terms and concepts from cognitive psychology, such as sensory memory, short-term memory, and long-term memory, are defined and discussed. The relevance of these concepts for foreign language acquisition is highlighted by numerous examples designed to show why and under what circumstances difficulties are encountered by students learning another language.

Padilla and Sung also discuss bilingual information processing and concepts of separate and shared memory. The chapter concludes with recommendations for language educators based on principles taken from information processing that are applicable to foreign language instruction. The implication is that sound foreign language pedagogy can be informed by research whose primary intent has been to test various cognitive models of language and memory in monolinguals. The recommendations, although not unfamiliar to language educators, are shown to be based on empirically sound evidence, rather than on common sense or folklore, about how best to learn a second/foreign language.

Mary McGroarty and Rebecca Oxford, in "Language Learning Strategies: An Introduction and Related Studies" (Chapter 4), provide an assessment of the research on the relationship between foreign language learning strategies and foreign language acquisition. Three emphases emerge: (a) The strategies that students employ in learning a foreign language are vitally important; (b) different learning strategies have differential effectiveness; and (c) the efficacious strategies can and should be integrated into classroom activities.

McGroarty and Oxford then review the findings from two studies that examined the cognitive learning strategies employed by two samples of university students learning a foreign language (either beginning Japanese or beginning Spanish). The strategies most related to effective foreign language acquisition were guessing meaning from context, active questioning, selective attention, using media, risk taking, and practicing language output. The ineffective strategies were making inappropriate guesses, pretending to understand, interrupting oneself, and memorizing or cramming. McGroarty and Oxford also note important attitudinal influences in foreign language acquisition and conclude with suggestions to teachers.

Nancy Rhodes and Lynn Thompson, in "An Oral Assessment Instrument for Immersion Students: COPE" (Chapter 5), review research findings on immersion education and note the lack of a standardized instrument to assess language proficiency of immersion students. The available instruments are not typically suitable for elementary school children, and most foreign language tests are more oriented to the formal aspects of language rather than communicative proficiency.

The CLEAR Oral Proficiency Exam (COPE) addresses both students' academic language (the ability to effectively discuss subject matter) and their social language (the ability to discuss their families, recreational activities, and social lives). The instrument is targeted to fifth and sixth grades in total or partial immersion programs. The authors review the development of the instrument and describe its contents and administration. They note that an important contribution of the COPE is the ability to identify students' strengths and weaknesses in separate language skill domains instead of only assessing overall proficiency. Charles W. Stansfield and Dorry Mann Kenyon, in "Extension of ACTFL Guidelines for Less Commonly Taught Languages" (Chapter 6), note the origins of foreign language proficiency guidelines with the Foreign Service Institute's Oral Proficiency Interview. With increasing interest in this area by academicians, the development of proficiency guidelines is beginning to include "less commonly taught foreign languages" (i.e., languages other than Spanish, French, and German).

Stansfield and Kenyon review the development of proficiency guidelines for Arabic, Indonesian, Hindi, and the African Language Group. Each of these languages raises important issues that Stansfield and Kenyon argue are recurrent in the development of proficiency guidelines for the less commonly taught languages. For Arabic, the problem deals with the numerous Arabic dialects and their appropriateness in different locales or contexts. For Hindi, the issue has to do with code-switching between Hindi and English and how that code-switching is interpreted differently in social versus formal situations. For Indonesian, the issue concerns a number of sociolinguistic factors and how Indonesian phrases carry information pertinent to social relationships. Finally, for African languages, the issue has to do with limited resources for an extremely linguistically diverse continent. In sum, Stansfield and Kenyon emphasize the fact that proficiency guidelines must reflect the cultural milieu of the language under consideration and that these guidelines continue to evolve.

# 3

# Information Processing and Foreign Language Learning

AMADO M. PADILLA
HYEKYUNG SUNG

Cognitive psychology is one of the most active and complex areas within the general discipline of psychology today. Cognitive psychology includes the study of perception, thinking, reasoning, memory, and problem solving. In cognitive psychology, we are interested in the knowledge that the individual possesses about the world. Further, because the study of language has so many connections with all of the themes covered by cognitive psychologists, it plays a central role in the study of these processes. As such, cognition and its associated processes explain how sensory information is received and stored, how stored information is retrieved, how comparisons and decisions are made to solve problems, and how outputs are produced in the form of actions (Anderson, 1985).

Of what relevance is cognitive psychology and information processing to the second-language educator? In answering this question we first affirm that exciting research on first-language production, comprehension, and use is being done by cognitive psychologists using an information processing paradigm (Houston, Hammen, Padilla, & Bee, 1989). For instance, comprehension can be thought of as occurring in three stages: perception, parsing, and utilization. The first of these stages, perception, concerns translation of auditory signals to word representations. In other words, how signals are translated into mental representations of communication by the hearer. Parsing is the cognitive processing concerned with translation of word representation to meaning representation. Because communication is about meaning, parsing is a higher-order mental activity that allows us to interpret the messages we receive. Finally, utilization concerns the use that we make of the meaning of the message that we hear. In the utilization of meaning, an integral component involves relating information in the message to the information already in memory.

Normally, we don't pay much attention to the three stages of linguistic processing described above, unless we are cognitive psychologists. Language acquisition and use, and the underlying cognitive processes involved, are taken for granted by the layperson. On the other hand, the second/foreign language educator may be much more attuned to how the learner translates, comprehends, and utilizes a second language. However, because the language educator is usually not a cognitive psychologist, he or she may not be familiar with principles and strategies from cognitive psychology that could make teaching language easier. Therefore, the purpose of this chapter is (a) to present the basic components of an information processing model; (b) to summarize a few essential points for how information processing concepts might have special relevance in second-language learning; and (c) to suggest some tips for how the language educator can maximize the learning of a second/foreign language through an understanding of an information processing approach to language instruction.


INFORMATION PROCESSING MODEL


Although a number of information processing models are available today, they all share a set of basic assumptions. Among these is the view that the person is an information processing system. According to this way of thinking, cognition involves the flow of information through the human mind, beginning with encoding and storage and ending with retrieval of stored information. A common representation of an information processing model is provided in Figure 3.1.

In this model, information is presumed to move through three memory systems. Perceived information first enters sensory memory; it may then be transferred to short-term memory (STM) and finally to long-term memory (LTM). Once information is in LTM, it is assumed to be learned and available for use in any situation or context. According to this type of

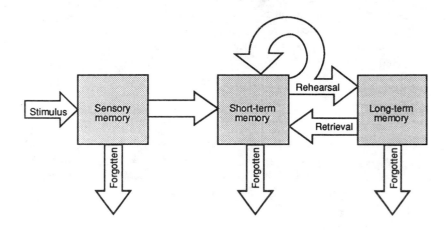

**Figure 3.1**   A Schematic of an Information Processing Model Showing the Three Major Components of Memory and the Relationship Between Short- and Long-Term Memory

NOTE: As can also be seen, forgetting can take place at any of three points in this model.

framework, the goal of foreign language instruction ought to be to develop LTM capacity in the new language, which means possessing vocabulary, grammar, and semantic representation in the new language. As the LTM in the second language grows larger, the language learner becomes more proficient in the second language and thus processes information more efficiently in the new language. In this way the learner is gradually and effectively able to operate with his or her new language. Unfortunately, this is easier said than done. Now, let's examine each of the major components of our information processing model and comment on the significance of how each operates when learning a foreign language.

### Sensory Memory

Whenever we experience something, such as seeing a poster on a bulletin board or hearing someone speak, the information enters our sensory memory. However, cognitive psychologists have shown that new information that enters our sensory memory decays, or fades, in about 30 seconds. Thus in order to operate on information in sensory memory the information must be transferred to short-term memory (STM). If the information in sensory memory is not transferred to STM, where it can be maintained for a short while, it will be lost.

To get a good idea of how this sensory memory system works, imagine listening to someone speaking a language you do not know. You hear the sounds that the speaker is making, but you cannot understand because you cannot process these sounds. The reason that you cannot process and transfer the information received in sensory memory to STM is because of the lack of prerequisite knowledge of the language. Let's take, as an example, an English speaker showing a Japanese businessman around who speaks almost no English at all. The English speaker asks, "Do you want to go to the sushi restaurant?" Our businessman can catch the word *sushi*, even though he does not understand anything else that he has heard. In the large flow of information that he is hearing, he might hear something like, ".... .... ..... sushi ......" because he is familiar with only the word *sushi*. Here, we conclude that for our businessman only the Japanese word *sushi* can be filtered in his sensory memory and the rest cannot be processed and, therefore, is lost.

Is it any wonder, then, that the first task in foreign language instruction is learning the basic sound system (phonemes) of the target language, combining these phonemes into morphemes (which are meaningful parts of speech) and then into a few basic words? Without at least a basic knowledge of the sound system in the new language, it is impossible to process the words through the sensory memory system. We can envision this stage as involving the learning of "feature detectors," which enable us to make sense of the multitude of auditory signals to which we are exposed. These feature detectors are formed on the basis of prior exposure to a language and consist of the basic sounds of that language.

In second-language learning we often make interesting and sometimes comical errors in filtering a new language through our sensory memory because we may not yet have fully developed detectors to process our second language. If the detectors are not quite developed in the second language, we process the auditory signals using our first-language detectors. For example, if your French instructor said, "Pas du Rhône que nous," a native English speaker who was just learning French might hear, "Paddle your own canoe." In this example, the student is filtering the French sentence through his English feature detectors because English is the dominant language for the hearer. Filtering in this way happens easily when the pronunciation of the French closely approximates well-known features of English. Another example is when a native Spanish speaker in an adult ESL class hears the instructor say, "Please watch the card," and interprets it as, "Please wash the car." In Spanish the /ch/ sound is pronounced nearly like the English /sh/ (e.g., like the /ch/ in *machine*). Thus the native speaker filters the word *watch* as *wash*. Similarly, /d/ final sounds in Spanish are infrequent and when they do occur they are like the English /th/ sound and not likely to be filtered, resulting in the perception of *car* rather than *card*.

Another problem that occurs because of our inability to perceive certain sounds in a second language is that we have difficulty in producing the sounds. Take the native Chinese-speaking restaurant owner who recommends to his English-speaking customers his special dish that comes with fried rice, which he pronounces as "flied lice"! In the Chinese speaker's case, the English sounds /r/ and /l/ are not differentiated and, therefore, he uses /l/ where /r/ is required when he speaks English.

## Short-Term Memory

If we attend to the information in sensory memory, the information can then be transferred to short-term memory (STM). Information that is transferred to STM is lost within about one minute unless it is rehearsed, repeated, or meaningfully encoded (see Figure 3.1). If the information is rehearsed and is meaningful, it can be transferred from STM to long-term memory (LTM). Information that gets to LTM does not have to be rehearsed to be maintained because it is permanently stored.

If information in STM is not sufficiently rehearsed, it is quickly forgotten. An example of the use of information in STM is when we hear a new phone number, practice (rehearse) it just long enough to dial it, and then forget it. In contrast, when we dial a phone number that we already know, we are retrieving the number from LTM. When information is in STM, we are generally conscious of it. However, when information has been transferred to LTM, we are no longer conscious of it unless we need it for something that we are doing at the moment.

Another major difference between STM and LTM is that the storage capacity of STM is quite limited. There is just so much information that we can hold in STM at any given moment. Studies of STM show that if, in a rote memory lesson on vocabulary, the teacher reads words to students at a rate of about one every second, students are only able to hold between 5 to 9 of them in STM. This is sometimes referred to as the "7 plus or minus 2" rule of STM. At that point, the teacher must stop adding words until the students are able to rehearse the words long enough to transfer them to LTM. If the teacher continues reading words beyond 7 plus/minus 2, each new word will "bump out" one of the previously read words. Thus, in teaching vocabulary in a foreign language, the instructor must be sensitive to both the capacity limitations of STM and the student's need to rehearse and make the information meaningful so that it can be transferred to LTM.

In a discussion of STM and its relevance to learning a second language, it is also important to note that such learning requires effort, which means that it becomes fatiguing after a while. Therefore, pauses in learning a foreign language are helpful in order to assist the student in recovering from the fatigue. Let's think of the student who has to attend to the incoming foreign language information with extra diligence in order to properly process the message in STM. Because transfer of information to LTM is not an automatic process, the student must expend extra energy during second-language learning. It is not surprising, then, to see the exhaustion in students who have been immersed in a foreign language class for a few hours.

## Long-Term Memory

The best way to think of long-term memory is as a storehouse where information is stored permanently when we are not using it. Unlike STM, the capacity of LTM is relatively unlimited, and we can continue to add new information to this storehouse throughout our lifetimes.

We are constantly accessing information from LTM and moving it to STM, where it is used to recall or recognize something. An appropriate probe, such as a question, makes us search through our permanent store and return the appropriate information to STM, or consciousness. For example, think of a country that is surrounded on all sides by the Pacific Ocean and that is a major producer of electronic equipment and automobiles. If you said "Japan," what you just did was bring information back out of LTM into STM. Thus information can be in both LTM and STM at the same time.

A very important feature of LTM that requires some discussion is that, when information is stored in LTM, it is done in an organized manner. We do not store information passively, rather we structure, relate, and interconnect it automatically. Like a librarian, we try to categorize our knowledge so that storage and retrieval are most efficient. It is interesting that we do most of this complex organizing without even being aware of it.

Some of the most interesting research on LTM has to do with how semantic information is stored in LTM, which has led to a number of semantic-network models for describing this process. In one way or another these models all assume that the best way to think about semantic storage is in terms of multiple, interconnected associations, relationships, or pathways. Information is assumed to be embedded in an organized, structured network composed of semantic units and their functional relationships to one another. Let's examine one of the many semantic-network models.

In a semantic-network model called the spreading-activation model (Collins & Loftus, 1975), the relationship between words is assumed to be very complex. For example, the word *red* might activate *fire engine, roses,* and *apples.* In turn, *fire engine* might activate *truck, ambulance,* and *house,* while *roses* activates *violets* and *flowers.* Similarly, *apples* might call forth *cherries* and *pie.* In some of these connections, the relationship to the word *red* might be stronger or more meaningful than in other cases. In addition, the spreading-activation model stipulates that an activated word can be more easily processed than an unactivated one (Anderson, 1983). For example, suppose you are given the word *bird* to get you started and then shown one of three target words *canary, box,* or *pielf* (a nonsense word) for a very brief period of time. You are instructed to decide as quickly as possible if the new word belongs to the same category as *bird* or whether it is a word at all. If you are like others given this task, you will show the fastest reaction time to the word *canary,* followed by *box,* and finally *pielf.* This occurs because the starter word (*bird*) activates material in the network; the closer this word is to the target, the more activated, and thus the more easily processed, that target is.

These are just a few of the ways in which LTM has been studied in monolinguals. When it comes to bilinguals, it is considerably less clear how information is processed and stored in LTM. We will turn our attention now to information processing in bilinguals in order to demonstrate how much more complicated language processing might be when two languages are involved.

## BILINGUAL INFORMATION PROCESSING

In the area of bilingual information processing a debate has ensued over whether there is a separate or shared LTM store. Kolers (1968) summarized this discussion by describing two competing views of how bilinguals process information. In the first model, known as the independent hypothesis, each language of the bilingual is believed to be stored separately in LTM. According to this view, information is stored in its own language-appropriate LTM. In addition, the two memory stores are kept in communication with each other via a translation mechanism. When information is required in working memory, the bilingual goes directly to the appropriate language LTM and retrieves the desired information. If the information that needs to be retrieved is stored in the other language, then the bilingual must retrieve it by using the translation mechanism and calling it forth in the appropriate language.

There are obvious advantages to a separate memory system for each language. One such advantage is that the bilingual with separate memory stores is less likely to experience negative interference between languages. Negative interference occurs when, for example, the person uses the semantic network of one language to process information in the other language. A concrete example would be the case of a Spanish-English bilingual who has the Spanish word *compromiso* (a social obligation) and the English word *compromise* (an agreed-upon settlement) stored in her respective language LTMs. Conceivably, it is very easy to confuse the meaning of these two words because they look and are pronounced somewhat alike. However, because of their different meanings, less confusion might occur if they were stored separately than if they were stored in the same LTM.

In the other model, known as the interdependent hypothesis, both languages are believed to occupy the same "cognitive space" in LTM. That is, information in the second language (L2) is encoded in the same LTM storehouse as information from the first language (L1). However, at the time of processing into LTM the information is tagged for its language (e.g., English, Korean) along with other attributes such as modality (e.g., speech, writing), frequency, and spatial and temporal aspects (Hamers & Blanc, 1989). Language, then, is just one of several tags by which the bilingual is able to access her or his two linguistic systems using a switching mechanism that calls forth the language-appropriate information. One possible drawback to processing information using a common memory store is that interference between L1 and L2 may occur with greater frequency than if information is stored in separate memory bins. Going back to our example of *compromiso* and *compromise,* we might very well expect more semantic errors to occur between these two words if something like a common LTM is operating in bilinguals. Although there are no studies that demonstrate this point, observations of Spanish-English bilinguals by Padilla support this explanation.

McCormack (1977), on the basis of a review of the research generated by Kolers's (1968) article, concluded that the common store or interdependent hypothesis is the most suitable of the two alternative explanations for how bilinguals process information in their two linguistic systems, and this has probably been the more accepted interpretation by researchers. For example, Mägiste (1979, 1980) found support for the interdependence hypothesis when she showed that the reaction times of Swedish-German bilingual students were significantly longer than reaction times of either German or Swedish monolinguals. Magiste believed that the slower reaction times of the bilinguals could be due to either of two factors: (a) interlingual interference between the language systems and (b) the overall less frequent usage of two languages on the part of the bilinguals compared with the monolinguals. In the Mägiste study, the first explanation (interlingual interference) supports the interdependent hypothesis.

However, the controversy of whether there is a separate or shared memory store is still unresolved. In an excellent and current review of the literature on information processing in bilinguals, Hamers and Blanc (1989) conclude that the controversy between the two opposing points of view is still very much of an open question and that existing data can be marshalled to support cither position. In another rcvicw, Grosjcan (1982) states that the question of independence versus interdependence was perhaps fated for mixed findings from the beginning.

In considering this question, Hakuta (1986) says that at some level we have a common store for both languages. Otherwise, it would be impossible, for example, for him to describe in English his trip to Japan during which he did not speak a word of English. It is also obvious that the two language systems must be independent at some level because bilinguals experience relatively little interference between their languages.

For our purpose here, it has been important to communicate the complexity involved in LTM processing when two languages are involved. Although no resolution between the two models is apparent, it is important to present these models because they have relevance to how a language instructor, by knowing something about information processing and bilingualism, can sequence units of material in an effort to maximize the learning of a foreign language. Moreover, by knowing how language is processed in cognitive terms, it makes understanding the types of errors that language learners are likely to make more comprehensible.

In the next section of this chapter, we will discuss how language educators can use some of the concepts and facts from research on information processing when they carry out instruction in a second/foreign language.

## IMPLICATIONS FOR LANGUAGE EDUCATORS

We have examined three components of an information processing model and how each component operates when people learn a foreign language. We have claimed that it is important for language instructors, especially second/foreign language educators, to know about an information processing paradigm. In this section, we discuss a few things that have been learned from research on information processing that have direct relevance for language educators. We begin with a discussion of processing time in foreign language learning, proceed to an examination of the similarity and dissimilarity between L1 and L2 and their effects on language learning, and conclude with some recommendations for foreign language teaching strategies.

### Processing Time

As we know, it takes time to master a second language, but the time involved in information processing is quite different and requires some discussion. Learning any difficult material may take anywhere from a few minutes of study to several hours. If the material is very difficult we might have to study it for several hours over several sessions. On the other hand, processing time in an "information" sense is much shorter and usually refers to seconds and even fractions of seconds.

Based on our earlier discussion of sensory memory, the input linguistic signals in a foreign language cannot be correctly filtered unless the feature detectors in the language are sufficiently developed. Therefore, it is obvious that in the beginning stage of learning a foreign language, learners need enough time to process the new linguistic signals. Because of this, two recommendations follow: (a) Instructors need to pace their rate of language input to the processing speed of the learners, and (b) instructors must make every effort to use clear pronunciation of the target language during their instruction.

Unfortunately, many foreign language instructors are not very conscious of the rate of their speech when lecturing in the classroom. Even when the student has achieved an intermediate or high level of foreign language proficiency, instructors still need to be sensitive to how much new information learners fail to understand because instruction may be taking place faster than they are able to integrate and retain it. Recall how quickly unprocessed information in sensory memory is lost. To prevent information loss in sensory memory and to help the transferring process to STM, instructional speed (pacing) is important. Similarly, clear articulation facilitates both the acquisition of the sounds of the new language and the processing of the language in sensory memory. The learner of a new language often needs to acquire new sounds and to differentiate between similar sounds. This task is made easier when the teacher and other language models use precise pronunciation.

In summary, we have learned that rehearsal is necessary in order to transfer information to LTM. Instructors should now more fully comprehend why second/foreign language learners need more time to process new linguistic information. Learners require enough time to rehearse the incoming information so that it becomes meaningful and is transferred to LTM. Accordingly, to help in the rehearsal process, instructors should employ methods of repetition of material at a speed of presentation that allows adequate rehearsal to take place. By practicing rehearsal strategies in the second language, learners can improve their ability to process foreign language input from sensory memory to STM and then to LTM. With practice and continued instruction, students will show a decrease in processing time as they gain proficiency in L2.

In the area of reading comprehension and reading speed, processing time really becomes noticeable in second-language instruction. Second-language learners cannot read with the same comprehension and speed as can monolinguals or proficient bilinguals. This means that, at the most elementary level, stimulus cards with vocabulary items must be presented for a longer period of time than might be normal with monolinguals. Similarly, at the more advanced levels, reading assignments must be geared to the learners' developing proficiency in the foreign language.

We also know that students expend lots of energy in processing new and unfamiliar information. Students are often mentally and physically exhausted even after brief periods of intense foreign language instruction. Therefore, students need well-spaced rest periods. These pauses during foreign language learning are effective both for reducing mental exhaustion and for providing enough time to recover so that learning can continue again. We know from work in information processing that having periods of rest from the task does not mean that we are not engaged in problem solution. Moreover, even though we are at rest we frequently continue to work on the problem at an unconscious cognitive level. In fact, students frequently report that following a period of rest they generally have new insights into a problem, see the material to be learned in new ways, and are ready to attack the task of learning the new material with renewed enthusiasm.

### Similarity/Dissimilarity Between L1 and L2

Does the similarity or dissimilarity between the native language and the new language affect language instruction? Dulay and Burt (1974) have studied the second-language learning of children and have shown that there does not appear to be a difference in total time taken to learn a language either when the two languages are closely related and belong to the same language family (e.g., English and Spanish) or when the two languages are very different (e.g., English and Chinese). This appears to be most accurate only in the case of successive acquisition of two languages in early childhood. However, findings from these studies may not be easily extended to the case of second/foreign language learning with adults. After LTM is quite fully developed in one language, learning another language is not comparable to the situation of the successive acquisition of a second language that is observed with children. In second/foreign language learning, similarity or dissimilarity between L1 and L2 may very well affect the rate of learning the new language.

Two languages that share many linguistic features (e.g., phonemic system, syntactic structure, and semantic usage), such as Spanish and Portuguese or Korean and Japanese, are conducive to faster rates of learning than two languages that are very dissimilar (e.g., English and Korean). Processing time is slower when two languages are very dissimilar in their linguistic features because the learner must learn most of the linguistic features of the new language.

On the other hand, if two languages are very similar there might also be a disadvantage. A student learning a second language that is very closely related to his or her native language may experience considerable interference between the two languages. This may occur at both the phonetic and the semantic levels. Remember our example earlier of *compromiso* and *compromise*. The similarity between these two words may lead the learner of Spanish to make incorrect semantic connections if the Spanish *compromiso* is processed through their native English semantic network for *compromise*.

## Teaching Method

Many foreign language instructors rely heavily on the translation method in their classes. However, you will recall from our discussion of LTM that it is desirable to develop LTM in the foreign language. By relying only on the translation method in teaching a foreign language, the instructor is actually prohibiting the development of LTM in the foreign language because everything is being processed through the first language LTM. Therefore, we recommend that the method of translation in teaching of foreign languages be minimized, and, in its place, we recommend that an immersion type of instruction be planned in teaching foreign languages (see Lindholm, 1990; Lindholm & Fairchild, 1990; Lindholm & Padilla, Chapter 9, this volume). Other instructional strategies that attempt to maintain separation of L1 and L2 are the Direct Method and the audio-lingual method (Larsen-Freeman, 1986). In these techniques, every effort is made to develop L2 as a separate system, unlike the Grammar-Translation Method, which relies heavily on L1 and is not devoted to developing oral proficiency in the foreign language.

## Classroom Environment

We know from work on information processing that noise can disrupt learning of unfamiliar information, including things to be learned in a nondominant language (Dornic, 1980). The disruption takes two forms. In the first, the learner finds it difficult to use inner speech (thinking) when there are many environmental noises and the situation demands processing in the nondominant language. In the second, distractions, including noise, seem to elicit second-language processing through the dominant language.

This means that the foreign language learner relies more heavily on translating from the weaker to the stronger language. This creates a situation where the student is slow to respond to classroom activities because it is taking that person longer to make sense of the auditory information that he or she is receiving in L2. These responses possibly lead the teacher to believe that the student is not attending to the material or has not mastered it when the problem is more a situation of an environmental stressor (e.g., distracting noise in the classroom) causing the learner to revert to older learned habits, thereby processing the L2 through her or his native language.

In this discussion, it is important to clarify that the noise that we are targeting for reduction is extraneous noise from the environment, for example, traffic on a busy thoroughfare. We are not including, for reduction, noise by the students in the classroom that occurs when learners are engaged in the active practice of the new language. Noise from students actively practicing their new language skills is important.

In conclusion, we have offered some recommendations for instructors of foreign languages. These recommendations may not appear innovative. This was not our intent. Rather, we wanted to show how general principles from information processing could be applied to foreign language education. What is known about language processing from an informational standpoint has been learned primarily from work with monolinguals. However, we believe that such knowledge has clear and important extensions to foreign language pedagogy and second-language learning and use.

## REFERENCES

Anderson, J. R. (1983). A spreading activation model of memory. *Journal of Verbal Learning and Verbal Behavior, 22,* 261–295.

Anderson, J. R. (1985). *Cognitive psychology and its implications* (2nd ed.). New York: Freeman.

Collins, A. M., & Loftus, E. F. (1975). A spreading activation theory of semantic processing. *Psychological Review, 82,* 407.

Dornic, S. (1980). Information processing and language dominance. *International Review of Applied Psychology, 29,* 119–140.

Dulay, H. C., & Burt, M. K. (1974). Natural sequences in child second language acquisition. *Language Learning, 24,* 37–53.

Grosjean, F. (1982). *Life with two languages.* Cambridge, MA: Harvard University Press.

Hakuta, K. (1986). *Mirror of language*. New York: Basic Books.

Hamers, J. F., & Blanc, M. H. A. (1989). *Bilinguality & bilingualism*. Cambridge: Cambridge University Press.

Houston, J. P., Hammen, C., Padilla, A., & Bee, H. (1989). *Invitation to psychology* (3rd ed.). San Diego: Harcourt Brace Jovanovich.

Kolers, P. A. (1968, March). Bilingualism and information processing. *Scientific American*, pp. 78–86.

Larsen-Freeman, D. (1986). *Techniques and principles in language teaching*. New York: Oxford University Press.

Lindholm, K. J. (1990). Bilingual immersion education: Criteria for program development. In A. M. Padilla, H. H. Fairchild, & C. M. Valadez (Eds.), *Bilingual education: Issues and strategies*. Newbury Park, CA: Sage.

Lindholm, K. J., & Fairchild, H. H. (1990). Evaluation of an elementary school bilingual immersion program. In A. M. Padilla, H. H. Fairchild, & C. M. Valadez (Eds.), *Bilingual education: Issues and strategies*. Newbury Park, CA: Sage.

Mägiste, E. (1979). The competing language systems of the multilingual: A developmental study of decoding and encoding processes. *Journal of Verbal Learning and Verbal Behavior, 18*, 79–89.

Mägiste, E. (1980). Memory for numbers in monolinguals and bilinguals. *Acta Psychologica, 46*, 63–68.

McCormack, P. D. (1977). Bilingual linguistic memory: The independence-interdependence issue revisited. In P. A. Hornby (Ed.), *Bilingualism: Psychological, social, and education implications*. New York: Academic Press.

# 4

# Language Learning Strategies
## An Introduction and Two Related Studies

MARY McGROARTY
REBECCA OXFORD

Many recent calls for educational reform decry the state of foreign language education in the United States. Few students at the secondary or postsecondary levels now take second-language classes, and fewer still attain any usable level of proficiency. At the same time, within the foreign language teaching profession, interest in understanding and improving instruction through more sophisticated understanding of the teaching/learning cycle is growing. One means to this increased understanding is more comprehensive knowledge of the processes learners use as they acquire a second language; another is greater appreciation for the attitudinal factors that contribute to second-language learning.

Second-language learning strategies are keys to language mastery. Recently, these strategies have attracted a great deal of attention from researchers, teachers, and students. This chapter provides a review of research related to language learning strategies, and an overview of the methods used to assess them. Following this introductory overview, two studies of strategies used by foreign language learners at the university level are presented as one possible approach to identifying how to promote effective foreign language learning.

## WHY LEARNING STRATEGIES ARE IMPORTANT

Research has shown that second-language learning strategies are important for four key reasons. First, appropriate learning strategies are related to successful language performance. Second, using appropriate learning strategies enables students to take responsibility for their own learning. Third, learning strategies are teachable. Fourth, addressing learning strategies in their programs gives teachers and students an expanded role.

### Relationship to Language Performance

Research comparing technical experts with novices indicates that experts use more systematic and useful problem-solving and comprehension strategies. The same finding occurs with expert language learners. Successful language learners generally use appropriate strategies, and these strategies help explain their outstanding performance. Whether or not they are aware of what they are doing, good language learners tend to use strategies that are appropriate to their own stage of language learning, personality, age, purpose for learning the language, and type of language. Just as appropriate learning strategies help explain the performance of good language learners, inappropriate strategies help explain the frequent failures of poor language learners and the occasional weaknesses of good language learners. If students and teachers know how learning strategies are most appropriately used, both groups can benefit greatly. Research provides a number of clues about how language strategies enhance second-language performance.

### Shifting Responsibility to the Learner

Using appropriate learning strategies enables students to take more responsibility for their learning by enhancing autonomy and self-direction. Why is it important for language learners to be active and independent? One answer comes from findings in cognitive psychology. All learning—especially language learning—requires learners to actively assimilate new information into their existing mental structures, thus creating increasingly rich and complex structures. Active language learners develop their own understandings or models of the second language and its surrounding culture. As they work with the second language over time, active language learners gradually refine their own linguistic understanding and, with practice, increase their proficiency in the second language. Appropriate learning strategies that encourage independent learning should be developed during classroom instruction. If this is done, the learner is able to continue learning independently even when he or she is no longer taking formal language instruction or when a large part of the language learning takes place outside of class.

## Teachability of Learning Strategies

Learning strategies provide a basis for remediating many difficulties in second-language learning and for improving the skills of all language learners. Unlike most other characteristics of the learner, such as aptitude, attitude, motivation, personality, and general cognitive style, learning strategies are teachable. While teachers cannot do much about some of the learner's other characteristics, research has shown that teachers can train students to use more effective learning strategies. Students can also train themselves to improve their own strategies through a variety of self-help materials.

## An Expanded Role for Teachers and Students

Shifting responsibility to the learner does not mean that the teacher forfeits employment or importance in the language teaching/learning process. On the contrary, it means that the teacher has an expanded role. That role not only includes imparting information, providing practice opportunities, and offering comprehensible input to the learner, it also includes determining which strategies the learner is using, assessing how appropriate those strategies are, and teaching the learner how to use strategies that foster enhanced learning. The teacher's role thus expands to encompass a needs assessment and the stronger encouragement of appropriate learning strategies.

The student's role, in turn, becomes one of active involvement in the learning process rather than the passive reception of didactic instruction. Furthermore, as students develop awareness of their preferred strategies, they can devise individualized methods of attaining and improving proficiency.

We have shown that learning strategies are important for four reasons. They improve language performance, encourage learner autonomy, are teachable, and expand the roles of the teacher and student in useful ways. More arguments supporting the importance of learning strategies may be discovered through further research. Based on our understanding of the importance of learning strategies, we can now ask: "How can we identify second-language learning strategies?" This question is the focus of the next part of this chapter.

## METHODS FOR INVESTIGATION: HOW ARE STRATEGIES IDENTIFIED?

Research on second-language learning strategies has evolved from simple lists of learning strategies to more highly sophisticated investigations using various forms of data gathering and analysis. We focus on the most widely used methods to show what each of them offers to understanding learning strategies and their effectiveness.

### List Making

Most of the early work on learning strategies consisted of simple lists of learning strategies (Oxford, 1986). Many published lists of second-language learning strategies, particularly those that were published more than a decade ago, were based on folklore, common sense, and the unstructured personal observations and experiences of the list makers. A strategy list might include, for example, "take an active approach," "search for meaning," "be willing to practice," "organize," "use memory devices," or "learn from errors." Some of these items are intuitively useful for learning any new kind of knowledge, whereas others pertain specifically to language. Although these lists were not systematically validated at the time they were presented, many of the strategies also appeared in later empirical studies (see Oxford, 1986). Such lists are important because they have been widely publicized and have consequently shaped a great deal of pedagogical practice.

## Formal Observation and Interviews

Instead of merely making lists, some researchers have examined strategies as they are applied in the actual learning process by means of observation of classes and interviews with learners. Using classroom observations as a basis for labeling strategies proved to be problematic because many strategies are internal and cannot be observed. Better studies were those using interviews with learners who are asked either to provide retrospective data about their language learning over the course of many years or to engage in introspective simulated-recall activities (such as explaining how they deal with unknown words as they are reading aloud) as they cope with an actual text or communication problem in the new language. If learners are able to verbalize their coping processes—and most studies indicate that, after training, nearly all can do so—then interviews and structured introspective methods can offer an assessment of the internal processes involved.

## Note Taking and Diaries

Some investigators have asked students to write notes or diaries on the strategies they used as they were learning a new language. This form of unstructured, introspective (as opposed to retrospective) note taking can be considered a written analog to introspective oral self-reporting or thinking aloud. Second-language learning diaries, written records of second-language learning kept over the course of time, can also provide valuable clues to the acquisition process, particularly as it changes with a learner's developing proficiency and expanded experiences in the new language. Hence, systematic notes and learner diaries have the potential for capturing the ongoing process of strategy adoption in language learning over weeks, months, or even years. The longitudinal and highly individual aspect of these studies makes them particularly helpful for gaining an appreciation of the variety of individual approaches that learners find useful depending on situation and proficiency level.

## Self-Report Surveys

Information from strategy lists, think-aloud studies, and learner notes and diaries has been compiled into lists of self-report strategies. Generally, items in such surveys are written in the form of behaviors (e.g., "When reading the new language, I try to get the gist of a passage before looking up all the new words," or "When speaking, I try to guess meaning from the words and expressions of the speaker") to which students respond in one of two ways: either by giving yes/no answers or providing an estimate of frequency of use based on a scale from "never" to "always" with appropriate intermediate points. Results from such surveys yield quantifiable descriptions of strategy use that can then be used in further statistical analysis aimed at identifying effective learning strategies.

Among the statistical methods most often used to examine self-report data are correlational analyses relating behavior items to proficiency or achievement and factor analyses that seek to group similar strategy items into clusters of behaviors that reflect a common underlying construct, such as reliance on memory or using functional practice. Studies using self-report surveys can provide a wealth of data that are easily collected and relatively comparable across subjects. Thus this technique is less sensitive to individual nuances of the learning experience but more efficient in gathering a substantial body of data to make comparisons within or across groups.

## LANGUAGE LEARNING STRATEGIES IN THE UNIVERSITY

The Center for Language Education and Research undertook a descriptive research project aimed at documenting the learning strategies and opinions of students in elementary Spanish and elementary Japanese classes at the university level (see McGroarty, 1988). By describing the strategies and opinion factors associated with student progress and achievement, we hoped to offer students and teachers further keys to understanding and improving instruction.

### Research Questions

The primary research questions were as follows: *(1) Which self-reported second-language study strategies are associated with success on classroom achievement measures or on proficiency tests?* By knowing more about these relationships, we could provide some validation of the

many strategies now encouraged and show students and teachers some possible keys to more effective instruction.

*(2) Which attitude and motivational factors predict success in second-language learning, and what is the relationship between attitudinal factors and study strategies?* Although it is difficult to manipulate attitudinal factors, it is nonetheless valuable, from a descriptive point of view, to know how they may underlie successful second-language study.

*(3) What distinguishes students who continue throughout one year of second-language study from those who drop out?* Given the effort expended on language learning by both students and teachers, it would be helpful to know who is more likely to persist in study and, therefore, make more informed choices among instructional alternatives.

## METHODOLOGY

Two large groups of student volunteers (88 for Spanish, 121 for Japanese) were contacted during the fall quarter and asked to complete several questionnaires and tests. These students represented a typical university sample; nearly all were undergraduates from a variety of majors. Students of all ethnic groups on campus participated, with proportionately more Anglo students in elementary Spanish and more Asian American students in Japanese (see McGroarty, 1988, for details).

The two main questionnaires concerned (a) strategies for second-language learning and (b) opinions related to language study in general and to the specific study of Spanish or Japanese.

To assess initial levels of skill, students in both languages took a comprehension test; elementary Spanish students also completed an oral interview. Students' exam scores and course grades were collected after each quarter, and at the end of the academic year those who remained enrolled were retested with language proficiency tests to assess progress in functional skills. We also examined traditional achievement as reflected in exam scores and grades. The results of the achievement and proficiency tests were correlated with the study strategies and factors derived from opinion questionnaires in order to identify the patterns that characterized successful learners at this level.

Thus the research offers a record of the first year of language learning through a series of psychometric "snapshots" taken at three points in time. A more complete description of the study, including the technical details of our research design, data gathering procedures, and data analysis, can be found in McGroarty (1988). The present report summarizes the general trends and discusses their implications for the teaching and learning of foreign languages at the university level.

## RESULTS

### Effective Strategies

The most important practical implications of the study came from the correlations among learning strategies, student achievement, and language proficiency. Achievement was measured by student exam scores and grades; language proficiency was assessed by tests of second-language comprehension and production. The relationships observed between these variables are summarized in the following paragraphs.

*Guessing meaning.* Four general categories of *seeking input* showed positive associations with learning and proficiency. *Making guesses about meaning from context in class* was associated with higher comprehension scores in both languages and with Spanish grades; *guessing meaning from gestures in conversation* was linked with higher grades for students of Japanese. Thus making educated guesses about meaning clearly has a place in beginning second-language instruction, particularly with respect to comprehension skills.

*Active questioning.* The second type of effective learner strategy consisted of *active questioning* behaviors used in class. All of the positive associations observed here pertained to the Spanish classes. *Asking the teacher about exceptions to grammatical rules* demonstrated links with both grades and aural/oral skills. *Asking the teacher when a new form is used* was associated with better oral interview scores. *Asking the teacher to repeat* was ambiguous: It was negatively associated with exams and grades in Japanese but was positively related to oral skills in Spanish. Thus the value of asking for repetition in class may vary depending on the nature of the class and the form of achievement being assessed.

*Selective attention.* The third category of input strategies dealt with *selective attention to the formal structure* of the new language. It is not surprising that most of the positive relationships were observed with the achievement measures—exams and grades—that involved a certain degree of accurate control of linguistic forms. *Repeating new words to oneself in class* was linked with exam scores and grades in Spanish. *Focusing on the main point and ignoring the rest of the lesson,* a selective attention strategy, was associated with better grades in both Spanish and Japanese and with better comprehension and production skills in Spanish. Two strategies oriented to control of form, *taking notes on new words in class* and *noticing grammatical rules in talk,* demonstrated positive relationships with grades in Japanese. Selective attention to the oral and written forms of the new language was, therefore, positive with respect to achievement and proficiency.

*Using media.* Using *different types of media* to support second-language learning, the fourth method of seeking input, was valuable in several ways. Students who were higher on *listening to the radio in the second language* had better exam scores in Japanese. *Watching TV in the second language* was associated with better grades and higher comprehension scores in Japanese and with better oral interview skills in Spanish. *Going to second-language movies* and *reading the new language to practice* were associated with better comprehension in Japanese. *Attending extra language lab,* however, was ambiguous: It was positively associated with grades but negatively related to comprehension scores in Spanish and exam scores in Japanese. Discussions with the Japanese instructors revealed that the quality of the lab materials was uneven, suggesting that the usefulness of attending extra language lab sessions may have depended on the adequacy of the materials available.

*Practicing output.* The second major category of strategy use consisted of ways to practice producing output in the second language. For the first strategy type, *using the language,* almost all of the positive relationships were observed with the aural/oral proficiency measures, thus providing convincing evidence that actual use of the new language enhanced conversational skills, although it may have had no clear relationship with improved achievement. The one strategy that showed a positive link with achievement, *thinking first in the second language,* which was related to Japanese exam scores, described a kind of private rehearsal rather than interpersonal use of language. *Using the second language voluntarily in class* was linked with better comprehension of Japanese. *Using the second language at a job* (a behavior observed for a small number of students in Spanish and almost no students in Japanese because of local employment conditions) was related to both comprehension and production of Spanish. *Socializing with second-language speakers outside class* showed links with Spanish oral skills and Japanese comprehension; *practicing the second language with bilingual persons who also spoke English* was characteristic of students with higher Japanese comprehension scores. *Thinking first in the second language* was positively related to comprehension scores in both languages.

Risk-taking behavior, long thought to make a difference in second-language learning, was linked with achievement as well as proficiency. *Not being afraid to volunteer in class* was correlated with grades in Japanese and with Spanish comprehension scores. *Not being afraid to make errors during natural conversations outside class* was linked with Spanish grades and with higher comprehension scores for both languages.

The third subcategory of output strategies, those related to *self-monitoring,* were also relevant to both achievement and proficiency. *Interrupting oneself if an error was made in conversation* was ambiguous, showing positive relationships with Spanish exam scores but negative ones with Japanese grades. *Correcting one's own pronunciation when studying in private* was positively linked with grades in Spanish. *Correcting answers aloud in class* coincided with better production skills in Spanish. *Thinking of alternative ways to say things* was typical of students with higher grades in Japanese. Finally, *saying the correct answer to oneself in class* was positively related to exam scores and grades in Spanish and to aural and oral proficiency in both languages.

Taken together, these effective learner strategies provided a portrait of students who made active efforts to generate and comprehend input by asking questions in class, using different types of media, and making guesses about meaning. Additionally, they practiced producing the new language by using it in class, on the job where possible, and in social situations. They were not afraid to risk making errors and using several strategies to check on their own accuracy in grammar and pronunciation. Finally, they expanded their awareness by making efforts to generate alternative expressions and to think in the new language.

### Ineffective Learner Strategies

The following paragraphs highlight the strategies with significant negative correlations with achievement and proficiency. Again, these relationships do not show cause and effect, but they do illustrate the strategies that predicted lower scores on the outcome measures.

*Guessing meaning.* Of the input-seeking strategies, certain kinds of guessing were associated with lower scores on exams and the Spanish oral interview. Weaker students *made inappropriate guesses about examples,* or *pretended to understand even when they did not*. As noted previously, an active questioning strategy, *asking the teacher to repeat*, was mixed: It correlated negatively with achievement in Japanese but positively with oral skills in Spanish, suggesting that its usefulness may vary with instructional circumstances.

*Selective attention.* The results for the third category, *selective attention to form,* are the most striking of the ineffective strategies: The negative relationships observed here were, with one exception, related to comprehension and oral production. Students who *made vocabulary lists, looked up all new words before reading,* and *went over material after class,* all behaviors that denoted assiduous and possibly excessive concern with grammatical form, performed less well on the tests of functional oral skills. The one strategy that was negatively related to achievement and proficiency was *analyzing first- and second-language contrasts.* Contrastive analysis, a long-established technique attractive to structural linguistics, co-occurred with relatively lower achievement and proficiency for these elementary language students.

*Using media.* The use of media in the form of *attending extra language lab* showed mixed results. In the case of Spanish, it is likely that attending extra language labs demonstrated a conscientious effort to improve on the part of students with low initial comprehension scores. As noted earlier, instructors in the Japanese classes suggested that the quality of the materials used in the lab, particularly after the first quarter of study, was less than optimal. Hence, we may speculate that extended practice with inadequate materials may have actually depressed achievement on exams.

*Practicing output.* The second major category of sometimes ineffective strategies, those related to ways to practice output, showed most of their negative relationships with the proficiency measures, as would be expected; inappropriate ways of practicing the oral language had far less impact on achievement than on functional skills. This pattern was clearest for the first and second subcategories, *using and avoiding the second language,* in comparison with Spanish proficiency scores. For students of Spanish, *changing known forms to fit a new situation* was inversely related to comprehension, suggesting that efforts to focus on known forms and then change them in interaction indicated generally weaker understanding. Because the results regarding *practicing areas missed in class* showed the effect of both missing class and practicing outside class, they are difficult to interpret; they probably indicated that students who missed things in class had lower comprehension scores. *Reviewing the lesson in English before class* had an inverse relationship with oral skills in Spanish, and *using English at social events where both languages were used* also had negative associations with comprehension and production in Spanish. These behaviors showed that students who continued to rely on English, instead of making efforts to use Spanish, had weaker functional skills.

The subcategory of self-monitoring strategies that appeared ineffective reflected excessive self-interruption. Students of Spanish who frequently interrupted themselves during natural language interaction had lower grades and lower aural and oral proficiency scores, again indicating insecurity in the new language. However, *interrupting oneself in class if an error had been made* was positively related to Spanish exam scores but negatively related to grades for Japanese students. This mixed outcome suggested that self-interruption in class was not necessarily counterproductive, and called for additional research to link self-correction to instructional processes and to specific features of the language being studied.

*Memorizing.* Finally, two strategies that could be called "cramming" approaches to second-language mastery emerged as negative influences on Spanish achievement and proficiency. *Memorizing forms without analysis* was typical of students with lower exam scores, a reasonable result given that exams require, at least in part, an accurate understanding and manipulation of language structure. *Memorizing sentences as units without breaking them down into parts* was negatively linked with Spanish comprehension, showing that students who could not yet segment the new language appropriately could not understand it well.

In general, these ineffective learner strategies were not uniform in their relationships with achievement and proficiency. It would, therefore, be incorrect to claim that any particular strategy (with the possible exception of contrastive analysis) should be avoided in elementary language study. However, the overall pattern shows that students of Spanish who made inappropriate guesses, often interrupted themselves in talk, and/or avoided using the new language in social situations or in individual study had lower achievement and proficiency scores. In the Japanese classes, the lower-achieving students were those who *frequently asked the teacher to repeat* and *interrupted themselves when speaking in class.* For both languages, strategies that exhibited excessive attention to form, as manifested in *contrasting the first and second language, making vocabulary lists,* and *looking up all new words before trying to read,* were associated with weaker functional skills in comprehension and production. Consequently, in beginning language classes where development of functional skills is a goal, teachers should caution students against overreliance on such strategies.

## Attitudes Affecting Second-Language Study

The second area of research concerned the identification of the attitudes and motivations characteristic of students who did well in beginning language courses. Although such considerations cannot be taught directly, they are valuable in understanding attitudinal and motivational predispositions that may influence foreign language study. The opinion scales as a whole, and the separate factors underlying them, illustrated some of the attitudinal dimensions affecting second-language achievement and proficiency in Spanish and Japanese.

*Attitudinal influences: Spanish.* For the beginning Spanish students, the total score for the opinion questionnaire—a measure that combined attitudes toward foreign language study in general, specific integrative and instrumental use of Spanish, attitudes toward the language class itself, and social support for language study—showed positive relationships with the comprehension and production pretests and with the strategy scales related to use of classroom and individual study behaviors. Positive attitudes were thus typical of students who had higher proficiency scores even at the beginning of the course. Moreover, such students were also more likely to make more frequent use of study strategies in class and in individual study of Spanish. Once the total opinion questionnaire had been analyzed into separate factors, additional patterns emerged. The four distinct factors identified in the Spanish questionnaire were these:

(1) an overall interest factor reflecting a generally favorable evaluation of foreign language study and of Spanish in particular;
(2) a specifically integrative factor related to the importance of Mexican American language and culture in the Southwest;
(3) a language-class-related factor showing lack of anxiety and willingness to take risks in class; and
(4) a social support factor showing perceived parental and peer interest in the study of Spanish.

The most robust set of relationships occurred with the language-class factor, which showed significant positive associations with all of the pretests, with exam scores and grades, and with the scale related to use of classroom strategies. These findings underscored the strength of personality traits, especially risk taking, which came into play in language classes (Ely, 1988). The perceived social support factor was related to all of the pretests, to grades for one quarter, and to the strategy scales for classroom and individual study behaviors. The first factor—interest and positive evaluation of languages and of Spanish—was associated with all of the pretests but with none of the achievement measures. The integrative factor related to local Mexican American language and culture was correlated with exam grades for one quarter.

For students of beginning Spanish, then, the order of importance of the attitudinal dimensions showed that attitudes related to enjoyment of the language class and to perceived social support for the language influenced both choice of language and success in study. Overall interest in foreign languages and in Spanish was typical of students who did well on the proficiency pretests, but it had no perceptible relationship with achievement. The motivational cluster related to the local importance of Spanish was the weakest influence; it had no impact on functional skill and only one association with achievement. For beginning Spanish students, then, the language-class-related factor had the strongest impact on achievement and proficiency.

*Attitudinal influences: Japanese.* The total opinion questionnaire score for the Japanese classes showed significant positive links with all three of the strategy scale scores: Students with more positive overall attitudes toward Japanese used study strategies more often in class, in interaction with others, and in individual study. The opinion total, however, showed no significant correlation with any of the achievement or comprehension measures. Perhaps, for this group of students, the total opinion score was more important in influencing initial choice of a language and efforts to study and use it consistently rather than in shaping progress in the language once enrolled.

Three distinct factors emerged from the factor analysis of the Japanese opinion data:

(1) an overall interest factor related to interest in foreign languages generally and Japanese in particular;

(2) a specifically instrumental factor related to present importance and expected future use of Japanese; and

(3) perceived parental and social support for the study of Japanese.

The first and third factors were comparable to those found for Spanish, while the second—instrumentality of the second language studied—

emerged only for Japanese. Unlike Spanish, no distinctive language-class-related factor was found, an unexpected result that probably reflected instructional arrangements. Instead of having section meetings five hours per week with the same instructor, students of Japanese had two large group lectures and three section meetings per week. Also, the section instructors were changed in the middle of each quarter in order to expose students to different speakers. Because of this variety of classroom formats, questionnaire items about student attitudes toward classroom activities were less applicable for the Japanese students. Of the three factors in the Japanese data, only the third—perceived social support—showed any links with proficiency (here, the comprehension pretest); none demonstrated any association with the achievement measures. However, both the first and the third factors were correlated with the scale measuring interactive behaviors, and all three factors were significantly related to the individual study strategy scale.

These results suggested that, for the students of beginning Japanese, attitudinal considerations were important in influencing the initial choice of a language to study. The factor reflecting perceived parental support for language study demonstrated the greatest number of significant associations with one proficiency test, with interactive behaviors, and with study behaviors. Higher scores on the second factor—instrumental value of Japanese—were also linked with greater use of interactive behaviors. All three factors were correlated with greater use of individual study strategies. Although attitudinal considerations showed no direct association with achievement, and only one with proficiency, the pattern of correlations with the study strategy scales implied that they had an indirect influence on learning: Students with higher scores on the attitudinal factors were more likely to make use of study strategies in interaction and in private study. Because these study strategies were also linked with achievement and proficiency in Japanese, the attitudinal factors may have promoted learning by increasing strategy use.

### Persistent and Nonpersistent Students

Because persistence in second-language study is a prerequisite to further development of functional and formal skills in the second language, we sought to identify the characteristics that distinguished those students who remained enrolled from those who left the course before the end of the first year of instruction. Two types of comparisons were done. The first consisted of a series of comparisons of background characteristics (including age, verbal and nonverbal IQ, and prior study of and exposure to the language being studied); pretests of language skills; and precourse opinions regarding language study. For Spanish and for Japanese, no differences between persistent and nonpersistent students were obtained on any of the background variables. The pretests of language proficiency also showed no differences between the groups with one exception: In Spanish, persistent students showed a tendency to have higher pretest comprehension scores than those who later dropped out. Whereas the Japanese comprehension pretests were comparable for persisters and nonpersisters, the results for the opinion questionnaire were not. Students who stayed in the Japanese course for a year had significantly more positive overall attitudes toward language study and the study of Japanese than those who dropped out of the course, again attesting to the important role of attitudes in predicting persistence in foreign language study.

The second set of comparisons of persistent and nonpersistent students used Rasch modeling, a technique that assessed how well the response patterns of persisters and nonpersisters fit the constructs measured by the comprehension pretests, study strategy scales, and opinion measures. For both Spanish and Japanese, results showed that the responses of persisters and dropouts on the comprehension tests were no different from each other. In Spanish, however, the students who persisted saw themselves as using the interactive language strategies more often than those who left the course. This suggests that persistence in beginning Spanish study may, in part, be predicted by a self-perceived propensity to use the language in natural interaction. In Japanese, the only difference between the groups was that persistent students fit the positive attitudinal profile reflected in the opinion questionnaire better than those who later dropped out. This comparison corroborates the previous comparison based on the opinion questionnaire total, once more showing that motivational considerations affected long-term progress in the language by promoting persistence.

DISCUSSION

The results of our investigations on foreign language learning strategies provided more keys to understanding effective learning at the beginning level of university language study. In both Spanish and Japanese, certain behaviors denoting active participation in class, such as *asking the teacher about exceptions, saying answers to oneself,* and *guessing meaning from context during instruction,* were valuable. Additionally, interaction behaviors, such as *using the second language at a job* and *not being afraid to take risks* showed positive links with learning outcomes, as did various behaviors related to seeking additional input through print or electronic media. In contrast, *conscious comparison of the new language with the native language* and *frequent self-correction during interaction* were consistently negative with respect to learning outcomes. Effective learners in these university classes drew on both cognitive and social behaviors to create a balance between attention to form and the development of functional skills. Whereas different strategies emerged in the correlations for Spanish and for Japanese, results for both languages showed that certain strategies related to seeking input and practicing output in the new language contributed to traditional achievement and to functional proficiency.

The attitudinal results and persistence comparisons revealed additional influences on language study, and these were different for Spanish and Japanese. For Spanish, *positive evaluation of language study, social support for second-language study,* and *enjoyment of the language class* were linked with various achievement and proficiency measures. Students who persisted throughout a year of beginning Spanish had better initial comprehension skills and considered themselves more likely to use interactive learning behaviors. In the Japanese classes, only *social support for language study* was related to functional comprehension. Although similar in personal characteristics and initial language skills, persistent students of Japanese had significantly more positive attitudes toward language study, in general and specifically toward Japanese, than those who dropped out. Although a positive disposition toward language study was a common element in successful language learning, the nature of the relevant underlying factors was different for each language. This suggests that specific attitudes toward the language chosen and the instructional situation had a differential impact on beginning language study (also see Gardner, 1987).

Taken together, the results indicated that effective language learning at the university level consisted of an optimal combination of strategies that helped students seek appropriate exposure to the language and practice the language in class or in interaction. Precise motivational factors varied according to language studied and instructional context, although a positive attitude toward language study and the language chosen was a constant, if sometimes indirect, influence on successful learning (see Ely, 1988).

Because these results are based on correlations, it is not possible to posit a direct cause-and-effect relationship between these strategies and better comprehension. Students with higher test scores used certain behaviors, so it is reasonable to think that their use contributed to better skills. However, some of these behaviors, such as *being able to focus on the main point* and *asking the teacher about exceptions in class*, depended on already having sufficient comprehension skills to identify main points and exceptions. Thus these results are useful in a descriptive sense, for they tell us which strategies were used by good students. We then infer that use of the strategies indicated more effective learning processes, a reasonable inference but one that demands further empirical and practical proof. The strategies linked with test scores and proficiency, therefore, serve as initial guidelines for constructing theoretical and pedagogical models of effective language learning (in this connection, see Oxford & Schleppegrel, 1988).

What can teachers do to help beginning language students master a new language? Results from this study showed that strategies such as *making guesses from context, repeating answers in class, making efforts to use the new language in real communicative situations*, and *using a variety of media to increase one's exposure to the language* predicted positive results. In contrast, *excessive attention to linguistic detail, continual efforts to make conscious comparisons between the first language and the second language*, and *reliance on English even when it was possible to try using the other language* were all strategies that retarded achievement and proficiency. By identifying and modeling the effective strategies described, and cautioning students against the ineffective ones, teachers can help students to make their second-language study more efficient.

Even the effective strategies revealed in this study demand further investigation and pedagogical experimentation to establish their usefulness in a particular classroom setting. Further research, linking learning strategies and teaching conditions and processes, is needed to provide a fuller understanding of university foreign language learning (see Wenden & Rubin, 1987). Additional studies to refine the connections between student strategy use, attitudes, instructional contexts, and learning outcomes will assist language teachers and students in finding additional avenues to second-language mastery.

## REFERENCES

Ely, C. M. (1988). Personality: Its impact on attitudes toward classroom activities. *Foreign Language Annals, 21*(1), 25–32.

Gardner, R. C. (1987). *Social psychology and second language and second language learning.* London: Edward Arnold.

McGroarty, M. (1988). *University foreign language learning: Spanish and Japanese* (CLEAR Technical Report No. 10). Los Angeles: University of California, Center for Language Education and Research.

Oxford, R. (1986). *Second language learning strategies: Current research and implications for practice* (CLEAR Technical Report No. 3). Los Angeles: University of California, Center for Language Education and Research.

Oxford, R., & Schleppegrel, M. (1988). *Strategies for second language learning.* New York: Newbury House.

Wenden, A., & Rubin, J. (1987). *Learner strategies in language learning.* Englewood Cliffs, NJ: Prentice-Hall.

# 5

# An Oral Assessment Instrument for Immersion Students
## COPE

NANCY RHODES
LYNN THOMPSON

Spanish immersion programs for English-speaking children have been in existence in the United States since 1971, when the first program was initiated in Culver City, California. Various research studies in the United States and Canada have consistently shown the cognitive, affective, and academic benefits of immersion (Genesee, 1987; Lambert, 1978; Lambert & Tucker, 1972). Anecdotal evidence collected from parents of children in immersion programs and from immersion class teachers has also continued to illustrate that these students are speaking the language fluently and can get along in a Spanish-speaking country with little, if any, difficulty.

But until recently there has been no standardized way to judge exactly how well students in immersion programs are speaking the language. Are they comparable to native Spanish speakers of the same age? Can they manage in a social situation talking about sports as well as they can in an academic setting describing a science experiment? Are their skills in comprehension, fluency, vocabulary, and grammar at approximately the same level or are they stronger in some areas and weaker in others?

The Center for Language Education and Research (CLEAR) identified the need for an oral interview-type test for fifth and sixth graders that would elicit normal speech and would yield global ratings of proficiency. There were two major problems with the tests already in existence. First, the available proficiency tests were not suitable for elementary-age students, and, second, the foreign language tests, like most language tests, did not measure students' academic language.

The CLEAR Oral Proficiency Exam (COPE) test is intended to address both students' academic language (their ability to discuss subject matter—social studies, geography, and science—effectively in the language) and students' social language (the ability to discuss their family, recreational activities, and social life in the language). The test developers aimed first to produce an oral proficiency test for students in Spanish immersion programs and then to adapt it for English as a second language (ESL) students in the same grades. The purpose of this chapter is to provide a brief overview of testing procedures that have been used in the past with immersion students and then provide details on the test specifications, development, piloting, validation, and administration of the Spanish immersion CLEAR Oral Proficiency Exam.

## TARGET STUDENT POPULATION

The COPE is designed for students who are enrolled in a Spanish immersion program and are currently in fifth or sixth grade. Language immersion is an approach to foreign language instruction in which the regular curriculum is taught in a foreign language. The new language is used as the medium as well as the object of instruction. Immersion programs vary in the amount of time devoted to instruction in the foreign language—there are both total and partial immersion programs.

In *total immersion*, the foreign language is used for the entire school day during the first two or three years (see also the chapters by Snow in this volume). Reading is taught through the foreign language; instruction in English is introduced gradually and the amount of English is increased until the sixth grade, where up to half the day is spent in English and half in the foreign language. In *partial immersion*, instruction is in the foreign language for at least half the school day from the very beginning. The amount of instruction in the foreign language usually remains constant throughout the elementary school program.

The following are the goals for partial and total immersion programs:

(1) functional proficiency in the foreign language (children are able to communicate in the foreign language on topics appropriate to their age level);

(2) mastery of subject content material of the school district curriculum;

(3) cross-cultural understanding; and

(4) achievement in English language arts comparable to or surpassing the achievement of students in English-only programs.

A two-way immersion program, a variation of the programs described above, is similar to regular immersion programs except that included among the students are native speakers of the target language as well as native speakers of English (see Chapter 7 of this volume for more details on two-way immersion). The goals of two-way immersion, in addition to subject content mastery, are that the English-speaking students become functionally proficient in the foreign language and that the native speakers of the foreign language become functionally proficient in English. The COPE has been pilot tested with students in two-way immersion programs as well as in total and partial immersion programs.

## WHAT'S BEEN DONE IN THE PAST

Three areas of immersion education need to be assessed with standardized measures: subject matter knowledge (in all subjects), English language knowledge, and foreign language knowledge. The use of standardized measures with immersion students is especially important for ongoing comparisons with nonimmersion students in the school district as well as with students in other immersion programs across the country.

Subject matter knowledge in the areas of social studies, science, and mathematics has traditionally been tested with standardized tests in English, whether or not the subject was taught in English. That the tests are administered in English has more to do with the lack of content-appropriate tests in Spanish than with a specific decision by the schools to test only in English. Results of subject area tests consistently show that immersion students perform as well as their nonimmersion counterparts in all subjects (Lambert & Tucker, 1972; Lapkin, Swain, & Argue, 1983; Swain, 1979).

English language skills, including reading comprehension, spelling, punctuation, and vocabulary, have also been regularly tested. Fifth- and sixth-grade students consistently perform as well or better than nonimmersion students, particularly in the areas of reading comprehension and vocabulary knowledge (Swain, 1979).

Foreign language skills, on the other hand, have not been a major focus of attention for testing. From the inception of immersion programs in the United States, it was assumed that the children would learn the foreign language fluently as they learned social studies, science, and mathematics, so there were few attempts to assess the language skills of these students separately. In addition, there were few, if any, tests available that were appropriate for assessing the language of immersion students. The few standardized tests available were typically designed for students in bilingual education programs (who are native speakers of the target language), not for advanced-level fifth- and sixth-grade immersion students. Further, the existing tests did not examine academic as well as social language. They tended to focus on Spanish language skills such as vocabulary, comprehension, conceptual development, and oral production.

Because a common yardstick for oral language did not exist, teachers who were interested in assessing overall language proficiency often attempted to devise their own evaluation measures to compare students with one another. Such locally developed instruments, however, tended to be program-specific and did not allowed for comparison across programs. Therefore, teachers and researchers suggested to CLEAR test developers that an instrument was needed to specifically address the assessment of academic and social language skills of immersion students.

## DEVELOPMENT OF THE COPE

### Background Information

As a model for the development of an objective and accurate oral proficiency measure, we looked first at the ACTFL/ETS Oral Proficiency Interview (ACTFL, 1986), which is designed with the academic foreign language learner in mind. The ACTFL/ETS Oral Interview is a 30-minute session involving a trained interviewer and a subject. The oral interview is designed to determine the subject's proficiency level at a given point in time. Because the oral interview evaluates proficiency through performance on a range of near-natural communication tasks, the student's competence in the language, rather than knowledge of a particular course or curriculum, is being evaluated. The objective nature of the oral interview thus makes it ideal for inter- and intraprogram assessment.

The ACTFL/ETS Oral Interview has its origins in the Interagency Language Roundtable (ILR) oral proficiency scale, which has been used by the U.S. government, with periodic refinements, since 1956 to assess the oral proficiency of participants in intensive government language training programs. In this test each subject is interviewed by one or two trained testers who ask a series of open-ended questions designed to elicit, by the end of the interview, the highest level of speech competency. The resulting speech sample is scored on a scale of 0 to 5, based on explicit descriptions of comprehension, fluency, vocabulary, grammar, and pronunciation. Evidence for the construct validity of this earlier government oral interview procedure has been demonstrated by Bachman and Palmer (1981).

Experimentation with the ILR scale in the academic context, where students did not tend to reach the same level of proficiency as graduates of intensive government language programs, showed that a scale geared to the academic context was needed. The ACTFL/ETS Oral Interview procedure was developed from the ILR protocol for use in academic contexts, providing a global rating of the subject's communicative competence, based on the same five factors used by ILR interviewers. It differs, however, in that it allows for finer distinctions at the lower levels of the ILR scale, where most academic foreign language students tend to cluster. In addition, the oral interview uses descriptive terms in place of numbers for each level, with major categories (each with subdivisions) called "novice," "intermediate," "advanced," and "superior."

Both of these instruments were designed and implemented with the adult foreign language learner in mind. In recognition of the need for a rating scale appropriate for younger students, the ACTFL/ETS rating scale was adapted by Educational Testing Service researchers in 1983 for junior high school students. The major modifications were adjustments in the descriptors for grammar and the omission of pronunciation as an assessment parameter, because the researchers found that this aspect of language ability "ceases to be a matter of much concern with students exposed to (a foreign language) from the early grades" (Rabiteau & Taft, n.d.). Because this rating scale was developed through interviews with immersion program participants only slightly older than those for whom we wished to design an instrument, this modified scale was used as a starting point for developing an oral proficiency test for fifth- and sixth-grade students in Spanish immersion programs in the United States.

## Test Specifications

Four requirements were added to the modified ACTFL/ETS rating scale as test development procedures began. First, the test should not require more than 15–20 minutes to administer so that it is possible to use in the school context. Second, the format should provide a stimulating and realistic context for both examinee and examiner. Third, the test should assess cognitive/academic as well as social/survival skills. Fourth, procedures for test administrators appropriate for the new COPE scale should be developed along with the appropriate test format.

The first and second requirements were addressed in the following ways: two students are interviewed at a time and the entire interview is contextualized. The precedent for these modifications in the ACTFL oral interview can be found in Alice Omaggio's (1983) discussion of teaching and testing language. She suggested the value of "contextualizing" the testing situation and described paired interviews with two students taking turns asking and responding to questions drawn from conversation cards. An additional precedent for paired testing is found in Reschke's (1978) suggested modifications of the FSI oral interview for secondary and college students. He suggested interviewing up to three to five students at a time. Our experience, however, showed that no more than two elementary school students should be interviewed at a time.

Thus the format for the COPE interview required creating an imaginary but realistic situation where two students could carry out a series of brief conversations based on instructions contained in a set of dialogue cards. In the Spanish COPE interview, students are asked to play the roles of a Mexican student visiting an American school and a North American student acting as the guide during the visit. Both students receive cues for a variety of brief conversations from a set of dialogue cards that the interviewer reads to them (see Appendix A for sample transcript).

The third requirement consequently relates directly to the contents of the dialogue cards. These cards were developed on the basis of observations of school and classroom activities, interviews with sixth-grade students to find out their interests, textbook contents, and several ideas from a 1984 set of ETS situation cards. Topics include academic areas (science, social studies, and geography), school-related topics (fire drills, using the cafeteria), and social topics (movies, parties, social life). Specific topics in the final version of the COPE include the following:

(1) *greetings* (welcoming the Mexican student);

(2) *program of studies* (discussing the Spanish program and other course offerings;

(3) *the cafeteria* (directions, vocabulary for food, likes and dislikes);

(4) *time lines* (telling time, describing daily activities);

(5) *the library* (vocabulary specific to library, explaining and giving advice on library procedures);

(6) *fire drill* (asking for/giving clarification and assistance);

(7) *two trips* (describing places, intended activities, and means of transportation);

(8) *school buses* (asking for and giving directions and schedules);

(9) *the movies* (the American invites the Mexican to go to a movie; social language—invitations);

(10) *social life* (vocabulary relating to entertainment and fashion—expressing likes and dislikes);

(11) *a party* (social language and cultural behavior—discussion of an invitation to a party);

(12) *science project* (scientific language—discussion of good versus bad nutrition);

(13) *future careers* (vocabulary for professions, future tense);

(14) *an accident* (describing an accident, expressing emotions, interviewing, use of past tense);

(15) *a fight* (describing a fight, making generalizations);

(16) *unfair rules* (discussion of school rules, expressing opinions); and

(17) *science equipment* (identifying and describing the utility of science equipment).

Each dialogue card contains explicit instructions to follow and language to use for the interviewer. These 17 cards are organized in order of difficulty (see Appendix A for samples of dialogue cards).

In tandem with the development of the dialogue cards and procedures for conducting the interviews, test developers worked to adapt the modified ACTFL/ETS rating scale for elementary-age students. To make scoring easier, descriptions of the new rating scale were organized at each level by the categories of comprehension, fluency, vocabulary, and grammar. Technical terminology was simplified and descriptions were augmented as needed by consulting the "Student Oral Proficiency Rating" (SOPR) (Zehler et al., 1987) and a short version of the ACTFL/ETS Guidelines prepared for elementary schools. These descriptions were then placed in a matrix that is divided into Junior Novice (low, mid, high); Junior Intermediate (low, mid, high); and Junior Advanced (advanced, advanced plus, and superior) on the horizontal axis and Comprehension, Fluency, Vocabulary, and Grammar on the vertical axis. The brief general descriptions of the oral proficiency categories presented below provide an outline of the points highlighted in the COPE matrix.

*Comprehension* refers to the ability to understand the spoken language in a range of situations, including formal, instructional situations in which there are few contextual cues to meaning as well as informal conversational situations. Comprehension also refers to being able to understand normal speech—speech that has not been adjusted in pace or repeated.

*Fluency* refers to the rhythm and pacing of the speech produced by the student. It involves the degree to which speech is produced smoothly without hesitations and without pauses to search for vocabulary and expressions.

*Vocabulary* refers to the student's knowledge of the words and expressions needed to communicate. This knowledge includes both the range of vocabulary used appropriately and the use of idiomatic words and phrases.

*Grammar* refers to the accuracy of the speech used by the students in terms of word formation and sentence structure. When judging the student's accuracy, all of the following are considered: the frequency of grammatical errors, the degree to which they interfere with a listener's ability to understand, and the range of grammatical structures used by the student.

The fourth requirement for the test, that procedures for test administrators be developed, has been addressed in the test administrator's manual. The administrator's manual helps ensure consistent and accurate administration and scoring of the interview by walking the potential interviewer through these categories and explaining how to rate each student. It is necessary to be thoroughly familiar with the entire rating scale before conducting any testing.

### The Interview Procedure

Testing requires approximately 15–20 minutes for each pair of students, and it should take place in a quiet room without distractions. Ideally, the interview should be conducted by two test administrators to ensure accurate rating of the interview. The first test administrator can act as the "interviewer" and the second as the "rater." The interviewer should give the instructions to the examinees while the rater assumes the responsibility for rating student performance.

The two test administrators should create a relaxed, informal atmosphere, seating each pair of students comfortably without a desk in between the test administrators and the students. The four can sit around a small, round table or the end of a long one. Once the students are comfortably seated, the interviewer greets them in Spanish. Each student is then asked his or her name and grade (in Spanish) and this information is written down on the rating sheets (one per student). The interviewer, continuing in Spanish, asks the students who would like to play the role of the Mexican and who would like to play the role of the North American. Once the roles are assigned, the interviewer gives general instructions for the interview in Spanish: Students are told that they will be asked to engage in a number of short dialogues and are encouraged to say as much as they can and use their imaginations. The interviewer then starts the interview with the first card (greetings) and continues with up to six additional cards identified as core cards. If at any time students experience a high degree of difficulty, the interviewer moves to one or two of the supplementary cards at that level or the level below in order to "fine-tune" the rating. Rating sheets are filled out by the rater for each student as soon as possible after the completion of the interview. When rating a student, each category is considered separately and the level that best represents the student's performance in that proficiency category is selected. An "x" is then drawn across the description for that level.

In our pilot testing and subsequent test administrations described below, test administrators were trained in the following manner. First, they reviewed the "Instructions for Using the CLEAR Oral Proficiency Exam (COPE)" with a trained test administrator and then they rated a number of previously recorded interviews. Their ratings were then compared with the "on-the-spot" ratings. In addition, the trainees conducted several interviews under the supervision of the trained test administrator. In this way, interrater reliability was maintained.

### Pilot Testing

Both the Spanish and the English versions of the COPE test were pilot tested with Spanish immersion and ESL students in California, Maryland,

Virginia, and Wisconsin. This initial administration allowed us to evaluate the mechanics of the test construction and the rating procedures. Substantial revisions were made on the dialogue cards and rating scale and clinical testing of the instrument took place during the 1987–1988 school year in Washington, D.C., and Minnesota. To determine the appropriate population for the COPE, three different types of programs were used in the clinical testing: partial immersion, two-way partial immersion, and content-based FLES. (Content-based FLES programs are language classes in which subject content is taught in the foreign language—see Chapter 13, Curtain & Martinez, this volume. Less time spent teaching subject content through the language distinguishes this model from the immersion models. In the program tested, social studies was the subject taught in the foreign language.) Another oral proficiency test, the IDEA Proficiency Test (IPT), was administered as a criterion measure against which the COPE could be validated. The correlation between the IPT and the COPE is reasonably good (r = .62) considering that the IPT is very different from the COPE in many respects (format, content, context). Bearing this in mind, the fact that the COPE has a concurrent validity index of .62 provides us with a fair degree of assurance that the COPE validly measures oral proficiency as intended. It was found that the COPE is a valid measure of oral proficiency for partial and two-way partial immersion students. In addition, some evidence was found to support the use of the COPE with content-based FLES students. Following suggestions of teachers and test administrators, additional revisions were made to the dialogue cards and rating scale.

*Test Administration*

In fall 1988, the COPE was administered to students at two total immersion sites and one partial immersion site as part of a study comparing different types of elementary foreign language programs. Fifth and sixth graders from three FLES programs were also given the COPE. Test administrators found that the COPE was most appropriate for partial and total immersion programs. Given differing program emphases and intensity, the COPE proved, as expected, to be inappropriate for regular, nonintensive FLES students. At the same time, however, teachers and test administrators recognized the value of some type of interview format for FLES students as well. In terms of overall results, the total and partial immersion students scored in the Junior Intermediate high to Superior range while FLES students ranged from below scale to Junior Novice high. Within the immersion group, a pattern emerged with the students' ratings in the four subscales of proficiency skills. They scored the highest in comprehension, and then their ratings decreased gradually for each of the other three skills: fluency, vocabulary, and grammar. Their strengths were as predicted by their teachers and substantiated anecdotal evidence: The students' comprehension of oral Spanish was outstanding, their fluency and vocabulary were good, and their grammar ranked the lowest of the four skills.

## CONCLUSIONS AND RECOMMENDATIONS

On the basis of pilot testing and test administrations at nine sites, there is considerable evidence that the COPE is an appropriate instrument for testing oral proficiency of fifth- and sixth-grade students in total and partial immersion and in two-way partial immersion programs. It is the first test developed for this age group that addresses both academic and social language. Most important, the COPE has given us the ability to identify students' strengths and weaknesses in separate language skills instead of assessing only overall language proficiency.

Results show that, on the one hand, immersion students' comprehension is close to that of native speakers of the same age, while, on the other hand, their use of grammar clearly identifies them as non-native speakers. This finding concerning grammar is a critical one that has implications for future research. Future studies on the COPE should include detailed error analyses of immersion students' language in order to identify specific grammatical problems. The results of these analyses can be used in the classroom to directly address the grammatical errors that are common to immersion students.

Future research should also include larger samples of students and focus on the differences in productive skills of partial and total immersion students. In addition, further study should include additional test administrations to students in a variety of types of content-based FLES programs in order to determine if and how the COPE may be a useful instrument for students in those programs as well.

It is recommended that the COPE continue to be administered by specially trained interviewers and continue to be validated and tested for interrater reliability. There is a possibility that in the future the COPE can be adapted so that classroom teachers can use it as a teaching tool, first to assess students' proficiency and then to address specific needs identified on the test.

# APPENDIX A:
# Transcript of Spanish COPE Test

ADMINISTRATION WITH TWO FIFTH GRADERS
IN A TWO-WAY BILINGUAL PROGRAM

The following is an excerpt from an actual interview conducted during spring 1988. The three dialogue cards with their English translations have been included for your reference. The three dialogues transcribed here are "The Cafeteria," "A Fight," and "Scientific Equipment."

Note about the two students and their program: The student playing the role of a visiting Mexican student comes from a bilingual family; the student playing the role of a North American has a Hispanic mother but doesn't speak much Spanish at home. Half of their classes at school are taught in Spanish and half in English.

The test administrator reads the following:

* * *

*COPE Dialogue Card: La Cafetería*

*Es la hora del almuerzo, y el mexicano quiere saber cómo funciona la cafetería de la escuela.*

*(Al mexicano:) Pregúntale qué hay que hacer para almorzar. Pregúntale cómo se va a la cafetería, cómo se seleccionan los varios platos, y dónde puede sentarse para comer el almuerzo.*

*(Al norteamericano:) Pregúntale qué le parece la comida aquí y cómo son las comidas en las escuelas mexicanas.*

* * *

Translation:
It's lunchtime, and the Mexican student wants to know how the school cafeteria functions.
(To the Mexican:) Ask what there is to eat. Ask how to get to the cafeteria, how to choose the various selections on the menu, and where you sit to eat lunch.
(To the American:) Ask your Mexican friend how he/she likes the food here and what the meals are like in Mexican schools.

\* \* \*

Student responses:
Note: "M" is playing the role of the Mexican student and "N" is playing the role of the North American student.

M: *¿Cómo se usa la cafetería aquí?*

N: *Solo va y le coja la comida que tiene en la mesa . . . y eso es.*

M: *¿Y dónde se puede sentar?*

N: *En cualquer . . . hay come cuarto mesas para el quinto grado y tiene que sentar en uno de esos mesas. ¿Y cómo le parece la comida?*

M: *Zico.*

N: *¿Cómo?*

M: *Zico. Good.*

(laughter)

N: *¿Y cómo es la comida en Mexico?*

M: *Para ( ? ) a la cafetería y selecciona lo que quieras y se sienta donde quiera.*

\* \* \*

*COPE Dialogue Card: Una Pelea*

*Ustedes estan hablando durante el recreo.*
*(Al norteamericano:) Dile al mexicano que ayer en el patio de recreo dos niños estaban peleando. Dile cómo comenzó la pelea; qué estaba haciendo el niño cuando el otro le pegó; y qué castigo recibieron.*
*(Al mexicano:) Dile qué pasa en México cuando los niños pelean en la escuela.*

\* \* \*

Translation:
You are talking during recess.
(To the American:) Tell your Mexican friend that yesterday on the play-ground you saw two kids fighting. Tell him how the fight began, what the one kid was doing when the other hit him, and what punishment they received.
(To the Mexican:) Tell what happens in Mexico when kids fight in school.

\* \* \*

N: *Habiá un pelea entre dos niños y un niño estaba hablando de mamá del otro. Y después el otro le pegó en la cara, y el otro le patió. Y después el profesor fue muy enojado y dijo que los dos no podían venir a la escuela para dos días.*

Interviewer
to North
American: *Pregúntale a ella que pasa en México cuando los niños pelean en la escuela.*

N: *¿Qué pasa en México cuando los niños pelean en la escuela?*

M: *Cuando los niños pelean en la escuela se tiene que mover a otra escuela.*

\* \* \*

*COPE Dialogue Card: Equipos Científicos*

*Aquí tienen ustedes dibujos de equipos que se usan en la clase de ciencias. Quiero que Uds. hablen de cómo se llama cada objeto y cómo se usa.*
*(A los dos:) Cada uno puedo nombrar y describir cuatro objetos.*
*(Los materiales dibujados son: balanza, imán, lupa, aguja, tenacillas, frasco con tapadera, regla, y microscopio.)*

\* \* \*

(Give each student the science equipment card.)
Here you have drawings of pieces of equipment that are used in a science class. I want you to name each object and tell how it is used.
(To both:) Each one can name and describe four objects.
(The objects drawn are: a scale, a magnet, a magnifying glass, a needle, tongs, a test tube, a ruler, and a microscope.)

\* \* \*

N:  (picture of magnet) *El imán se usa para . . . algunas veces para encontrar si algo es magnético or si no es. También algunas veces se usa para recoger cosas que son magnéticos.*

M:  (picture of tongs) *La pinza es para recoger cosas pequeñas que no se puede recoger con la mano.*

N:  (picture of a ruler) *La regla es para medir cualquer cosa.*

M:  (picture of a scale) *Y la balancia es para medir las cosas.*

N:  (picture of a needle) *La aguja es para coser.*

M:  (picture of a magnifying glass) *Um, ¿Qué es esto en español?*

Interviewer:  *¿No sabes? Bueno, ¿Sabes cómo se usa?*

M:  *Sí. Esto se usa para ver cosas pequeñas.*

N:  (picture of microscope) *No se cómo se llama, pero esta también se usa para ver cosas pequeñas, pero muy pequeñas.*

\* \* \*

This transcript represents approximately 5 minutes of a 15-minute speech sample on which the students' ratings would be based. As can be seen in the *Una Pelea* dialogue, the interviewer must sometimes deal with one student who does not offer as much information as the other, although the student may be as proficient if not more proficient than the other. Students are encouraged to elaborate on topics, as is shown in the *Equipos Científicos* dialogue. Students were asked to expand on and explain the use of a piece of scientific equipment, even when they didn't know the name for it. Overall, these two students received ratings ranging from Advanced Plus to Superior.

# APPENDIX B

**Figure 5.1** Clear Oral Proficiency Exam (COPE) Rating Scale for Spanish

STUDENT'S NAME _____  GRADE _____  SCHOOL _____

CITY AND STATE _____  RATED BY _____  DATE _____

| | Jr. Novice Low | Jr. Novice Mid | Jr. Novice High |
|---|---|---|---|
| Comprehension | Recognizes a few familiar questions and commands. | Understands predictable questions and commands in specified topic areas, though at slower than normal speed. | Can sometimes understand simple questions and commands when applied in new contexts. May understand familiar language at normal speed. |
| Fluency | Conversations are limited to an exchange of memorized sentences or phrases. | Operates in a limited capacity within predictable topic areas. Long pauses are common. May start sentences correctly but frequently completes them with gestures or other non-verbal means. | Uses high frequency utterances with reasonable ease. There are signs of emerging originality and spontaneity. Able to complete most sentences verbally. |
| Vocabulary | Uses memorized utterances and words belonging to learned categories. Does not recognize words or phrases outside the context in which they have been learned. | Has vocabulary for common activities and objects but frequently searches for words. Recognizes known forms outside of learned contexts. | Basic formulae and words for regular activities come readily. Vocabulary adequate to minimally elaborate utterances. |
| Grammar | Utterances are usually memorized forms. | Usually achieves correct grammar in familiar patterns but accuracy is easily upset. May have a high rate of self-corrections. Reliance on patterns is greater than reliance on memorized utterances. | Grammar is largely correct for simple familiar language. Isolated forms such as past tense, but and simple connectors, and direct and indirect object pronouns may be used but cannot be generalized across grammatical structures. |

**Figure 5.1** Clear Oral Proficiency Exam (COPE) Rating Scale for Spanish (continued)

| | Jr. Intermediate Low | Jr. Intermediate Mid | Jr. Intermediate High |
|---|---|---|---|
| Comprehension | Follows fairly normal conversation with frequent clarifications (non-verbal as well as verbal). | Comprehension problems seldom evident on everyday topics. Carries out commands without prompting. May show some difficulty on unfamiliar topics. | Usually understands speech at normal speed, though some slow-downs are necessary. Can request clarification verbally. |
| Fluency | Satisfies everyday social and academic needs adequately but not fully. Maintains simple conversation by answering questions. | Shows evidence of spontaneity in conversation. Maintains simple narratives. Sometimes initiates talk without relying on questions or prompts. | Maintains conversation with remarkable fluency but performance may be uneven. Uses language creatively to initiate and sustain talk. |
| Vocabulary | Makes statements and asks questions adequately to satisfy basic social and academic needs but has difficulty explaining or elaborating them. | Permits limited discussion of topics beyond social and academic needs. Attempted circumlocutions may be ineffective. | Broad enough for relatively complete discussion of familiar social and simple academic topics. Sometimes achieves successful circumlocutions. |
| Grammar | Talk consists primarily of uncomplicated original sentences with correct word order. Makes little use of modifiers. Can use basic connectors such as *but* and *because* accurately. Attempts to use more complex forms are often incorrect. | Sentences show some complexity but may be inaccurate. Uses a variety of verb tenses in specific forms but does not employ the full range of possible conjugations. Pronouns still show evident inaccuracies. | Able to use the complete range of conjugations across tenses for regular verbs but does not have full control of irregular forms. Use of complex connectors, direct and indirect object pronouns usually correct. |

**Figure 5.1** Clear Oral Proficiency Exam (COPE) Rating Scale for Spanish (continued)

|  | Jr. Advanced | Jr. Advanced Plus | Superior |
|---|---|---|---|
| Comprehension | Understands academic talk and social conversation at normal speed. May have trouble with highly idiomatic speech. | Understands complex academic talk and highly idiomatic conversation, though confusion may occur in rare instances. | Has no difficulty in conversation or in academic talk. |
| Fluency | Shows high degree of ease of speech. Reports facts easily. Explains points of view and abstract concepts in an uncomplicated fashion. | Handles most academic and social requirements with confidence. | Able to participate fully in social and academic talk. Responds with ease to highly idiomatic conversation, hypothetical situations, and discussions of abstract concepts. |
| Vocabulary | Uses a variety of idiomatic expressions. Uses circumlocutions effectively. | Complete enough to fully discuss most academic and social topics. Flow of talk is rarely interrupted by inadequate vocabulary. | Vocabulary is extensive and groping for words is rare. Shows familiarity with idiomatic expressions and facility with less common vocabulary which permit discussion of topics in unfamiliar situations. |
| Grammar | Most forms largely but not consistently correct. Has good control of pronouns and sequencing devices—*the first, but, then,* etc. Shows expanded use of adjectives and adverbs. | Uses all tenses comfortably with a high degree of accuracy, though occasional errors are evident. | Control of grammar and syntax is strong enough that no major patterns of error are revealed. |

## REFERENCES

American Council on the Teaching of Foreign Languages (ACTFL). (1986). *ACTFL Proficiency Guidelines*. Hastings-on-Hudson, NY: Author.

Bachman, L., & Palmer, A. S. (1981). The construct validation of the FSI oral interview. *Language Learning, 31*(1), 365–396.

Curtain, H. A., & Pesola, C. A. (1988). *Languages and children—making the match. Foreign language in the elementary school*. Reading, MA: Addison-Wesley.

Educational Testing Service. (1984). *Situation cards: Designed and assembled with the assistance of the Interagency Language Roundtable participating agencies*. Princeton, NJ: Author.

Genesee, F. (1987). *Learning through two languages: Studies of immersion and bilingual education*. Cambridge, MA: Newbury House.

Gutstein, S., & Goodwin, S. (1987). *The CLEAR Oral Proficiency Exam (COPE) Project Report*. Washington, DC: Center for Language Education and Research, Center for Applied Linguistics.

Lambert, W. E. (1978, February). Cognitive and socio-cultural consequences of bilingualism. *Canadian Modern Language Review, 34*(3), 537–547.

Lambert, W. E., & Tucker, G. R. (1972). *Bilingual education of children: The St. Lambert experiment*. Rowley, MA: Newbury House.

Lapkin, S., Swain, M., & Argue, V. (1983). *French immersion: The trial balloon that flew*. Ontario, Canada: Ontario Institute for Studies in Education.

Omaggio, A. C. (1983). *Teaching language in context*. Boston, MA: Heinle and Heinle.

Rabiteau, K., & Taft, H. (n.d.). *Provisional Modified ACTFL/ETS Oral Proficiency Scale for Junior High School Students*. Princeton, NJ: Educational Testing Service.

Reschke, C. (1978). Adaptation of the FSI interview scale for secondary schools and colleges. In J. Clark (Ed.), *Direct testing of speaking proficiency: Theory and application: Proceedings of a two day conference*. Princeton, NJ: Educational Testing Service.

Swain, M. (1979). What does research say about immersion education? In *So you want your child to learn French!* Ottawa, Ontario: Canadian Parents for French.

Wang, L. S., Richardson, G., & Rhodes, N. (1988). *The CLEAR Oral Proficiency Exam (COPE). Project report addendum: Clinical testing and validity and dimensionality studies*. Washington, DC: Center for Language Education and Research, Center for Applied Linguistics.

Zehler, A. et al. (1987). *Student Oral Proficiency Rating (SOPR)*. Arlington, VA: Development Associates.

# 6

# Extension of ACTFL Guidelines for Less Commonly Taught Languages

CHARLES STANSFIELD
DORRY MANN KENYON

### DEVELOPING PROFICIENCY GUIDELINES

The assessment of foreign language proficiency, originally articulated by the Foreign Service Institute's Oral Proficiency Interview, is now of critical interest to academicians who are concerned with foreign language instruction. This shifting of concern into academia was largely goaded by three entities: the American Council on the Teaching of Foreign Languages (ACTFL), the Educational Testing Service (ETS), and the Interagency Language Roundtable (the ILR is a committee comprising representatives from various government agencies interested in foreign language testing).

In 1981, ACTFL and ETS, with assistance from ILR representatives, undertook the writing of proficiency testing guidelines in all skill areas for the commonly taught languages (i.e., Spanish, French, and German). A year later, ACTFL published the first set of generic guidelines for foreign language testing (Hiple, 1986).

The ACTFL Proficiency Guidelines are a scale of language proficiency at nine different levels. The lowest level is absolute zero, or no knowledge of the foreign language. The next level is Novice Low, which represents knowledge of only a few words (20, for example) in the foreign language. At the Novice Mid level, the learner knows more vocabulary (60 words, for example) but lacks any ability to use even the most rudimentary elements of the grammar of the language. At the Novice High level, the learner knows still more everyday vocabulary and begins to use simple sentences, although inconsistently.

At the three Intermediate levels, the learner can create simple sentences by combining and recombining learned elements of the language. At the Intermediate Low level, the learner can ask and answer simple questions, although in a highly restricted manner. At the Intermediate Mid level, the learner can talk about self and family members and can participate in simple conversations regarding personal history and leisure time activities. At the Intermediate High level, the learner can initiate, sustain, and close a general conversation and can use connected discourse for simple narration or description.

The ACTFL Guidelines contain two advanced levels, Advanced and Advanced Plus. These two levels are characterized by the speaker's ability to narrate and describe with paragraph-length discourse. At the Advanced level, the speaker can satisfy both the requirements of everyday situations and routine school and work requirements. At the Advanced Plus level, the speaker shows emerging ability to support opinions, explain in detail, and hypothesize.

The highest level on the ACTFL scale is called Superior. At this level the speaker can participate effectively in most formal and informal conversations on practical, social, professional, and abstract topics and support opinions and hypothesize using nativelike discourse strategies (ACTFL, 1986).

In the ensuing years, guidelines were developed for a larger variety of languages, including "non-Western" languages. As a result, a number of new issues in developing language-specific guidelines began to emerge.

The Center for Applied Linguistics (CAL; located in Washington, D.C.) and ACTFL recognized the need for these issues to be explored by research scholars and jointly undertook a project to provide (a) teachers of the less commonly taught languages (LCTLs) with information about the nature of proficiency testing guidelines and to clear up common misconceptions and (b) identify the issues involved in adapting existing guidelines for the commonly taught languages to the LCTLs.

The project goals were achieved through the organization and sponsorship of special workshops for teachers of four targeted languages: Arabic, Hindi, Indonesian, and African languages (particularly Hausa). In addition, the project published and distributed a special volume of articles and working papers that provide a foundation for future work in this area (Stansfield & Harman, 1987).

## Workshops

The teacher workshops were held in conjunction with conferences of relevant associations: the Association of Asian Studies (workshops on Hindi and Indonesian), the South Asian Studies Conference (workshop on Hindi), and the first annual symposium on Arabic Languages and Literature (workshop on Arabic). (No workshop was held for the African languages.) Although the format of each workshop varied, they generally consisted of a demonstration of the ILR Oral Proficiency Interview in the target language and discussions of the application of the generic proficiency guidelines to the teaching and testing of oral proficiency in that language.

## The Volume

The project volume (Stansfield & Harman, 1987) is a collection of reprinted articles and specially commissioned works published under the auspices of the Center for Applied Linguistics. It contains the 1986 generic ACTFL proficiency testing guidelines, introductory articles for those who are new to proficiency testing, and articles presenting the current thinking in adapting the guidelines to the LCTLs.

The volume also includes an updated version of the 1984 "Topical Bibliography of Proficiency Related Issues," which provides invaluable information on the development of the guidelines and their application to classroom instruction and testing as well as on proficiency concepts and the issue of accuracy. The issue of accuracy has become controversial in recent years due to differences of opinion as to its importance in a scale of communicative competence.

The final project activity was the distribution of the volume to over 200 professionals in the field of foreign language education, particularly in the LCTLs.

## RECURRENT ISSUES IN EXTENDING
## ACTFL GUIDELINES TO LCTLs

A number of issues raised during the course of the project may interest a wider audience in foreign language education. We realize that these issues, discussed in the following pages, are not all of the issues that may arise in extending the ACTFL guidelines to all languages. However, each of these issues is relevant to a number of LCTLs in addition to the ones discussed here.

### Arabic and the Problem of Diglossia

In developing oral (and aural) proficiency guidelines, Arabic presents the problem of a diglossic situation in which separate standards are invoked for the spoken and written language. Although Modern Standard Arabic (MSA)—the language taught by Arab speakers in schools and widely used in the media—presents a standard for the written language, there is no one dominant form of spoken Arabic in the Arab world.

The "educated native speaker" of Arabic (the standard on which the oral proficiency guidelines are usually based) typically uses the local colloquial dialect, whether in Morocco, Egypt, Lebanon, or another Arabic-speaking region. In writing the guidelines for Arabic oral proficiency, it is clearly impractical to produce or administer tests for all of the various Arabic colloquial dialects.

A practical and admittedly compromise solution chosen by Roger Allen (1985) was to use MSA for all language skills, including oral proficiency. This has the advantage of allowing a uniform set of standards to be written. In addition, MSA is the most commonly taught form of Arabic in the United States. Nevertheless, these guidelines do not adequately reflect the "real-world" use of spoken Arabic in which the local colloquial dialect is learned first and used in everyday situations. Indeed, many native speakers of Arabic do not speak MSA at all, which is a kind of lingua franca reserved for very formal or pan-Arab communication.

Another solution would be to prepare oral proficiency guidelines for a major colloquial dialect, such as Egyptian, while using MSA for the testing of reading and writing proficiency. However, the choice of the major dialect is problematic in that it may be merely a reflection of political or arbitrary considerations.

Standard procedure for the oral proficiency interview in Arabic is to present the stimuli in MSA, but to accept appropriate responses in any colloquial Arabic as well as in MSA. Although MSA is not the language of daily conversation, the use of MSA can be reasonably accepted as a mark of an educated native speaker at the highest levels of proficiency when required by the context (for example, giving a formal speech, delivering an academic lecture, or during formal introductions). Ultimately, as Allen (1987) pointed out, oral proficiency ratings need to reflect the use of both MSA and colloquial dialects in various sociolinguistic situations in accordance with the sociolinguistic rules followed by educated native speakers themselves.

In the final analysis, before a solution to the problem of the diglossic situation in Arabic can be reached, agreement is needed among Arabists regarding how far the Arabic guidelines should reflect the multidialectical realities, cultural politics, and linguistic aspirations of native speakers throughout the Arab world. Until agreement on these issues is reached, no definitive form of proficiency guidelines for Arabic can be written.

## Hindi and the Problem of Code-Switching

Hindi presents a challenge to the development of proficiency testing guidelines in a way similar to that of Arabic. In this case, the diglossia is in a different form, namely, Hindi-English code-switching. While code-switching may in some languages be an indication of low-level ability, appropriate Hindi-English code-switching is the mark of an "educated" native Hindi speaker.

The prevalent observation of Hindi-English code-switching is due to the dominant presence of English in India, where it has the status of a national language. For example, an engineer or a diplomat living in Delhi or Agra would likely use Hindi at home, in the street, with friends, and in informal settings. However, for professional purposes or in more formal settings, English typically takes precedence.

Moreover, a number of definite "rules" for Hindi-English code-switching exist that are relevant to the context of the dialogue. Thus code-switching could represent low-level proficiency in informal contexts but high-level proficiency in more formal ones. Thus, if a speaker were discussing a high-level topic, such as nuclear disarmament, the ability to carry out at least part of the conversation in Hindi would be an indication of high-level proficiency in Hindi.

One solution to this problem is to define oral proficiency testing guide-lines in terms of the purpose for which the nonnative speaker is learning Hindi. Thus, while educated native speakers of Hindi may not, on the whole, have the opportunity to develop their more formal linguistic skills in Hindi, foreigners studying Hindi for literacy and cultural research may be expected to attain a mastery above the norm even for educated native speakers. At the opposite extreme, in the context of national and interna-tional business conducted in India, English may be so commonly used as the language of communication that the need for any Hindi proficiency is excluded altogether.

In Hindi, as in other LCTLs, we have insufficient experience with the guidelines to judge their validity in the language-specific domains of pho-nology, morphology, and syntax. That is, we do not know how these lan-guage domains should appear in a description of proficiency at each level in the Hindi guidelines. Nor are we confident of the general guidelines' suitability for assessing control at the discourse and sociolinguistic levels.

As a solution to this problem, Gambhir (1987) proposed an approach to developing skill-level descriptions that may be useful to Hindi and to other LCTLs as well. The approach involves two stages. First, a linguistic analysis could be carried out on a large number of interviews in order to rate them according to the generic proficiency guidelines at different lev-els. The results could be used to form tentative descriptions of linguistic control at each proficiency level. Next, trained teachers and scholars would collectively adjust these descriptions based on their observations and experience. This approach would be objective in that it is data-based, yet it would be in accord with the intuitions and observations of experi-enced language specialists.

## Indonesian and the Importance of Sociolinguistic Factors

In developing guidelines for Indonesian, as for Hindi, research is needed to determine which features of grammar, vocabulary, and syntax are characteristic at each proficiency level. Some features that are typi-cally a problem in learning European languages are not a problem in Indonesian.

For example, tense poses very little problem to students of Indonesian as time is marked by adverbs rather than by verb forms. Also, Indonesian grammar focuses on the verb and the object. Therefore, Indonesians put less emphasis on the doer (subject) in their speech. On the other hand, competence in Indonesian involves the ability to make use of appropriate style and register and of the sociolinguistic rules that are both rigid and necessary for basic proficiency in Indonesian. As Wolff (1987) pointed out:

> Whereas a linguistic *faux pas* may be the cause of amusement or discomfort in Europe, in Indonesia it can be the cause of serious tensions. Unfortunately, Indonesian is one of those languages in which almost every time one opens one's mouth, a strong statement is made about human relations, social status, and the kind of person everyone involved in the conversation is.

Because of the extreme importance of the sociolinguistic function of the language, oral proficiency testing for Indonesian must develop stimuli that allow the examinee to demonstrate a mastery of sociolinguistic routines in a wide variety of contexts, including some contexts that are peculiar to the Indonesian culture. Although Indonesian does not require a total merging of language and culture, the language does involve sociolinguistic rules in a more pervasive way than in Western languages.

## African Languages and the Problem of Limited Resources

During the familiarization phase of the ACTFL/CAL project, we decided to concentrate on the problems confronting the African languages as a whole rather than concentrating on a single language. The African Language Group poses a rather difficult problem for the development of different sets of language-specific proficiency guidelines: Between 1,500 and 2,000 different languages are spoken in Africa. Moreover, the demand for instruction in these languages in the United States is quite low, and resources for instruction in these languages are very limited.

As a result, it is likely that guidelines can only be drafted for a relatively small number of African languages, and some work in this direction has begun on the part of African language specialists and the Title VI African Studies Centers.

First, agreement has been reached on categorizing 82 primary African languages into three groups according to priority. These groups represent the degree of importance that African language scholars attribute to each language. Thus the languages in the first group would be the first to be addressed through the development of proficiency guidelines. Next, a list of scholars was compiled to review proficiency interview protocols. In addition, a survey and evaluation of language teaching materials has been completed (see Dwyer, 1986a, 1986b).

Given the tremendous resource limitations, we selected the ACTFL Team Testing model (Dwyer & Hiple, 1987) in order to establish appropriate proficiency testing guidelines. In this approach, the oral interview is conducted by two persons instead of one: a native speaker of the target language who is not necessarily a trained proficiency evaluator and an ACTFL trained and certified evaluator who is not necessarily proficient in the target language.

This model parallels the linguist/native speaker-informant method often used to teach the less commonly taught languages. In this connection, African linguists agreed to a three-year plan that includes the organization of standard ACTFL workshops in English, French, and/or Arabic to certify African linguists. Future workshops are designed to prepare instructions for the native speaker and his or her role in the above-mentioned team testing model and to establish language specific guidelines for Hausa and Swahili.

There is no doubt that the language-specific guidelines must reflect the cultural milieu of Africa and the unique manner in which language is used there. It may be that certain high- or low-level tasks associated with the guidelines for Western languages are inappropriate in certain African contexts.

## CONCLUSIONS

The preceding discussion makes it clear that much work remains to be done in extending the proficiency guidelines beyond the commonly taught languages. The task raises issues not encountered when working with many Western languages. However, some practical suggestions for solutions have emerged from our experiences with the four languages detailed above.

As the introduction to the new set of generic ACTFL proficiency testing guidelines (published in 1986) states:

The 1986 guidelines should not be considered the definitive version, since the construction and utilization of language proficiency guidelines is a dynamic, interactive process. The academic sector, like the government sector, will continue to refine and update the criteria periodically to reflect the needs of the users and the advances of the profession.

Thus the development of both the generic and the language-specific proficiency testing guidelines is clearly an ongoing process. The recently completed joint ACTFL/CAL project for the familiarization of teachers of the LCTLs with the ACTFL proficiency guidelines has been one significant part of this process.

## REFERENCES

American Council on the Teaching of Foreign Languages (ACTFL). (1986). *ACTFL Proficiency Guidelines.* Hastings-on-Hudson, NY: Author.

Allen, R. (1985). Arabic proficiency guidelines. *al-'Arabiyya, 18,* 45–70.

Allen, R. (1987). The Arabic guidelines: Where now? In C. W. Stansfield & C. Harman (Eds.), *ACTFL Proficiency Guidelines for the Less Commonly Taught Languages.* Washington: Center for Applied Linguistics. (ERIC Document Reproduction Service No. ED 289 345)

Dwyer, D. J. (Ed.). (1986a). *The design and evaluation of African language learning materials.* (ERIC Document Reproduction Service No. ED 281 357)

Dwyer, D. J. (1986b). *A resource handbook for African languages.* (ERIC Document Reproduction Service No. ED 280 274)

Dwyer, D., & Hiple, D. (1987). African language teaching and ACTFL Team Testing. In C. W. Stansfield & C. Harman (Eds.), *ACTFL Proficiency Guidelines for the Less Commonly Taught Languages.* Washington: Center for Applied Linguistics. (ERIC Document Reproduction Service No. ED 289 345; also available in *Foreign Language Annals, 21,* 35–39, 1988)

Gambhir, V. (1987). Some preliminary thoughts about proficiency guidelines in Hindi. In C. W. Stansfield & C. Harman (Eds.), *ACTFL Proficiency Guidelines for the Less Commonly Taught Languages.* Washington: Center for Applied Linguistics. (ERIC Document Reproduction Service No. ED 289 345)

Hiple, D. (1986). A progress report on ACTFL guidelines, 1982–1986. In H. Byrnes & M. Canale (Eds.), *Defining and developing proficiency: Guidelines, implementations and concepts.* Lincolnwood, IL: National Textbook.

Stansfield, C. W., & Harman, C. (Eds.). (1987). *ACTFL Proficiency Guidelines for the Less Commonly Taught Languages.* Washington: Center for Applied Linguistics. (ERIC Document Reproduction Service No. ED 289 345)

Wolff, J. (1987). The application of the ILR-ACTFL test and guidelines to Indonesian. In C. W. Stansfield & C. Harman (Eds.), *ACTFL Proficiency Guidelines for the Less Commonly Taught Languages.* Washington: Center for Applied Linguistics. (ERIC Document Reproduction Service No. ED 289 345)

# PART III

# Immersion Education: Design, Implementation, and Evaluation

*Part III describes the state of the art concerning contemporary models of language education. These chapters cover the range of issues from program ingredients to program evaluation.*

Marguerite Ann Snow, in "Language Immersion: An Overview and Comparison" (Chapter 7), notes the historical origins of immersion education in the United States as deriving from the importation of similar programs in French immersion from Canada. She notes the four key features of immersion programs: (a) the delivery of subject matter (e.g., math, social studies) in the foreign language, (b) the separation of second-language students from native language speakers, (c) the promotion of additive bilingualism, and (d) the changing sequence and intensity of foreign language instruction as children move through the grade levels. Snow also notes the importance of participating in the immersion program for at least four to six years, strictly separating the languages of instruction into different time periods, and the role of home-school collaboration. Snow's overview chapter also identifies the goals of immersion education, including language proficiency, content mastery, and positive self- and cross-cultural attitudes and behaviors.

Snow reviews the literature on program effectiveness and on the variations in the immersion models. Her chapter concludes with a detailed description of three Spanish immersion programs that varied according to a number of features of program implementation. She reports that the best program was one that emphasized content instruction, was intense, involved the entire school, used separate English-speaking and Spanish-speaking instructors, and was associated with positive community integration into the program.

Nancy Rhodes, JoAnn Crandall, and Donna Christian, in ""Key Amigos": A Partial Immersion Program" (Chapter 8), trace the development of a partial immersion program at Key Elementary School in Arlington, Virginia. Their chapter includes a detailed program description, particularly with respect to the division of language instruction during the course of the program and the role of peer models. Their evaluation, covering a two-year period, demonstrated high satisfaction on the part of students, teachers, and parents as well as significant achievement gains. Although not without methodological limitations, this study supports the concept of bilingualism as a cognitive asset.

Kathryn J. Lindholm and Amado M. Padilla, in "A High School Bilingual Partial Immersion Program" (Chapter 9), underscore the value of two-way immersion programs for both native English speakers and non-native English speakers. The immersion program goals are to develop oral and academic Spanish proficiency, to increase school retention, to generate normal or above average academic achievement in traditional content areas, and to develop positive interpersonal and intergroup attitudes and behaviors. The underlying assumptions include the idea that bilingualism is a cognitive advantage, that content mastery transfers between languages, that purposeful instruction maximizes second-language learning, and that classroom heterogeneity and cooperative learning enhance teaching outcomes.

Lindholm and Padilla describe a high school partial immersion program and compare that program both with programs geared toward Spanish for native Spanish speakers and with a traditional Spanish instruction program that focuses on grammar and literature. In an analytical comparison, Lindholm and Padilla report a number of consistent differences among the three programs. Of course, native Spanish speakers obtained the highest proficiency scores, but, more important, the partial immersion students consistently outperformed the traditional Spanish-track students and reported much greater exposure to Spanish in the broader linguistic environment (including the media). They conclude that bilingual immersion programs can be tailored to meet the individual learning needs of students, particularly within the immersion framework.

Marguerite Ann Snow, in "Instructional Methodology in Immersion Foreign Language Education" (Chapter 10), is concerned with the teaching methods used in immersion foreign language education. She describes the strategies and techniques used by experienced immersion teachers and draws on insights from similar programs that are of benefit to the immersion model.

Snow's focus on instructional methodology includes discussions on vocabulary development, the role of culture, the personal attributes of teachers, and cooperative learning, among others. She highlights the multiple skills required of immersion teachers and summarizes the features of immersion classrooms that enhance learning. Snow concludes with an itemization of the important issues that educators and administrators must address in implementing an immersion foreign language program.

Snow, in "Spanish Language Attrition of Immersion Graduates" (Chapter 11), concludes this part of the volume with the description of a pilot assessment of foreign language attrition (i.e., loss of skills) on the part of immersion graduates who completed an elementary school immersion program. She noted that the type and intensity of continuing exposure to the foreign language was most important in predicting language retention and maintenance.

# 7

# Language Immersion
## An Overview and Comparison

## MARGUERITE ANN SNOW

This chapter provides an overview of the immersion model of foreign language education, including key instructional features of the model. A detailed description of three examples of the immersion model is provided. The programmatic and instructional features of the three sites are described and the educational outcomes of Spanish and English are compared. An exemplary version of the immersion model is proposed that maximizes the advantages of the model and offers a successful formula for achievement in both languages.

### HISTORICAL OVERVIEW OF THE IMMERSION MODEL

In 1963, dissatisfaction with current practices of teaching French, and a growing realization of the importance of French in Canadian life, were rallying points for a group of concerned Canadian parents to consider alternative approaches to the teaching of French as a second language (Lambert & Tucker, 1972). These parents felt that their children, like themselves a generation before, had been inadequately prepared by the school system to use French for any authentic real-life purpose outside of the classroom. The efforts of the parent group and a team of psychologists from McGill University were finally rewarded in 1965 with the creation of a new alternative—a French immersion program—that provided a total French environment when the children entered kindergarten. Today, the French immersion model, with its humble beginnings in the Montreal suburb of St. Lambert, has spread throughout the 10 Canadian provinces and boasted, in 1987, an enrollment of approximately 200,000 English-speaking children (Tourigny, 1987).

During the late 1960s, word spread to the United States, where several University of California, Los Angeles professors succeeded in finding local support for the establishment of a Spanish Immersion Program in Culver City, California, in 1971. Since the early 1970s, immersion programs have spread across the United States as well, albeit in a more limited way, so that presently there are at least 30 immersion programs representing a diversity of foreign languages, such as Spanish, German, French, Cantonese, and Japanese (Rhodes, 1987).

## KEY FEATURES OF
## THE TOTAL IMMERSION MODEL

Immersion education grew out of a grass-roots movement of English-speaking parents who sought a more effective approach to the teaching of French as a foreign language in the elementary schools in Canada. It is important to keep in mind, therefore, that this chapter is concerned with describing an educational approach for the teaching of *foreign languages* to *language majority* students. It is not the purpose of this chapter to treat the many varied and interesting approaches to bilingual education and ESL instruction in the United States that are designed for *language minority* (non-English-speaking) students.

### Four Key Features

The immersion model rests on four key features that provide a strong theoretical and pedagogical foundation for its application both as a model of foreign language education specifically, and more generally and importantly, as an effective model of elementary education:

(1) The second language is used for the *delivery of subject matter instruction.* That is, the second language is the medium of instruction for school subjects such as mathematics, science, and social studies. Immersion education is based on the belief that children are able to learn a second language in the same way they learned their first language: (a) by being exposed to authentic input in the second language and (b) by needing to use the second language for real, communicative purposes. Viewed from this perspective, subject matter teaching is also second-language teaching. The standard school curriculum becomes the basis for meaningful input, because the purpose of school is to teach subject matter. Immersion programs capitalize on this content learning for language acquisition purposes and provide an authentic need for students to communicate information about the subject matter. Immersion education actually provides a two-for-one opportunity: Students learn the regular school subjects that all youngsters must study in elementary school while "incidentally" learning a second language.

A key feature of immersion education is that language learning occurs through the vehicle of content instruction. There is little or no explicit teaching of the second language compared with other, more traditional foreign language teaching methods. Thus incidental learning is a feature of the model, but is not to be interpreted as "casual" or "haphazard." On the contrary, in the actual delivery of instruction, language teaching aims can indeed be very purposeful.

(2) Second language *learners benefit from being separated from native speakers* of the target language. Because the learners are all in the same "linguistic boat" (Krashen, 1984), they receive instruction especially prepared and designed for their developing levels of proficiency in the second language.

(3) *Immersion programs reflect the broader perspective of the world outside of school*, specifically in the United States. English-speaking children in immersion programs, although they receive the majority of their elementary school education in their second language, are in no danger of losing their first language. English is pervasive in their world—on TV and radio, in conversations with parents and friends, even in international travel to many foreign countries. In technical terms, immersion education promotes *additive bilingualism* (Lambert, 1984), because immersion students are adding to their linguistic repertoire and sense of identity through the experience of being schooled in the foreign language. The opposite situation is experienced by many language minority children, for example,

native Spanish-speaking children, who are thrust into a *subtractive* environment. In a subtractive school environment, the new language (English) is learned at the expense of the native language. Powerful sociocultural influences and differences in academic achievement levels are believed to result from these contrasting types of school experiences.

(4) The *sequence and intensity* of first- and second-language instruction changes over time. In the standard total immersion program, all initial instruction (starting in kindergarten) is provided in the second language. Instruction in the first language is added to the curriculum to some degree (e.g., English language arts and/or a selected content area such as social studies) in grade three, and gradually more and more instruction is delivered in English in the upper elementary grade levels. Of course, there are many variations of the total immersion model (some will be discussed later in this section), but the key features that distinguish a total immersion program from other types of foreign language instruction programs are the early onset of second-language instruction and the fact that the second language is used for subject matter teaching.

## Other Important Features of the Immersion Model

(5) *Programs have a duration of at least four to six years.* Second-language learning is a gradual process. It takes many years to develop a strong academic and social foundation in the second language. Results of immersion programs must be evaluated over the entire period of elementary school. Parents, students, and teachers must be aware of this fact so that reasonable expectations are set from the beginning of immersion education.

(6) *The two languages are separated for instruction.* This principle is applied in two important ways in the immersion classroom. The same material is *never* repeated in the two languages. There is no translation of content instruction from the immersion language to the first language, nor is there repetition of delivery in one language and then the other. The second application of this principle is the strict language domains of the instructors. It is always preferable, especially in the earlier grades, to have both an English-speaking model and a second-language model. This is usually accomplished by setting up English-speaking exchange teachers to conduct the English language arts component in the lower grades. In addi-

tion to maintaining separate language models, specialization of instruction in this way provides an important role for monolingual English teachers.

(7) *Home-school collaboration is emphasized.* Since the inception of immersion programs, parents have played a very important role in setting up new immersion programs and providing continuing support for established programs.

## GOALS OF IMMERSION EDUCATION

The theoretical features of immersion education provide the basis for the articulation of the specific goals of immersion programs.

(1) Immersion students will make normal progress in achieving the objectives of the standard elementary school curriculum.

(2) They will maintain normal progress in development of the first language (English).

(3) They will develop functional proficiency in speaking, listening, reading, and writing the foreign language.

(4) They will develop positive attitudes toward themselves as English speakers and toward representatives of the ethnic or linguistic community of the foreign language they are learning.

A fifth goal may be desirable or mandatory in some American immersion settings:

(5) They will have the opportunity to be schooled in an integrated setting with participants from a variety of ethnic groups.

### How the Goals Measure Up

Unlike the parents of St. Lambert, who were willing to risk enrolling their children in an experimental program in 1965 with only great enthusiasm to sustain themselves, there is a great deal of research evidence currently available regarding the effectiveness of immersion education. The past 20 years have produced an accumulation of research studies initially aimed at allaying parental fears and, ultimately, designed to answer the broader questions of the effectiveness of the immersion model. The following are brief summaries of the research findings concerning the four general goals of immersion education.

*Scholastic achievement.* Immersion students have been tested using standardized tests in different subject matter areas (e.g., English reading, mathematics, science). These tests have typically been administered in English even though the subject matter may have been taught exclusively or mainly in the second language. The results from controlled comparison studies in Canadian and American programs consistently indicate that immersion students do as well as, or better than, their monolingual peers in the subject areas tested (Campbell, 1984; Lapkin & Swain, 1984).

*English language development.* The overall findings from standardized testing of English language arts are that immersion students perform on par with their monolingual counterparts. In the first few years of an immersion program, there is generally an expected lag in performance because the students have not yet been exposed to English language arts in the curriculum. The lag disappears once English language arts are introduced into the curriculum at grade two, three, or four (depending on the program). Indeed, it is interesting that the lag is so consistently small. This finding provides tentative evidence of the positive influence of the use of English outside of school and the degree to which skills (especially reading skills) are transferred from the second language to the native language.

*Second-language development.* The research findings on second-language development have been examined from two different perspectives. Studies have been conducted comparing students from more traditional foreign language programs of the 20–30 minutes per day variety (referred to as "core French" in Canada and "FLES," foreign language in the elementary school, in the United States; see Campbell, Gray, Rhodes, & Snow, 1985). In these studies, immersion students scored significantly higher across the board in all the skill areas tested. However, comparisons of this type become almost impossible in the upper grades. The differential in attained proficiency becomes so great that the same tests cannot be given as they become too difficult for the "core French" and FLES students and, conversely, too easy for the immersion students.

Increasingly, it has become clear that a more appropriate comparison group is native speakers of the second language. This kind of comparison study has been possible in Canada, where, in certain provinces, there exist native French speakers attending French-medium schools. The results are generally examined in two categories: receptive skills (listening and reading) and productive skills (speaking and writing). The Canadian findings consistently indicate that the French receptive skills of immersion students are nativelike by the end of elementary school. The same is not true of their productive skills, however. Findings from virtually all immersion programs, whether in Canada or the United States, indicate that the productive skills of immersion students are not nativelike. Immersion students achieve a level of fluency rarely, if ever, attained in any other type of foreign language program; however, their speech and writing lack the grammatical accuracy and lexical variety of native speakers.

*Attitudinal development.* Studies have shown no evidence of any problems in emotional or social adjustment among students in any of the different types of immersion programs. Several studies have examined such social-psychological factors as attitudes toward representatives of the second-language group and perceived psychological distance from the second-language group. In general, immersion students in the early grades demonstrate very positive attitudes toward themselves and representatives of the second-language group. Their attitudes become less positive, however, as the students progress through the immersion program in the upper grades. These changes have been attributed to increased peer pressure toward conformity as children grow older, continued socialization of ethnic prejudice, or general developmental changes in attitudes. Further study needs to address these important social-psychological effects of immersion schooling.

## VARIATIONS OF THE IMMERSION MODEL

The main focus of this chapter is the total immersion model, which was first established in Canada and is now in place in many American schools. As discussed, the two key features of total immersion are the time of onset of second-language instruction and the intensity of instruction throughout the elementary school program. In *total* immersion programs, 100% of instruction in kindergarten through grade two is provided in the second language. By the upper grades, at least 50% of instruction continues to be offered in the second language. Since 1965, several variants of the total immersion model have been implemented that may be more desirable or more feasible depending on local needs and resources. These variants are described in the following section.

### Early Partial Immersion

Early partial immersion is a program in which less than 100% of curriculum instruction during the primary grades is provided in the second language. The amount of second-language instruction varies from program to program, but 50% first-language instruction and 50% second-language instruction is the most common formula from kindergarten through grade six. Reading is generally taught in both languages.

### Delayed Immersion

Delayed immersion is a variation of the immersion model in which the second language is not used as a medium of instruction in elementary school until grade four or five. Accordingly, students in delayed immersion programs learn to read in their first language. Often, students in delayed immersion programs receive some second-language instruction earlier in elementary school when the second language is taught as a school subject (e.g., Core French or FLES).

### Late Immersion

Late immersion is a type of immersion in which intensive use of the second language does not occur until the end of elementary school (grade six) or the beginning of secondary school. Late immersion students usually receive some second-language instruction in the earlier grades, but the second language is not used as the medium of instruction for subjects in the regular school curriculum.

### Double Immersion

Double immersion is a program that employs *two* nonnative languages for instruction during the elementary grades. The two languages are usually selected for their sociocultural significance, perhaps one for economic or social benefits and the other for its religious or cultural importance. Double immersion programs can be classified as "early immersion" if they begin in the primary grades or as "delayed immersion" if instruction in the two languages is held off until the upper elementary grades.

IMPLEMENTATION OF THREE
SPANISH IMMERSION PROGRAMS

This section of the chapter examines three examples of the immersion model. The programmatic and instructional features of each site are described and the educational outcomes of Spanish and English are briefly summarized. The three programs are classified as immersion because they meet the criteria discussed earlier. Namely, in all three sites, the second language (Spanish) is used as the medium of instruction for substantial amounts of the regular elementary school curriculum. The programs, however, also differ in a number of notable ways in their implementation of the total immersion model.

### Site 1

Site 1 is the oldest immersion program in the United States. The program is divided between two different schools: kindergarten through grade five are located at an elementary school site; grade six is located at the local middle school. The kindergarten through grade five immersion program is a program within a school where there are traditional English-only classrooms on the same site. The predominantly Anglo population of students is enrolled on a voluntary basis starting in kindergarten.

In kindergarten and first grade, all instruction is given in Spanish. English language arts and reading are taught for one hour in grades two and three. In grades four to five, there is an approximate 60%-40% division of the curriculum in Spanish and English, respectively. The teachers at Site 1 perform the Spanish and English instructional functions. Although native Spanish speakers are accepted into the kindergarten through grade-five program, only a few have participated through the years. In the late 1980s, however, native Spanish speakers have been integrated into grade six at the middle school to create a two-way program (see Chapter 9, Lindholm & Padilla, this volume). A partial immersion program continues at the middle school in grades seven and eight in which two classes per day are offered in Spanish. Parental involvement has become more active in recent years with the establishment of a parent support group. Through the efforts of the parent group, exchanges have been set up in which a group of immersion students lives for one month in Guadalajara, Mexico, and a group of Mexican students studies in the middle school in Southern California.

**Table 7.1** Summary of Programmatic and Instructional Features of Three Spanish Immersion Programs

| Feature | Site 1 | Site 2 | Site 3 |
|---|---|---|---|
| 1. Program type | one-way immersion model | one-way immersion model | one-way immersion model |
| | established 1971 | established 1977 | established 1977 |
| | program within a school | total school program | program within a school |
| | grades K–5 (grade 6 now part of middle school) | grades K–6 | grades K–6 |
| | neighborhood school | magnet school (90% bussed, 10% local) | magnet school |
| | no partial immersion program available in grades K–5 | partial immersion program available for students entering in grades 3–6 | partial immersion program available for students entering in grades 3–6 |
| 2. Program goals | scholastic achievement in all subject areas | scholastic achievement in all subject areas | scholastic achievement in all subject areas |
| | development of L1 | development of L1 | development of L1 |
| | functional competence in L2 | functional competence in L2 | functional competence in L2 |
| | positive attitudes to L2 culture & people | positive attitudes to L2 culture & people | positive attitudes to L2 culture & people |
| 3. Interlocking features | native Spanish speakers accepted in K–5 program (not systematic program) | native Spanish speakers specifically excluded from program; noninterlocking in grades K–6 | native Spanish speakers specifically excluded from program; noninterlocking in grades K–6 |
| | interlocking in grade 6 | | |

**Table 7.1** Summary of Programmatic and Instructional Features of Three Spanish Immersion Programs (continued)

| Feature | Site 1 | Site 2 | Site 3 |
|---|---|---|---|
| 4. Participants | voluntary program parent selected<br><br>predominantly Anglo | voluntary program parent selected<br><br>integration formula not to exceed 49% minority | voluntary program parent selected<br><br>integration formula not to exceed 49% minority |
| 5. Amount of instruction in English (K–6) | grades K–1 100% L2<br><br>grades 2–3 1-hour English reading/language arts<br><br>grades 4–6 60%–40% Spanish-English | grades K–2 100% L2<br><br>grades 3–6 1-hour English reading/language arts 80%–20% Spanish-English | grades K–2 100% L2<br><br>grades 3–6 1-hour English reading/language arts 80%–20% Spanish-English |
| 6. Teacher variable | no separation of language role; teacher has *dual* language Spanish-English role<br><br>no instructional aides<br><br>no resource teacher | separation of language role; separate Spanish and English teachers<br><br>instructional aides<br><br>resource teacher on site | separation of language role; separate Spanish and English teachers<br><br>instructional aides<br><br>resource teacher on site |
| 7. Articulation | partial immersion in grades 6–8 | partial immersion in grades 7–12 | partial immersion in grades 7–12 |
| 8. Extracurricular activity | exchange program with John Kennedy School in Guadalajara, Mexico | field trips to Mexico; exchange programs with Mexicali, Mexico | field trips to Mexico; exchange program with Mexicali, Mexico |

**Table 7.1** Summary of Programmatic and Instructional Features of Three Spanish Immersion Programs (continued)

| Feature | Site 1 | Site 2 | Site 3 |
|---|---|---|---|
| 9. Parental involvement | parent support group (ALL) classroom volunteers | parent booster groups classroom volunteers | parent booster group classroom volunteers |
| 10. Evaluation | standardized testing: CTBS English CTBS Español | standardized testing: CTBS English CTBS Español (through 1985), now La Prueba | standardized testing: CTBS English CTBS Español (through 1985), now La Prueba |
| 11. Support/funding | district funded | district funded as magnet school | district funded as magnet school |

## Site 2

The immersion program at Site 2 was established in 1977 for kindergarten through grade six. It is a total school program, that is, all students attending the school are enrolled in the immersion program. The school serves as a voluntary magnet school for the district's integration plan, therefore, the majority (90%) of the students are bussed in from outside the school's boundaries. The integration formula specifies that the student population is not to exceed a 49% minority enrollment. In kindergarten through grade two, the students receive all their instruction in Spanish; in grades three through six there is one hour of English language arts and reading. The total ratio of Spanish to English is approximately 80%-20% by the end of elementary school. In Site 2 there are separate teachers for the Spanish and English components of the curriculum. A partial immersion program is available for those students entering the school in grades three to six.

Native Spanish speakers are excluded from the elementary immersion program. Site 2 offers an articulated program with partial immersion programs available in junior high school and high school. Junior high students can select from a variety of course offerings in Spanish, including science, mathematics, art, home economics, music, and physical education; in the high school, partial immersion students take three subjects taught in Spanish. Extracurricular activities in the elementary school include frequent field trips to Mexico and longer exchange programs with Mexican schools. A parent booster group sponsors fund-raising activities to aid the students in these activities.

## Site 3

The immersion program at Site 3 has generally the same instructional characteristics as Site 2; because both programs are located in the same district and there is close coordination between the two sites. There are, however, three programmatic features that distinguish the two schools. Whereas Site 2 is a total school program, Site 3 is a program within a school. Second, Site 3 is located in a low-income neighborhood whereas Site 2 is located in a middle-class area of the same district. Third, there is no partial immersion program at Site 3 for newly enrolled students.

## COMPARISON OF THREE PROGRAMS

The three immersion programs were selected for further study because they contrast in their implementation of the total immersion model. The first distinguishing instructional characteristic of the programs is the intensity of second-language instruction. This feature can be further divided into two elements: onset of first language instruction and use of the second language to teach subject matter in the core curriculum. When the three sites are compared on these features, there is a major programmatic difference between Site 1 and the design used in Sites 2 and 3. In Site 1, English is introduced in second grade and gradually incorporated into the curriculum for subject matter teaching. The ratio of time allocated to teaching in the two languages is approximately 60%-40% (Spanish-English). Thus, in Site 1, English takes on an expanded role in the upper elementary grades. In contrast, English language arts and reading are not introduced until the third grade at Sites 2 and 3, and, throughout the elementary grades, the use of English is confined to the teaching of English language arts. Therefore, for Sites 2 and 3, English is not the medium of instruction for the teaching of other core subjects as at Site 1 in the upper grades.

The second distinguishing feature of the three schools is the actual physical setup of the immersion programs. Sites 1 and 3 are programs within a school. In other words, there are traditional English-only classrooms within the same school. Consequently, the school environment remains largely English-speaking. Site 2, on the other hand, is a total school program. Students in Site 2 are part of a more intensive Spanish-oriented milieu in which the speaking of Spanish is a natural element of their school environment.

The role of the teacher is a third distinguishing instructional feature of the three programs. In Site 1, the teacher assumes the dual responsibility for both Spanish and English instruction after grade one, whereas separate instructors teach the Spanish and English components of the curriculum in Sites 2 and 3 in the early grades. The curricular design of Sites 2 and 3 sets up clear boundaries for language use in the classroom.

Finally, opportunity for interaction with native Spanish speakers is the fourth distinguishing feature of the immersion programs. Traditionally, immersion students have had few opportunities for authentic use of the second language with native speakers. The geographic proximity of Sites 2 and 3 to Mexico could create more opportunities for active use of the language than those available to students in Site 1. In addition, all three schools have organized field trips and exchanges to provide extracurricular activities for their students. Finally, the curricular design of Sites 2 and 3 retains the "sheltered" element of the immersion model by specifically excluding native Spanish speakers from participation in the immersion program. While native speakers have always been accepted into the program in Site 1, only a few have participated through the years.

## Spanish and English Language Achievement

Fifth- and sixth-grade students in the three immersion sites were administered the Modern Language Association (MLA) *Cooperative Test of Spanish* (1963). This test assesses Spanish proficiency in the skill areas of listening, reading, and writing. Results revealed relatively high percentile rankings on all three subtests. Students scored highest on the listening subtest, followed by reading and then writing. Thus the receptive skills of listening and reading were more developed in these students than the productive skill of writing; these findings corroborate immersion results from Canada. Furthermore, for all three subtests of the MLA, students from Site 2 scored significantly higher than those in Sites 1 and 3.

Further comparisons were possible with analyses of the district-administered CTBS-English and Español test results. Although Site 1 ranked first on the vocabulary subtest of the reading test and on the computation subtest of the mathematics test, Site 2 scored significantly higher on the total reading, total language, and total mathematics tests of the CTBS-English.

It is also interesting to note that grade-five students, at all three sites, are reading at least one grade or better above their grade level (5.8) in their first language, English. Likewise, the students are above grade level in English language achievement. The weakest of the language skills seems to be spelling; however, two of the three sites are still at grade level. The mathematics scores yielded a similar pattern. All groups are above grade level for the subtests of computation and application and on the total mathematics test. These findings thus provide further evidence that students can receive substantial amounts of the elementary school curriculum (in the case of Site 1), and all content teaching (Sites 2 and 3), through the medium of the second language without impairment of scholastic skills. Indeed, according to these findings, these programs may enhance academic achievement in some cases.

The CTBS-Español results provide an interesting comparison with the MLA Spanish scores. On the CTBS-Español, all sites fell below grade level in Spanish reading with the main deficiency being in vocabulary development. For Spanish reading achievement, Site 3 outranked the other two sites. In contrast, the Spanish mathematics scores for the two sites reported were well above grade level, even for the concepts and application subtests, which require the reading of word problems. Site 2 ranked ahead of Site 1 in mathematics on the CTBS-Español.

It is clear from the discussion of the MLA Cooperative Test of Spanish and the CTBS-English results that students in Site 2 demonstrated significantly higher achievement in both their first and second languages than their counterparts in Sites 1 and 3. Because variables such as sex, IQ, SES, and ethnicity cannot be controlled for in self-selected programs such as immersion programs, we cannot determine with certainty the causal variables leading to the superior success of Site 2 on these standardized tests. We can, however, treat Site 2 as an exemplary program and reexamine the programmatic and instructional features of the program that form the backdrop for the high levels of language development attained.

The objective of the study reported in this chapter was to examine the particular constellation of programmatic and instructional features that compose an effective foreign language program. It is proposed that five programmatic and instructional features of Site 2 combine to provide a successful formula for first-language achievement in English and second-language acquisition of Spanish among language majority students.

First, the intensity of instruction at Site 2 is great. The introduction of English is delayed a year until third grade and all core subjects are taught in Spanish throughout elementary school. Second, Site 2 provides a total-school Spanish milieu for its students. Thus the influence of the second language is carried beyond the classroom into the school grounds, offices, library, and so on. This setup provides an environment conducive to the use of Spanish for nonacademic, social purposes, thereby extending the range of uses to which the students can apply their Spanish. The third exemplary feature of Site 2 is the division of language functions between the Spanish teacher and the English teacher. This clear division facilitates control over the use of English and Spanish at appropriate times in the classroom. The fourth factor, which may contribute to the success of the immersion program at Site 2, is the attitudinal and language-use patterns of the students. On an attitude/motivation self-report questionnaire, 71% of the students at Site 2 rated their Spanish language experience as "good," indicating positive attitudes toward the learning process. All of

**Table 7.2**  Programmatic and Instructional Features of an Exemplary
Immersion Program Site—Site 2

Shared Assumptions of the Immersion Model:

1. The L2 used as the medium of instruction to teach the standard elementary
   school curriculum.
2. The immersion model serves the foreign language needs of English-speaking
   language majority students

Distinguishing Characteristics:

1. Intensity of L2 instruction/onset of L1 instruction:
   L2 only—kindergarten through grade 3;
   L1 for one hour—grades 4 through 6 (80%–20%, Spanish–English)

2. Physical setup: total school program creates a Spanish milieu

3. Role of instructors: separate Spanish/English teachers

4. Positive attitudes and language use outside of school

5. Sheltered student population: Spanish speakers excluded from participation

the students at Site 2 reported speaking Spanish away from home; they
also had the highest travel rate to Spanish-speaking countries. The final
distinguishing feature of Site 2 is the sheltered student population. Native
Spanish speakers are excluded from participation, allowing immersion students to receive language input appropriate to their ability.

CONCLUSION

The motivation for this study was the need for further evaluation of
existing immersion programs and a closer examination of the features that
combine to create effective foreign language programs. The programmatic
and instructional features that provide the setting for high levels of first-
and second-language development in three different sites were described
in depth. The results provide program and curriculum designers with a
model plan for implementing an exemplary program that combines all the
best features of the immersion model.

# REFERENCES

Campbell, R. N. (1984). The immersion education approach to foreign language teaching. In *Studies on immersion education: A collection for United States educators* (pp. 114–143). Sacramento: California State Department of Education.

Campbell, R. N., Gray, T. C., Rhodes, N. C., & Snow, M. A. (1985). Foreign language learning in the elementary school: A comparison of three language programs. *Modern Language Journal, 69*(1), 44–54.

Dolson, D. (1985). *The application of immersion education in the United States.* Rosslyn, VA: National Clearinghouse for Bilingual Education.

Krashen, S. (1984). Immersion: Why it works and what it has taught us. In *Language and society: The immersion phenomenon* (Vol. 12, pp. 61–64). Ottawa, Canada: Commissioner of Official Languages of Canada.

Lambert, W. E. (1984). An overview of issues in immersion education. In California State Department of Education, *Studies on immersion education.* Sacramento: California State Department of Education.

Lambert, W. E., & Tucker, G. R. (1972). *Bilingual education of children: The St. Lambert experiment.* Rowley, MA: Newbury House.

Lapkin, S., & Swain, M. (1984). Research update. In *Language and society: The immersion phenomenon* (Vol. 12, pp. 48–54). Ottawa, Canada: Commissioner of Official Languages of Canada.

Modern Language Association. (1963). *Cooperative foreign language test.* Menlo Park, CA: Addison-Wesley.

Rhodes, N. (1987). *Total and partial immersion language programs in U.S. elementary schools.* Washington, DC: Center for Applied Linguistics.

Tourigny, R. (1987). *Immersion in Canada: 200,000 students and going strong.* Paper presented at the Advocates for Language Learning Conference, Washington, DC.

# 8

# *"Key Amigos"*
## *A Partial Immersion Program*

NANCY RHODES
JOANN CRANDALL
DONNA CHRISTIAN

## HISTORY OF THE PROGRAM

During the 1985–1986 school year, staff of the ESOL/HILT program in the Arlington Public Schools began to exchange information and ideas with their counterparts in the Hartford (Connecticut) Public Schools Bilingual Program Office. These activities were prompted by the research in both school systems by the Center for Language Education and Research (CLEAR) and the Center for Applied Linguistics (CAL). At one point in spring 1986, two representatives from Hartford visited the program in Arlington; in May, a reciprocal visit was made to Hartford by two individuals from Arlington. The discussions in both cases were far ranging but dealt extensively with program models, methods for educating language minority students, and the second-language education of majority students. As a result of these meetings, a plan was set in motion to establish a partial immersion program at Key Elementary School. The idea was to begin with a first-grade classroom, with students from English-speaking and non-English-speaking backgrounds, and to establish the class within the "gifted and talented" track at that school. Instruction would be divided equally between English and Spanish. For the English speakers, this class would provide a partial immersion experience, in which they would develop Spanish language skills through the use of Spanish in the classroom. The Spanish speakers would continue to develop their English language skills, but would also have an opportunity to maintain and expand their Spanish skills. A search for teachers with appropriate qualifications was undertaken, and two teachers (one for the English component and another for the Spanish component) were identified.

By the end of the summer, the program was in place. CLEAR staff agreed to provide assistance in monitoring the program, providing staff development, and preparing a program review at the end of the school year. The first of many meetings took place involving Key Elementary and CLEAR staff just before the school year began. Visits were also arranged for teachers and interested parents to a local bilingual program (Oyster School in Washington, D.C.) and to local immersion programs (Montgomery County, Maryland). As a result, school staff gained access to a network of local educators who were concerned with similar issues.

## DESCRIPTION OF THE PROGRAM

### Program Design

The Key Partial Immersion Program was designed so that "second language learning is done in a way similar to how children acquire their first language: they learn it in order to take part in meaningful and interesting communication" (from a report on the program prepared by Katharine Panfil, Foreign Language Supervisor for Arlington Public Schools). Half of each day is conducted in English and half in Spanish, providing an "immersion" experience for the nonnative speakers of the language. Further, because the class includes native speakers of both languages, the students can turn to their fellow students as language learning resources.

Two first-grade classes were paired for the first year of the program. Both classes followed the regular first-grade curriculum, but one (the "immersion" class) received instruction for a half day in English and a half day in Spanish. With the students switching classrooms at the lunch break, the change from one language to another was easily demarcated. In the morning, the immersion students were instructed in language arts and mathematics in English. After lunch, they moved to the other teacher's room, where they studied science, social studies, and Spanish language arts in Spanish. The second first-grade class also switched rooms at lunch, but their instruction from both teachers was in English. Thus the second class could be viewed as a "control group" for evaluative purposes, although students were not randomly assigned to the two classes. Special classes (music, art, physical education, library) occurred as scheduled in the regular first-grade curriculum for both groups and were offered in English.

During the English portion of the day, the pilot class followed the regular first-grade curriculum and used materials comparable to other first-grade classrooms. During the Spanish portion of the day, the first-grade science and social studies curriculum was followed despite a comparative dearth in Spanish language materials for those subject areas. For Spanish language arts, there were some texts and readers, but again the supply was much more limited. Supplementary Spanish language materials, such as library books, audiovisual aids, and so forth, were also limited.

*Personnel*

A native speaker of Spanish provided the Spanish language instruction to the immersion class. The school principal assumed responsibility for all phases of implementation, and the ESOL/HILT Resource Specialist gave ongoing support for the teachers and students in the program. In addition, the foreign language supervisor assisted at the county level through support for staff and curriculum development. Other staff at Key, including the reading specialist and the department chairs, kept informed about the progress of the students and provided support as needed.

*Class Composition*

The partial immersion class began with an enrollment of 17 children. Of these, 9 were native speakers of Spanish and 8 were native speakers of English. During the school year, 5 students transferred into the immersion class: 3 native speakers of other languages (Armenian, Chinese, and Vietnamese) who had been mainstreamed into English-medium classes and two native English speakers. For the most part, then, the class contained 22 students: 9 Spanish speakers and 13 English speakers. The comparison class contained a smaller proportion of native English speakers and was smaller overall. Its composition changed during the year as well, but for most of the year, there were 14 students, including 5 native speakers of English, 5 native Spanish speakers, and 4 native speakers of other languages.

## Evaluation Procedures

Arlington staff requested that CAL/CLEAR provide an evaluation of the immersion program's first year of operation. A plan was developed to address the following questions:

(1)  What is the English and Spanish proficiency of students in the immersion program, and how does it change over the years?

(2)  How well do the immersion students do in content area subjects? Do they make academic progress comparable to other first graders?

(3)  Are cross-cultural and language attitudes enhanced by participation in the program?

(4)  How do parents and other members of the school view the program?

(5)  How might the program be improved?

In addition to ongoing involvement by CLEAR in a variety of advisory capacities, several types of information collection activities were specifically undertaken.

From January through March, CLEAR staff systematically conducted classroom observations of the immersion class, observing both the English (morning) and the Spanish (afternoon) instructional periods. The observations were staggered so that all the days of the week were sampled at least twice. In addition, several observations were conducted with the paired class to provide a basis for comparison of instruction in the immersion and all-English classrooms. CLEAR staff also had numerous opportunities to visit the classes at other times, before and after the observation period, and to talk informally with the immersion teachers and other Key staff.

A range of data were collected on the students to assess their academic progress and language development. In the fall and spring, the Language Assessment Scales (LAS) were administered to provide a measure of both English and Spanish proficiency for the immersion students. The Boehm R Test of Basic Concepts assessed the students' conceptual development in English and Spanish. Finally, the students' mastery of content-area subjects was examined from scores on end-of-unit tests in social studies, science, and mathematics. We also took into consideration daily attendance when looking at the success of the program as a whole.

In order to determine participants' perceptions of the program, the students were interviewed in small groups and asked about their feelings on learning in Spanish and in English. Teachers were also interviewed, including those teaching in the program, four teachers from other classrooms, the reading specialist, and the ESOL/HILT resource specialist. Although not formally interviewed, other staff members' perceptions were also tapped, including those of the principal. Finally, the parents of the immersion students were asked to describe their feelings, in phone interviews (either in English or Spanish), about the program.

The results of these information collection efforts are described in the following section.

## STUDENT PROGRESS AND SATISFACTION

### English and Spanish Language Development

The Language Assessment Scales (LAS) were used to measure English and Spanish language development through a five-part test that measured students' ability with minimal pairs (identifying words as being the same or different), vocabulary (naming an object represented by a drawing), pronunciation (repeating a word), comprehension (listening to a tape and then pointing to a picture that is described on the tape), and oral production (retelling a story). The first four parts of the test made up 50% of the total score, while the story retelling made up the other 50%. Students were rated on a scale from 0–5: scores 0, 1, and 2 indicated levels of a "nonspeaker"; 3 indicated a "limited speaker"; and 4 and 5 indicated a "fluent" (proficient) speaker.

*English speakers.* On the English test in the fall, of the 12 native English speakers and native speakers of languages other than English or Spanish, three were at level 3, seven at level 4, and two at level 5. By spring, two were at level 4 and the rest had moved up to level 5. The scores were comparable for the paired class.

On the Spanish test in the fall, all the nonnative Spanish speakers scored at level 1. By the spring, four students had moved up to level 2. It should be noted here that, although the scores do not show a dramatic improvement from fall to spring, the test administrator commented that there was a noticeable improvement in the students' comprehension and attentiveness during test taking, especially during the story portion of the test. In addition, individual component test scores showed a systematic increase, even though a change in overall level may not have occurred.

*Spanish speakers.* On the English test in the fall, among the 9 native Spanish speakers, one student was at level 1, two students were at level 3, three at level 4, and three at level 5. By the spring test, one student was at level 3, one was at level 4, and seven were at level 5.

In the fall on the Spanish test, one student was at level 3, three at level 4 and five at level 5. By spring, all were at level 5.

Three important conclusions can be drawn from the above findings: (a) The native English-speaking students in the pilot class performed as well in English as the students in the comparison class (who had been receiving all of their instruction in English); (b) the English-speaking students in the pilot class improved their Spanish from fall to spring, as demonstrated by their scores on the five parts of the LAS, even though their overall level may not have changed; and (c) the Spanish-speaking students in the pilot class improved their Spanish *and* English from fall to spring.

### Conceptual Development

The Boehm Test of Basic Concepts is designed to measure children's mastery of concepts considered necessary for achievement in the first years of school. Boehm test results may be used both to identify children with deficiencies in this area and to identify individual concepts on which the children could profit from instruction. The test consists of 50 pictorial items arranged in approximate order of increasing difficulty. The examiner reads a statement describing each set of pictures and instructs the children to mark the one that illustrates the concept being tested.

*English speakers.* On the English version of the Boehm in the fall, the native speakers of English in the pilot class averaged 45.9 items correct, while the native speakers of languages other than English or Spanish averaged 44.6. In the spring, their scores had increased to 48.1 and 47.0, respectively, an increase of 2.2 and 2.4 points. In the paired class, native speakers of English averaged 47.0 items correct in the fall and 49.2 in the spring, a gain of 2.2; and native speakers of other languages scored 45.0 in the fall and 48.0 in the spring, for a gain of 3.0. Thus the gains for these students on the English version of the Boehm were quite similar, between 2 and 3 points.

On the Spanish version of the Boehm, the native English speakers scored 27.2 in the fall and 29.2 in the spring, a gain of 2 points. Speakers of other languages increased by 7.3 points, from 23.0 in the fall to 30.3 in the spring.

*Spanish speakers.* On the English test, the native speakers of Spanish in the pilot class scored 41.5 items correct in the fall and 46.1 in the spring, for a gain of 4.6 points. On the Spanish version, they received similar gain scores, 41.4 in the fall and 45.9 in the spring, improving by 4.5 points. In the comparison class, the native Spanish speakers had an average of 45.3 in the fall and 47.7 in the spring on the English version of the Boehm, a gain of 2.4 points. They were not given the Spanish test.

We can make several observations on the basis of the Boehm scores: (a) All groups of students showed gains in their understanding of concepts from fall to spring; (b) the pilot class, group by group, had gains similar to those of the paired class from fall to spring on the English test; (c) the native Spanish speakers in the pilot class made the most progress, improving an average of 4.6 points on the English version of the test and 4.5 points on the Spanish. This final observation is particularly noteworthy, because it indicates that the conceptual development of the Spanish speakers was facilitated by continued development of their native language along with English.

## Social Studies, Science, and Math Achievement

Students in the pilot class were given 10 chapter tests in science and 7 chapter tests in social studies throughout the year. Because science and social studies are taught only in Spanish, the tests were, of course, in Spanish. The class scores for science (when each student's individual grades have been averaged) were 4 As, 11 Bs, 5 Cs, and 2 Ds (2.7 average on a 4-point scale). The class scores for social studies were 3 As, 12 Bs, 5 Cs, and 2 Ds (2.7 average). The average for the comparison class for both science and social studies, where the instruction and tests were given in English, was 2.8. Thus there were virtually no differences in science and social studies test results and final grades between the pilot and the comparison class.

On the math chapter tests, the paired class scored higher than the pilot class. Students in the pilot class averaged 2.3 and students in the paired class averaged 3.0. Both classes received math instruction in English.

## Student Satisfaction

The majority of the students expressed a great deal of satisfaction with the partial immersion class. They eagerly expressed their opinions of the class and appeared pleased that someone was interested in what they had to say. Their main reasons for liking instruction in Spanish included the following:

> "If you have a friend who speaks Spanish you can speak to him."

> "I like Spanish because it's fun. I like reading in Spanish and it's fun to do sometimes. I like to say things in Spanish to my friends."

> "I haven't learned it yet, but it's fun to learn something new. We get hard work."

> "We learn a lot. We color, we read, we watch movies, we have fun, we work, we use the computer."

When asked why some students in the class (native speakers) spoke more Spanish than others, their responses showed a keen awareness of the reasons people speak different languages:

> "They *know* Spanish. They're born somewhere Spanish. Their mommy knows it and when they're born, they know the language their mommy knows."

> "When they were little babies they started out with Spanish. When they grew up they knew how to speak Spanish. If their mother was a Spanish person, then they could speak Spanish. My mother wasn't a Spanish person so I can't speak Spanish."

We asked the students if learning in Spanish was any different from learning in English and most of them felt that it was. However, one student responded with this insight:

> "It's not that different. It's just that one (teacher) speaks English and the other speaks Spanish. When Miss C. speaks in Spanish, everyone knows in Spanish what she's saying in English. . . . What they say is the same but they just say it in different languages."

*Attendance*

The classroom teachers reported that student attendance in the pilot program was normal throughout the year and was comparable to attendance in the other first-grade classes.

## SCHOOL AND COMMUNITY AWARENESS AND PARENTAL ATTITUDES

*School and Community Awareness*

To obtain a general sense of how the immersion program fit into the entire Key School program, we interviewed staff members who were not directly involved with the immersion class, including two kindergarten teachers, a first-grade teacher, and a third-grade teacher. We were interested in finding out how much they knew about the pilot Spanish immersion program at the school. It turned out they knew quite a bit. Their general impressions were that (a) the teachers in the program had to do a great deal of planning, far beyond what's usually expected of classroom teachers; (b) in the team teaching approach, with one teacher teaching the children in the morning and the other in the afternoon, it was crucial that the teachers work well together; and (c) it's an appropriate type of program for Key School because of the multicultural nature of the student body.

The Arlington community has become very involved in Key's pilot program through the Arlington County Citizen's Foreign Language Advisory Committee. In a recent report to the Arlington Advisory Council on Instruction, their recommendations included (a) the continuation and expansion of the Key School Spanish immersion program and (b) implementing the Key School model at other schools and with other languages.

*Parental Attitudes*

Overall, parents have been very pleased with what their children have been learning in the partial immersion program. During our phone interviews, many mentioned that they had had reservations during the first month or two when the children had a lot of adjusting to do—not only adjusting to the day-to-day activities of first grade but also to a new language as well. But as time went on, they felt that it became a lot easier for the children, and by November and December they were settled into the regular classroom routine. A parent whose native language is neither Spanish nor English commented, "Our daughter *really* likes it and that's the most important thing . . . and neither of her parents speak any Spanish at all."

Some of the native English-speaking parents expressed concern that they couldn't help their child with Spanish homework and hoped to be able to take Spanish classes sometime in the future. The Arlington Foreign Language Supervisor has offered to provide these classes through the Adult Education Department as soon as there is a group of 10 interested adults.

The English-speaking parents offered various reasons for enrolling their children in the program, including the following:

"It gives him every chance possible to do well and have a good education."

"Immersion is a great way to absorb language with little effort."

"I thought it was an exciting program and I wanted it for my daughter since I've always found languages very difficult myself."

The Spanish-speaking parents expressed equal satisfaction with the program, but for different reasons. They felt that the immersion program gave their children a wonderful opportunity to keep up their Spanish. Parents commented:

"My husband and I feel that it's best for our child to stay in the program to learn Spanish instead of just trying to pick up Spanish at home. At school he learns better than at home. We want him to keep up his Spanish and we tend to speak too much English at home."

"I want my child to learn two languages, and it's very important that he doesn't forget his Spanish."

One parent summarized the general feeling of other parents by commenting:

"We would like our child to continue immersion in the second grade. Key School has run the program very well. They've kept us informed on the progress of the program which is crucial. I like the openness they've had—we could visit the classrooms whenever we wanted."

Thus it is not surprising that all but two of the parents were definitely planning on enrolling their child in the second-grade immersion class in the fall. (Of the two who did not express this intention, one family was leaving the area and the other was still undecided.)

## RECOMMENDATIONS FOR THE KEY SCHOOL PARTIAL IMMERSION PROGRAM

At the close of the first year of implementation, CAL/CLEAR staff offered a number of recommendations to the Key School program. The major recommendation was that *the program should not only be continued but also be expanded.* Here, we agreed with the Arlington County Foreign Language Advisory Committee, who also recommended that a kindergarten and second-grade class be added, while continuing the first-grade program, permitting students to continue in a partial immersion program for another year, and also expanding the opportunities for other students in the county to participate in innovative language education programs.

Other recommendations included:

(1) Summer curriculum development and teacher meetings should be encouraged. In the inaugural year, the two participating teachers were forced to develop curricula and plan activities throughout the year because there had been limited start-up time for the program. However, participating teachers should meet and work together in the summer months to design a carefully structured and integrated program. This will also reduce the demand for daily discussions and meetings to ensure that the program is integrated and complementary. A clearly articulated curriculum will be especially important if kindergarten and grade two are added to the sequence. All kindergarten, first- and second-grade teachers, resource personnel, and key staff should be involved in the summer meetings.

(2) A common planning period for paired teachers should be scheduled. In 1987–1988, the teachers did not have a set time when they could meet to coordinate their instructional programs and discuss problems. As a result, they gave up lunch time, arrived early and stayed late, and found brief intervals in which they could meet. In the future, paired teachers should have planning periods, with students from both classes assigned to another teacher or activity to keep the time truly free for planning.

(3) Paired classes should continue to meet near each other. It was help-ful that the paired teachers had classrooms next to each other, enabling them to briefly discuss particular students or plans without needing to leave the classroom area. This pattern should be retained in the future, with classes either next door to each other or in close proximity.

(4) Increased opportunities for acquisition and practice of Spanish should be provided by the program. Because there are limited opportuni-ties for English-speaking children to acquire or practice their Spanish out-side of class, more activities need to be provided for English-speaking children to learn and practice Spanish. These could include enhanced Spanish language arts instruction, which could be offered to the English-speaking students while the Spanish-speaking students are engaged in Spanish reading. Other opportunities are available within the classroom, where students can serve as resources to each other, but the teachers need to encourage and structure these interactions. In 1987–1988, there was a very limited amount of small group or paired interaction in the classes, when such cooperative learning could have been very beneficial for all students.

(5) An ongoing program of in-service education for teachers and re-source specialists should be provided. To enable teachers to continue to expand their repertoire of methods and activities for the partial immersion classes and to ensure articulation across grade levels, an ongoing series of staff development workshops should be planned, involving key personnel within the program. Others working in two-way programs in the area should also be invited to encourage sharing among teachers in this area. Summer immersion workshops are an excellent step in this direction. Par-ticipation in language conferences is also an excellent idea.

(6) Classes should encourage increased small group or peer-peer inter-action. When students have an opportunity to work together, both orally and on written tasks, their language and academic development are pro-moted. Although classrooms are small and relatively crowded, opportuni-ties for more small group or paired cooperative learning should be incor-porated as an integral part of the instructional program. Perhaps several staff workshops could be directed to helping teachers more easily incorpo-rate peer-peer instruction in their classes. It is particularly important in a program such as this one, given that a major goal of the program is in-creased understanding between student groups as well as improved ability to communicate in each other's languages.

(7) An increased budget for Spanish language materials for classroom use and the library is needed. The Spanish language materials available to

the program were quite limited, often requiring the Spanish teacher to adapt English language materials. For example, when she taught a science lesson in Spanish, she often had to use English-titled filmstrips and supplementary materials. Spanish language materials for classroom use, key reference works such as encyclopedias and dictionaries in Spanish, and Spanish language pleasure reading books are needed to support the efforts of the program to help English-speaking students acquire Spanish language skills.

CONCLUSION

As this chapter indicates, the Key Partial Immersion program made an excellent start in its pilot year. The preliminary findings on the effects of the program laid the basis for a great deal of enthusiasm for recommending program continuation and expansion.

# 9

# A High School Bilingual
# Partial Immersion Program

KATHRYN J. LINDHOLM
AMADO M. PADILLA

It is generally acknowledged that it is difficult to teach a foreign language to students using a traditional type of curriculum in such a way that students achieve proficiency in the target language. Despite this fact, traditional methods of foreign language instruction are usually included in the curriculum in many high schools.

In a recent national survey of foreign language programs, Rhodes and Oxford (1988) reported that 95% of the surveyed 1,349 secondary schools provided foreign language instruction, with Spanish as the most frequently taught foreign language (86% of secondary schools with a foreign language offered Spanish). In these schools, 96% provided standard foreign language classes, 20% offered exploratory courses, 2% taught subject matter (e.g., U.S. history) in the foreign language, and 4% provided language for native-speaker courses. What these statistics demonstrate is that foreign language instruction is frequently provided in secondary schools, but most schools rely on the traditional foreign language instructional approach, with only a few schools offering special types of programs to further stimulate foreign language learning on the part of their students.

Most research in foreign language learning and teaching has concentrated on teaching methods in foreign language education (Politzer, 1981; Stern, 1981) or on second-language learning issues (e.g., Alatis, Altman,

& Alatis, 1981; Krashen, 1981; McLaughlin, 1978, 1980), with only a few research studies focused on the relationship between second-language teaching and learning (Beardsmore & Swain, 1985; Campbell, Gray, Rhodes, & Snow, 1985; Krashen, 1981; Krashen, Butler, Birnbaum, & Robertson, in press).

Foreign language research that compares different forms of foreign language instruction programs are scarce, particularly at the secondary level. In one of the few comparative foreign language program studies to date, Campbell, Gray, Rhodes, and Snow (1985) compared the Spanish language reading, listening, and writing abilities of sixth-grade students enrolled in one of three types of foreign language programs: (a) foreign language in the elementary schools (FLES), (b) immersion, and (c) partial immersion. Their results indicated that the immersion students outperformed the partial immersion students who outscored the FLES students. These results were not surprising given the different levels of exposure to the foreign language that the students received. However, as the authors pointed out, the immersion model provided the best opportunity for students to acquire foreign language competence at a level sufficient to allow them to use the language for real-life social and academic purposes.

In another comparative study, Beardsmore and Swain (1985) examined the French language performance of eighth-grade students in the Canadian immersion program with eighth-grade students in the European school model program. The Canadian immersion model was designed primarily for enrichment while the European school model was developed for language maintenance, with both promoting French as a second language using totally different strategies. Test results showed that the students scored comparably on the French achievement tests. These results were interesting in light of the fact that the immersion students had completed approximately 4,500 hours of French instruction compared with the 1,300 hours of instruction received by the European school students. However, the European students, in contrast to the immersion students, had far more access to French language use in the community, through contact with French speakers and French language media. These authors discussed the findings in terms of the role of the environment and the opportunity to use the target language as decisive factors in determining the nature of the instructional model and the amount of target language input required in school.

Two significant points emerge from the two comparative studies: (a) the important role of content instruction in immersion programs in promoting second-language development through the focus on subject matter rather than language (Campbell, 1984; Swain, 1984) and (b) the importance of interactions with native speakers in promoting second-language learning (Lindholm, 1987; Lindholm & Fairchild, 1990; Long & Porter, 1985).

In chapters by Lindholm (1990) and Lindholm and Fairchild (1990) in Padilla, Fairchild, and Valadez (1990), we learned that foreign language programs can be designed for elementary-level students to simultaneously meet the needs of both English speakers learning Spanish as a second language and Spanish speakers learning English and developing their Spanish. These bilingual immersion programs can provide second-language (L2) students with greater second-language proficiency than that achieved by students in traditional foreign language courses and can enhance the first language (L1) literacy and communication skills of nonnative English speakers. The purpose of this chapter is to describe a unique high school bilingual partial immersion program. We will specifically examine and compare the Spanish reading, writing, listening, and speaking proficiency levels of students enrolled in the bilingual partial immersion program and students enrolled in a traditional Spanish language program.

## PROGRAM DESCRIPTION

The bilingual partial immersion program at Mount Miguel High School, a high school in the San Diego area that has a mixed ethnic student composition, is open to any interested incoming ninth grader. Program participants are divided into two tracks: Intensive Spanish as a Second Language (ISSL) and Spanish for Native Speakers (SNS). The ISSL track, where Spanish is used as the medium of instruction, demands a four-year commitment to Spanish (one hour per day, five days per week) enabling students to obtain more exposure to Spanish, particularly communicative input. For students in the SNS track, Spanish is also the medium of instruction. Because SNS students enter the program with varying degrees of oral-aural fluency (although few have had any formal education in Spanish), SNS classes are intended to provide an opportunity for the development of Spanish academic language and literacy skills. Thus the two tracks of formal instruction in Spanish were designed to fulfill the differing needs for achieving Spanish academic proficiency in the two

**Table 9.1**  Partial Immersion Program Curriculum Design

| Year 1 | Year 2 | Year 3 | Year 4 |
|--------|--------|--------|--------|
| ISSL 1 | ISSL 2 | ISSL 3 | ISSL 4 |
| SNS 1 | SNS 2 | SNS 3 | SNS 4 |
| | P.E. | History | Government/ Anthropology |

populations in this program. After the first year, ISSL and SNS students participate together in one content course taught in Spanish each semester. All of the content courses satisfy graduation requirements. The curriculum design is illustrated in Table 9.1. The third-year history course and the fourth-year government and anthropology courses are taught in alternating units of Spanish and English. Physical education is taught entirely in Spanish, which simply means that Spanish is the medium of communication while students are engaged in physical activity.

There are also traditional Spanish (hereafter SPANISH) foreign language courses taught at the high school that focus on Spanish grammar and literacy largely using English as the medium of instruction.

### Goals and Assumptions of the Program

The primary goal of both the ISSL and the SNS classes is to enable students to achieve a high level of Spanish language proficiency, including interpersonal communication skills and cognitive/academic language proficiency. Another goal is to conduct language instruction in a way that enhances the recognition and appreciation of Hispanic culture for both native and nonnative speakers of Spanish and that demonstrates the advantages of bilingualism.

Embedded within the philosophy of the program are also several extralinguistic goals. Among these are the social integration of Hispanic and non-Hispanic students in and out of class. Another goal is the status equalization of Hispanic and non-Hispanic students through the medium of Spanish language instruction. Finally, the inclusion of a Spanish language program for native speakers in the curriculum is intended to make Hispanic students feel more comfortable with the school and thus more likely to remain until graduation.

These goals rest on a set of assumptions that have to do with both the structuring of language exposure and the relative benefits derived from such instruction by native and nonnative speakers of Spanish. These assumptions are as follows:

(1) Acquisition of Spanish language proficiency by nonnative speakers is enhanced through interaction with native speakers.

(2) Heterogeneous grouping, in conjunction with cooperative learning strategies, results in enhanced levels of academic performance and prosocial attitudes and skills.

(3) Students can learn academic content through the medium of Spanish language instruction if input is organized and comprehensible.

(4) Language learners acquire the target language more efficiently when classroom language use has a purpose.

(5) There is a common underlying cognitive/academic proficiency that transfers between languages such that history knowledge taught in Spanish can be tested for in English and vice versa.

(6) Institutional use of Spanish for academic purposes (other than as a compensatory strategy for limited-English speakers) raises the status of the language in the school setting and assigns greater status to Hispanics, with positive effects on the self-esteem of Hispanic students and on the attitudes of non-Hispanic students toward Hispanic peers.

These assumptions are all derived from the literature on language education and serve as the basis for the development of the high school partial bilingual immersion program.

## Issues in Program Implementation

It is never easy to implement a new program in a school, even when a commitment to do so is apparent. This was true of the Mount Miguel High School partial bilingual immersion program. To make the program work it was first necessary to have teachers available with both the necessary linguistic competence and the academic preparation demanded for high school instruction. Further, the teachers had to be committed to become involved in the proposed educational innovation. Another consideration had to do with the availability of a "critical mass" of native Spanish-speaking students willing to enroll in a program of the type described here. Fortunately, there were both teachers and bilingual students willing to commit to the program.

Any school attempting a partial immersion program of the type described here for the secondary school level must also consider the availability of texts and other instructional materials in the target language that also address the required elements of the content-area curriculum. This is no small matter and requires very careful searching for relevant and usable materials.

Administrative personnel from the principal on down must be ready to support and maintain all needed language and content courses. In addition, the teaching staff must be granted time for planning and coordinating instruction. This type of instruction demands considerably more coordination if the desired outcomes are to be achieved.

Finally, if a partial bilingual immersion program is to work, there must be students willing to participate and parents who are supportive of such a program. The ISSL and SNS programs both require a four-year commitment from students. In addition, parents must be supportive of the idea that academic content can be learned through the medium of a second language for the nonnative Spanish speakers while the Hispanic parents must permit their children to serve as language role models in a context that has not generally been supportive of Spanish language maintenance.

Fortunately, the school in question was able to overcome all of these concerns and implemented its program. In doing so the staff requested technical assistance in the evaluation of the program from the research staff of the Center for Language Education and Research (CLEAR). In the next part of this chapter, we present the findings of the third-year evaluation of the program.

## METHODOLOGY

### Testing Procedures and Instruments

Each student was tested in his or her language class for three consecutive days toward the end of the spring semester. On the first day, students were administered the Modern Language Association (MLA) Cooperative Foreign Language Spanish listening test. On the second day, students were given the MLA Spanish reading test and completed a background questionnaire. The MLA Spanish writing test was administered to the students on the third day. In addition, the students were rated for Spanish speaking proficiency several days later.

The MLA Cooperative Foreign Language Test was designed to test the four language skills—listening, speaking, reading, and writing—in secondary schools and colleges. There are separate measures of listening, speaking, reading, and writing at two achievement levels—the lower level (L) corresponding to the first two years of language learning and the higher level (M) corresponding to the third and fourth years of language learning. The MLA test measures the learner's knowledge of structures that are common in speech and those that are common in writing; the test is also designed to measure a student's knowledge of vocabulary and idiom in their receptive and productive aspects. Students in all three language programs (ISSL, SNS, SPANISH) were administered the MLA listening, reading, and writing subtests. The American Council on the Teaching of Foreign Languages (ACTFL) Proficiency Guidelines were used to rate the students' speaking proficiency in Spanish.

The background questionnaire consisted of four sections. The first section contained questions that probed the Spanish language exposure and Spanish language use of the students. It included questions asking for the students' first language, language spoken in the home, the occupational and educational background of the parents, whether the students spoke Spanish outside of the home, how much they listened to Spanish radio or television programs, and whether they or their parents read Spanish books, newspapers, or magazines. The second section comprised questions about the students' attitudes toward Spanish and the Hispanic culture. Motivation to use Spanish, to be exposed to Spanish, and to further develop one's Spanish was assessed by questions in the third section. Finally, the fourth section of the questionnaire asked students to rate their ability to use Spanish along six dimensions.

### Description of Students

A total of 545 students participated in the data collection. Of these, 53 were in the Spanish for Native Speakers (SNS) track, 79 were in the

Intensive Spanish as a Second Language (ISSL) track, and 391 were in the traditional Spanish (SPANISH) track. In the SNS track, there were 21 first-year, 15 second-year, and 17 third-year students. Of the ISSL students, 35 were in their first year, 30 were in their second year, and 14 were in their third year of Spanish. Finally, 220 of the SPANISH students were first-year students, 111 were second-year students, and 69 were third-year students. A total of 22 students were in their fourth year of study. This one classroom of students was a combination of SPAN, ISSL, and SNS students. Characteristics of the three groups of students are described and compared on several background variables.

Characteristics that relate to Spanish language home background and exposure to Spanish help clarify the language proficiency outcomes attained by our three groups of students. As Table 9.2 shows, 84% of the SNS, 5% of the ISSL, and 3.3% of the SPANISH students spoke Spanish as their first language. When the home language was examined, 32% of the SNS spoke only Spanish at home and another 64% spoke both Spanish and English. Of the ISSL students, none used Spanish exclusively at home, but 11% conversed in both Spanish and English in the home. In the SPANISH group, fewer than 1% claimed to speak only Spanish in their home while another 10.5% used both Spanish and English. Another way to look at this is that only 4% of the SNS students used English exclusively at home compared with 89% of the SPANISH and 89% of the ISSL students. What these findings show is that most of the SNS students and a few ISSL and SPANISH students received exposure to and had opportunities to use Spanish in the home environment.

Another index of exposure to Spanish includes Spanish media such as TV, radio, and literature. In each of these forms of media, the SNS group received the most exposure, followed by the ISSL group and, finally, the SPANISH group. In fact, from Table 9.2, almost three times as many ISSL students reported watching Spanish TV, listening to Spanish radio, and reading Spanish books, newspapers, or magazines as SPANISH students.

These findings about student characteristics are important because they indicate differential exposure to and use of Spanish according to the classification of students as SNS, ISSL, or SPANISH. In general, the SNS students had the highest exposure to and use of Spanish, as would be expected for native speakers. Also interesting is the extent of Spanish media exposure by the ISSL group, which may be indicative of their motivation to acquire Spanish proficiency.

**Table 9.2**  Percentage of Spanish Language Exposure and Use by the Three Groups of Students: Spanish for Native Speakers (SNS), Intensive Spanish as a Second Language (ISSL), and Traditional Foreign Language Instruction (SPANISH).

| Language Exposure | SNS | ISSL | SPANISH |
|---|---|---|---|
| *Native Language* | | | |
| Spanish | 84.0% | 5.0% | 3.3% |
| *Home Language* | | | |
| Spanish | 32.0% | 0.0% | 0.5% |
| Spanish and English | 64.0% | 10.8% | 10.5% |
| (Total Spanish) | (96.0%) | (10.8%) | (11.0%) |
| *Spanish TV* | 82.0% | 45.5% | 17.1% |
| *Spanish Radio* | 46.0% | 27.7% | 9.0% |
| *Read Spanish* | 71.4% | 49.0% | 16.9% |

FINDINGS OF THE STUDY

*Listening Comprehension*

Table 9.3 presents the mean scale scores and norming percentiles for the three groups of students. All three groups of students (SPANISH, ISSL, SNS) performed well on the listening subtest, with each group's mean score above the mean score for the norming sample.[1] For example, the SNS group obtained a mean scaled score of 178, which corresponds to the 94th percentile for the norming group; thus 94% of the students in the norming sample scored lower than the SNS students on the listening subtest.

In order to determine differences between the three groups in Spanish listening comprehension and whether there were larger or smaller differences between groups across the three years of the program, a statistical analysis (two-way analysis of variance) was computed using the scaled scores. This analysis revealed a statistically significant difference between the groups in listening comprehension. In addition, listening comprehension improved significantly for all groups from the first through the third year of instruction.

A statistical (Scheff) test that compares the performance of two groups of students at a time was then computed for each possible group combination (i.e., SNS versus ISSL, ISSL versus SPANISH, SNS versus SPANISH) for each year. The results showed that on all comparisons the SNS students scored significantly higher on listening skills than both the ISSL and the SPANISH students. In addition, the ISSL group scored significantly higher on this measure than the SPANISH group in all but the third year. In the third year, the ISSL students scored higher, but not significantly so, than the SPANISH students.

In looking at the student performance over the years, in general, third-year scores were the highest, followed by second-year and, finally, first-year scores. Paired comparisons revealed that there were not generally statistically significant differences from year one to year two, and from year two to year three. Rather, first-year scores differed significantly from scores of second and third years, but second-year scores were not significantly different from third-year scores.

## Reading Comprehension

Table 9.3 shows the mean scores, and percentile rank, on reading comprehension for the three groups of students. All three groups performed well on the test with mean scores higher than those for the norming sample.

As was the case with listening comprehension, it is important to determine if the differences in mean reading scores between the groups shown in Table 9.3 are statistically significant. Therefore, a statistic was computed that compares the language group (SNS versus ISSL versus SPANISH) and year of instruction (first year versus second year versus third year). The findings showed significant effects for language group and year of instruction. However, the analysis also showed that reading comprehension did not improve in a steady and consistent fashion from one year to the next as was found with listening comprehension.

Scheffé comparisons showed that the SNS students scored significantly higher than both the ISSL and the SPANISH students over all years of the program. Also, the ISSL students outscored the SPANISH students in all three years. However, the differences in reading comprehension between the ISSL and SPANISH groups were significant only during years two and three of the program.

**Table 9.3** Mean Scale Scores and Percentile Ranks on the Modern Language Association (MLA) Subtests of Spanish Language Proficiency

| Groups of Students | Listening Mean | %ile | Reading Mean | %ile | Writing Mean | %ile |
|---|---|---|---|---|---|---|
| *Year 1* | | | | | | |
| SNS | 178.0 | 94 | 167.3 | 65 | 170.7 | 76 |
| ISSL | 158.5 | 88 | 149.0 | 76 | 152.2 | 87 |
| SPANISH | 150.2 | 73 | 146.1 | 66 | 144.0 | 47 |
| *Year 2* | | | | | | |
| SNS | 186.0 | 92 | 184.3 | 81 | 173.7 | 49 |
| ISSL | 165.2 | 85 | 158.4 | 71 | 160.3 | 77 |
| SPANISH | 159.0 | 72 | 153.5 | 59 | 156.6 | 65 |
| *Year 3* | | | | | | |
| SNS | 186.5 | 92 | 190.2 | 90 | 176.3 | 61 |
| ISSL | 169.3 | 66 | 169.1 | 89 | 168.1 | 89 |
| SPANISH | 161.0 | 49 | 156.5 | 65 | 158.0 | 71 |

In comparing changes in reading comprehension across years, Scheffé comparisons revealed that there were no statistically significant differences between year one and year two performance, or from year two to year three. Overall, the first-year reading scores differed significantly from second- and third-year scores, but year two scores were not significantly different from year three scores except in one comparison. The ISSL group improved significantly on reading comprehension between years two and three.

### Writing Ability

Table 9.3 presents the findings for the writing subtest. Comparison of the students' mean scores with those of the norming samples indicates that both the SNS and the ISSL groups received higher means than the norming sample, whereas the SPANISH group scored slightly lower.

A significant difference was found in writing performance between groups of students and across years of the program. In addition, improvements in writing were not uniform for all groups across years. To better understand these differences, Scheffé comparisons showed that, again, the

SNS students scored significantly higher than both the ISSL and the SPANISH students. The ISSL students significantly outscored the SPANISH students in years one and three. The ISSL students received higher scores than the SPANISH students in year two, but this difference was not statistically significant.

Although year three scores were the highest, followed by year two-and, finally, year one scores, Scheffé comparisons revealed that, unlike the listening and reading scores, year-to-year differences depended on the group. For the SPANISH students, year one writing scores were significantly lower than writing performance attained at the end of year two and also that attained in year three. However, a significant improvement in writing was not observed between years two and three. In contrast, all year-to-year comparisons for writing ability were significant for the ISSL students. That is, year three writing scores were significantly higher than scores obtained in years one and two; similarly, end of year two writing scores were higher than year one scores. For the SNS group, year three scores were higher than year two scores and year two scores higher than year one scores, but these differences were not statistically significant.

### Speaking Ability

Table 9.4 depicts the mean scores and standard deviations on the ACTFL rating scale for speaking ability. The differences in oral language proficiency between the groups, seen in the table, were found to be statistically significant. Also, as with the other language performance measures already discussed, Spanish oral proficiency improved across years in the program for all groups.

As expected, Scheffé comparisons for each year indicated that the SNS students had significantly better oral language proficiency than either the ISSL or the SPANISH students. Similarly, the ISSL students possessed better oral proficiency than the SPANISH students.

In assessing improvement in Spanish oral proficiency across years in the program, Scheffé comparisons revealed that there generally were not statistically significant differences from year one to year two, and from year two to year three. Rather, the greatest gains in Spanish oral proficiency occurred between the first and second years for all groups, with proficiency levels in the third year of the program being higher generally than in the second year but not significantly higher.

**Table 9.4** Mean Scores and Standard Deviations on American Council on
the Teaching of Foreign Languages (ACTFL) Proficiency
Guidelines for Rating Spanish Oral Proficiency

| Groups of Students | Mean | S.D. |
|---|---|---|
| *Year 1* | | |
| SNS | 7.0 | 1.5 |
| ISSL | 2.8 | 1.4 |
| SPANISH | 1.7 | 1.4 |
| *Year 2* | | |
| SNS | 7.9 | 1.5 |
| ISSL | 4.2 | 1.7 |
| SPANISH | 2.9 | 1.4 |
| *Year 3* | | |
| SNS | 8.4 | 0.6 |
| ISSL | 5.1 | 1.4 |
| SPANISH | 3.3 | 1.6 |

## DISCUSSION AND PROGRAM IMPLICATIONS

Results showed that type of high school Spanish program significantly
influenced the level of Spanish proficiency attained by nonnative speakers
of Spanish. Students enrolled in a bilingual partial immersion program
where Spanish language instruction was included in content material performed higher on all measures of Spanish proficiency across all three
years of the program than did students enrolled in a traditional Spanish as
a foreign language program. These findings are important because they
provide support for the bilingual partial immersion model at the secondary
level in promoting higher levels of Spanish proficiency among both native
and nonnative speakers of Spanish.

An important point occurs with respect to interpreting the higher proficiency scores of the ISSL over the SPANISH students. At entry into the
program, the two groups of students had nearly equivalent exposure to
Spanish in the home environment, with about 11% of each group having
exposure to at least some Spanish in their home. Only slightly more ISSL
students (5%) than SPANISH students (3%) learned Spanish as their first
language. Furthermore, on a measure of attitudes and motivation related

to the Spanish language and Spanish speakers, the two groups did not differ. However, the groups differed in their self-initiated exposure to Spanish language media. For instance, three times as many ISSL students as SPANISH students watched Spanish TV, listened to Spanish radio, and read books and magazines in Spanish. Thus the ISSL students were possibly more motivated to acquire Spanish and thus committed themselves to a more intensive Spanish course, or they became more motivated as a result of the activities they engaged in through their Spanish bilingual partial immersion program. It is also possible that both of these conditions were operating with the ISSL students. Therefore, the greater motivation of the ISSL group, coupled with their overall higher level of Spanish language exposure in and out of the classroom, may account for these findings.

The consistently higher proficiency scores of the SNS students is also noteworthy. Although SNS students would be expected to have higher listening comprehension and speaking proficiency scores than their nonnative Spanish-speaking classmates, the fact that the SNS students used their Spanish oral skills to develop their literacy skills is also evident. That is, the goal of promoting complete Spanish proficiency among students enrolled in the SNS program was accomplished. The significance of this is that native Spanish-speaking students often do not acquire reading and writing literacy skills in Spanish because high school language instructors assume that they already possess these literacy skills.

The special effort to design a program appropriate to the Spanish language capability of the native speakers, therefore, served three purposes. First, the SNS students performed significantly higher on all proficiency measures than the nonnative speakers of Spanish. Second, by concentrating on the Spanish language development of the SNS group, it was also possible to ensure that these students could serve as good language models for the ISSL group. Finally, although no measures of social integration were available in this study, it is likely that bilingual partial immersion served the purpose of bringing students closer together in and out of the classroom.

The importance of these results is that foreign language courses can be tailored to the needs of students in ways that promote greater language proficiency. Providing native Spanish speakers with the opportunity to develop their literacy skills acknowledges the oral proficiency that they currently possess and builds on that proficiency to develop literacy skills that are not usually as well developed (see Campbell & Lindholm, in press). The result is an individual who is fully proficient in Spanish. In addition, an intensive bilingual partial immersion foreign language course that provides peer models, instruction in the language being taught, and content/language integration results in greater language learning than does traditional foreign language instruction. Among other gains is the fact that bilingual immersion students also appear more motivated to engage in activities outside of the classroom that serve to further promote their language learning.

## NOTE

1. The norming percentile is useful for a comparison of the MLA scores of the students with the MLA scores of the norming subjects. Using the student mean score, it is possible to obtain the percentage of subjects in the norming sample that received a lower score than the students' mean score. This percentile is actually an estimate because there is a band, or range, of percentiles; thus the percentile that is presented is the average percentile. This difference is evident in the tables, where mean scores that differ by only one or two points may vary by several percentile points.

## REFERENCES

Alatis, J. E., Altman, H. B., & Alatis, P. M. (1981). *The second language classroom: Directions for the 1980's.* New York: Oxford University Press.

Beardsmore, H. B., & Swain, M. (1985). Designing bilingual education: Aspects of immersion and "European school" models. *Journal of Multilingual and Multicultural Development, 6,* 1–15.

Campbell, R. N. (1984). The immersion education approach to foreign language teaching. In California State Department of Education, *Studies on immersion education* (pp. 114–143). Sacramento: California State Department of Education.

Campbell, R. N., Gray, T. C., Rhodes, N. C., & Snow, M. A. (1985). Foreign language learning in the elementary schools: A comparison of three language programs. *Modern Language Journal, 69,* 44–54.

Campbell, R. N., & Lindholm, K. J. (in press). Conservation of language resources. In B. VanPatten & J. F. Lee (Eds.), *SLA-FLL: On the relationship between second language acquisition and foreign language learning.* New York: Newbury House.

Krashen, S. (1981). Effective second language acquisition: Insight from research. In J. E. Alatis, H. B. Altman, & P. M. Alatis (Eds.), *The second language classroom: Directions for the 1980's.* New York: Oxford University Press.

Krashen, S., Butler, J., Birnbaum, R., & Robertson, J. (in press). Two studies in language acquisition and language learning. *ITL: Review of Applied Linguistics.*

Lindholm, K. J. (1987). *Directory of bilingual immersion programs: Two way bilingual education for language minority and majority students* (Educational Report No. 8). Los Angeles: University of California, Center for Language Education and Research.

Lindholm, K. J. (1990). Bilingual immersion education: Criteria for program development. In A. M. Padilla, H. H. Fairchild, & C. M. Valadez (Eds.), *Bilingual education: Issues and strategies*. Newbury Park, CA: Sage.

Lindholm, K. J., & Fairchild, H. H. (1990). Evaluation of an elementary school bilingual immersion program. In A. M. Padilla, H. H. Fairchild, & C. M. Valadez (Eds.), *Bilingual education: Issues and strategies*. Newbury Park, CA: Sage.

Long, M. H., & Porter, P. A. (1985). Group work, interlanguage talk, and second language acquisition. *TESOL Quarterly, 19*, 207–228.

McLaughlin, B. (1978). The monitor model: Some methodological considerations. *Language Learning, 28*, 309–332.

McLaughlin, B. (1980). Theory and research in second language learning: An emerging paradigm. *Language Learning, 30*, 331–350.

Padilla, A. M., Fairchild, H. H., & Valadez, C. M. (Eds.). (1990). *Bilingual education: Issues and strategies*. Newbury Park, CA: Sage.

Politzer, R. L. (1981). Effective language teaching: Insights from research. In J. E. Alatis, H. B. Altman, & P. M. Alatis (Eds.), *The second language classroom: Directions for the 1980's*. New York: Oxford University Press.

Rhodes, N. C., & Oxford, R. L. (1988). *A national profile of foreign language instruction at the elementary and secondary school level* (Technical Report No. 6). Los Angeles: University of California, Center for Language Education and Research.

Stern, H. H. (1981). Communicative language teaching and learning: Toward a synthesis. In J. E. Alatis, H. B. Altman, & P. M. Alatis (Eds.), *The second language classroom: Directions for the 1980's*. New York: Oxford University Press.

Swain, M. (1984). A review of immersion education in Canada: Research and evaluation studies. In *Studies on immersion education: A collection for United States educators* (pp. 87–112). Sacramento: California State Department of Education.

# 10

# Instructional Methodology in Immersion Foreign Language Education

## MARGUERITE ANN SNOW

This chapter is concerned with the instructional methodology used by teachers in the immersion model of foreign language education. In immersion programs, language majority children receive the bulk of their elementary school education through the medium of a second language. For example, English-speaking children in Culver City, California, spend most of the school day learning subject matter taught in Spanish; similarly, in Milwaukee, Wisconsin, immersion students learn such subjects as social studies and math in their second language, German. The challenge of immersion teaching is imparting difficult, cognitively demanding subject matter to children via their second language. The purpose of this chapter is twofold: (a) to describe the strategies and techniques used by experienced immersion teachers in integrating content and language instruction and (b) to draw from the insights of work in other second-language education programs for instructional strategies that could be incorporated into immersion teaching.

In the early years of immersion education in both the U.S. and the Canadian settings, the prevailing attitude was that elementary teacher certification and native or near-native proficiency in the second language were the only criteria in the recruitment of immersion teachers. In fact, in the United States, teachers with no previous bilingual teaching experience

156

were often preferred because it was felt that the assumptions of the immersion model were very different from bilingual education methodologies. For example, initial reading instruction is provided in the students' second language in immersion programs, a feature of the immersion model that differs from bilingual education methods. Immersion teachers were instructed to teach the standard elementary curriculum as they would normally do, albeit through the medium of a second language.

In the 1960s and 1970s, research on immersion education focused almost entirely on student academic achievement. Parents wanted to know if their children were reading at grade level and if they were doing as well as their nonimmersion peers in mathematics concept learning. Principals and other school officials turned to the results of longitudinal and comparative studies using standardized achievement tests to evaluate whether the immersion experiment was working. On the basis of this research, we know that children enrolled in immersion programs can excel linguistically and academically.

Attention is now turning to other areas of interest in immersion, including instructional methodology. One reason for this shift is the need to train teachers for the increasing number of immersion programs in the United States. The second reason for the attention to instructional methodology is more long range but critical for the continued evolution of the immersion model of foreign language education. The accomplishments of immersion programs are well documented; however, their limitations are also quite clear. Students leave immersion programs as functional bilinguals, able to use the second language for any communicative purpose, but they are rarely mistaken for native speakers and writers of the second language. Their speech and writing contain persistent grammatical errors or nonidiomatic patterns that characterize their output as nonnative. In seeking to promote the development of the model, reasonable questions to ask are these: "How can the immersion model be made even more effective?" "What can be done to upgrade certain components of the immersion model so that the goal of producing nativelike speakers of the second language is more feasible?"

In contrast to the careful scrutiny that student achievement in immersion programs has received, very little has been written about immersion instructional methodology. Two resource handbooks produced by the Ministry of Education of the Province of British Columbia in 1981, *Early French Immersion: Teacher's Resource Book* and *Early French Immersion: Administrator's Resource Book*, provide the best examples of guides developed specifically for prospective immersion teachers and administrators in the Canadian context.

Lapkin and Cummins (1984), however, cited a survey by Olson and Burns in 1981, which found that 68% of the immersion teachers in their Northern Ontario sample did not have any specific training in French immersion methodology; 75% of the teachers indicated that they did not have any preservice training; and 88% indicated that they were not involved in an ongoing in-service training program. Furthermore, despite the plethora of research studies conducted in the French immersion context, most of the immersion teachers were unaware of all but the most general research findings.

This finding was the impetus for a major Canadian study conducted in 1983 by the Canadian Association of Immersion Teachers, an organization seeking to establish immersion teacher training as a high priority (Wilton, Obadia, Roy, Saunders, & Tafler, 1984). The general goal of the study was to identify the needs of French immersion teachers in the areas of preservice training and professional development. The results indicated that teachers who had undergone preservice training rated methodology courses as the most useful and valid of all the courses taken, but they felt the greatest needs in professional development still remained in the area of immersion methodology, specifically in the teaching of oral French, science, reading, and written French.

Immersion teacher training in the United States can best be characterized in one of two ways: "under the wing," with new immersion teachers being "adopted" by experienced teachers, or "by the seat of the pants," as new teachers learn through trial and error. In a very general sense, the role of the immersion teacher is no different from that of every other elementary school teacher—to teach the curriculum at that grade level. However, because such a large part of instruction is through the medium of the students' second language, immersion teachers really have a second charge—to be language teachers as well. Immersion teachers, therefore, really wear two hats at all times. Through their instruction, they must promote mastery of the subject matter and second-language development concurrently.

The remainder of this chapter identifies specific techniques and strategies for the immersion teacher, but, first, a caveat is necessary. It is difficult indeed to separate, both in theory and in practice, immersion instructional methodology from the general techniques and skills that any effective teacher draws upon to facilitate learning, whether in a monolingual or a bilingual setting. All effective teachers plan for instruction, deliver instruction, and evaluate concept mastery. Obviously, it is beyond the scope of this chapter to attempt to detail the constellation of factors that constitutes effective instruction. It is assumed that a fully certified teacher possesses the general instructional skills acquired in an accredited teacher training program. The purpose here is to describe the additional skills that are needed to make the regular classroom teacher an immersion specialist.

## STRATEGIES AND TECHNIQUES IN IMMERSION INSTRUCTION

In recent years, three terms have been extensively used in second-language acquisition literature. The terms *sheltered instruction, comprehensible input*, and *negotiation of meaning* each have important implications for understanding the principles underlying immersion methodology. *Sheltered instruction* refers to the grouping of second-language learners for purposes of instruction. Krashen (1984) maintains that separating second-language learners puts them in the same "linguistic boat" in terms of their social and academic needs and abilities. It also creates a learning environment where teachers can gear their instruction to the proficiency level of the learners, thereby providing *comprehensible input* in the second language. Input is also made comprehensible through the negotiation of meaning between teacher and student. *Negotiation of meaning* is an interactive, reciprocal process in which immersion teachers and students employ a variety of techniques to make sure that they understand each other. The three terms provide an excellent conceptual starting point in our attempt to understand the pedagogical principles underlying immersion methodology.

Because the purpose of this chapter is to examine the "what" and the "how" of immersion teaching, it is necessary to consider the application of these principles to the classroom situation. Toward this end, CLEAR conducted a survey of experienced immersion teachers from well-established immersion programs in the United States. In all, 58 teachers from five immersion programs completed a comprehensive questionnaire in which they rated the frequency with which they utilized certain instructional strategies and described any other techniques they successfully used in their immersion classes. Findings from the survey provided valuable information about how immersion teachers put these three important principles into actual classroom practice.

## Core Instructional Strategies

Experienced immersion teachers use a variety of instructional strategies and techniques to help their students learn via a second language. Ten specific techniques stand out as the core instructional strategies leading to effective instruction, and they are described in Table 10.1.

## How Else Is Immersion Teaching Different?

In addition to employing a number of instructional strategies and techniques to make input comprehensible, immersion teachers must be prepared for several additional responsibilities.

(1) *Preparation.* Immersion teachers require more preparation time for curriculum development and translation of materials. They need more planning time than teachers in monolingual programs, as one teacher who participated in the survey explained, "to find alternative ways of presenting material" and "to search for the perfect combination of visuals, books, vocabulary, and techniques." In addition, immersion teachers must have an excellent understanding of the subject matter because they have to spend so much preparation time on lessons and materials that promote comprehension. For immersion teachers, subject matter knowledge has to be practically automatic.

(2) *Vocabulary development.* Because immersion students lack both basic and specialized vocabulary, teachers must concentrate on vocabulary development in a systematic manner. One teacher succinctly summarized this concern: "Immersion teachers must emphasize vocabulary building so that students are able to converse, discuss, [and] express feelings and personal reactions so that they are able to make the connections between concepts and information, and themselves."

(3) *Culture.* Immersion teachers must know the culture of the second-language community and strive to integrate it into the curriculum, not only as a distinct subject matter but wherever relevant. This can be done within the context of subjects such as social studies, or cultural themes may constitute individual lessons.

(4) *Personal attributes.* Immersion teachers must be patient and flexible because lesson preparation and instruction take more time. They must be comfortable being "good actors" because of the need to use body language and pantomime. They must know the language well and feel completely comfortable using it for both academic instruction and interper-

**Table 10.1**  Core Instructional Strategies

| Strategy/Technique | Application |
|---|---|
| 1. Extensive use of body language | Teachers link the abstract with the concrete by associating language with pantomime, gestures, and facial expressions, especially in the early grades. |
| 2. Predictability in instructional routines (e.g., opeings/closings, assignments/ homework directions, and so on) | Immersion teachers must provide more direction and structure for learners so students can anticipate or guess meaning even when they don't understand the language. |
| 3. Drawing on background knowledge to aid comprehension | Immersion teachers try to link the known with the unknown, the familiar with the unfamiliar, to provide a schema, or frame of reference, for new material. |
| 4. Extensive use of realia, visuals, manipulatives | Immersion teachers help associate language with its concrete referent through pictures and real-life objects; hands-on activities promote multisensory experiences. |
| 5. Review of previously covered material | Before introducing new material, immersion teachers must ensure understanding by review and careful diagnosis of the levels of student comprehension. |
| 6. Building redundancy into the lessons | Immersion teachers use repetition, paraphrase, restatement, and synonymy to give students many chances to understand the language. |
| 7. Explicit teacher modeling | The immersion teacher is the primary and usually only language model for the learners; explicit enunciation and multiple repetitions provide students with comprehensible language input. |
| 8. Indirect error correction | Immersion teachers correct language errors by modeling the correct responses for the learners. |
| 9. Variety of teaching methods and types of activities | Immersion teachers recognize diversity of general learning styles and also of language learning styles. |
| 10. Use of clarification/comprehension checks | Immersion teachers must use frequent and varied methods to check comprehension. |

sonal interaction. In one teacher's words, they must "constantly fight the urge to communicate with students in English," especially for discipline and classroom management. Finally, they must create an environment in which the students feel comfortable using their second language for all communicative purposes in the classroom.

## What Have We Learned About Immersion Methodology?

Identifying the multiple skills of experienced immersion teachers is an important first step in defining immersion instructional methodology. Similarly, the additional points raised by teachers about increased preparation time, lesson pacing, and material coverage are important practical considerations. It is clear that there is something different about immersion teaching. It is no longer sufficient to instruct immersion teachers "just" to teach the standard school curriculum or "just" to provide comprehensible input and negotiate meaning. We now know that effective immersion teachers utilize many creative and varied instructional techniques to make subject matter comprehensible in a second language.

One way to describe what we have learned is that *at a minimum* immersion teachers must use numerous language and instructional techniques/strategies to teach the subject matter effectively in a second language. For immersion education to work, teachers must use body language, build redundancy and repetition into their lessons, and emphasize vocabulary development. But, if our long-range goal is to think about how the immersion model can work even better, where else can we turn in this tinkering process to upgrade this instructional model? How can the immersion model be exploited or maximized further for its language teaching potential?

These questions were considered by Swain and Lapkin (1986), who reviewed several studies carried out in Toronto, Ottawa, Saskatchewan, and New Brunswick, Canada, with secondary school French immersion students. They found continued overall development of French skills in the secondary school; however, the students continued to show the weakest development in speaking and writing, particularly with regard to grammatical acquisition. As is the case in virtually all immersion programs, the students had relatively little opportunity to use French outside of class. Significantly, however, it also appeared they had relatively little opportunity to use the language *in* class. To test these conclusions, the researchers left a tape recorder running for a day in each of 19 grade-three and grade-six immersion classes. Analysis of the grade-six recordings showed that 81% of all student utterances consisted of a single word, a phrase, or a clause. These findings are hardly surprising. Clearly the dominant pedagogical orientation of North American schools, whether mainstream, immersion, bilingual, or the like, is one that places the teacher in exclusive control of instruction. In this orientation, referred to as the transmission model (Cummins, 1986), teachers are viewed as the holders of all knowledge; their job is imparting knowledge to students in the form of instructional objectives. While it is beyond the scope of this chapter to debate the relative merits of this orientation, it is quite fair to say that it is not optimally conducive to second-language learning.

## OTHER WORK IN
## SECOND-LANGUAGE EDUCATION

Work in other second-language educational programs provides insights into how the immersion model can become an even more effective model of second-language teaching. Enright and McCloskey (1985) provided some useful ideas for immersion teachers. Their title hints at the orientation being recommended: "Yes, Talking!: Organizing the Classroom to Promote Second Language Acquisition." They noted at least four principles that are at the heart of communicative language teaching:

(1)  Children learn language through purposeful, real, here-and-now experiences with language.

(2)  Children learn language as a medium of communication rather than as a curricular subject; language is viewed as a verb (doing language, or communicating) rather than as a noun (knowledge of a language).

(3)  Children learn language through creative construction; errors are part of the natural acquisition process.

(4)  Children learn language through *interaction*; this involves *exposure* to language as communication as well as opportunities to *practice* language as communication in a *variety of contexts*.

Immersion education, in its present form, is already an excellent example of communicative language teaching in terms of points 1–3. However, point 4, concerning language interaction, may be the weak link. Further, the authors offered seven suggestions for organizing a communicative classroom:

(1) *Organize for collaboration*—collaboration involves "two-way" classroom experiences with teachers and students working together and students working with each other.

(2) *Organize for purpose*—communicative activities have specific purposes that require an authentic need to communicate.

(3) *Organize for student interest*—when students are truly interested, they have a reason to communicate.

(4) *Organize for previous experience*—communicative classrooms build on what the students already know.

(5) *Organize for holism*—communicative activities require an integration of all language and cognitive skills.

(6) *Organize for support*—second-language learners need to know that their efforts to communicate are valued.

(7) *Organize for variety*—communicative classrooms must include a variety of materials, purposes, topics, activities, and ways of interacting.

According to Enright and McCloskey (1985, p. 439), teachers can organize their classrooms with "an eye toward exploiting their language-learning potential in addition to accomplishing their original purpose [to teach subject matter]." To accomplish this, however, a fundamental change in the traditional, teacher-centered classroom must take place: "No Talking!"—the edict of traditional classrooms—must become "Yes Talking!"—the password to communicative classrooms.

With the general principles of communicative language teaching in mind, two kinds of classroom activities—group work and cooperative learning—which are strongly supported by research and could easily be adapted for use in immersion teaching, are considered.


## Group Work

One excellent way to convert to a more communicatively oriented classroom is through the use of group work. Group work involves the systematic grouping of students for the purpose of participating in structured tasks. Long and Porter (1985, p. 207) recommended group work as an "attractive alternative to the teacher-led, 'lockstep' mode and a viable

classroom substitute for individual conversations with native speakers."
They offered five pedagogical arguments for the use of group work in
second-language learning.

First, *group work increases language practice opportunities*. We know
that in teacher-centered classes students do not get much chance to talk.
Studies have shown that, in a typical class, teachers talk for at least half,
and often for as much as two-thirds, of the class period. Long and Porter
estimated that, in an average language class of 30 students in a public
secondary school, students have a chance to talk about 30 seconds per
lesson—or just one hour per student per year. Of course, immersion
classes are different because the second language is used as the medium of
instruction for all or part of the day; consequently, immersion students
have much more exposure to the second language. This increased exposure probably accounts for the fact that immersion students develop
nativelike receptive skills. The example noted previously of the tape-re-
corded classes in Canada (see Swain & Lapkin, 1986), however, illustrated the point that, even with more instruction in the language in the
immersion setting, students still have relatively limited opportunities to
*use* the language for any extended period of time. Group work is one way
to take language out of the mouths of teachers and give immersion students the chance to produce in the second language.

Second, *group work improves the quantity and quality of student talk*.
Studies have shown that second-language learners working in groups produce more talk with other learners than with native speakers. Nonnatives
were found to use a wider range of speech acts in order to negotiate their
ideas with their nonnative counterparts and they also corrected each other
more in small groups. Furthermore, nonnatives did *not* produce any more
accurate or grammatical speech when talking with nonnatives than in conversations with native speakers. These findings contradict the popular belief that nonnatives are not good conversational partners. Instead, nonnatives can provide each other with genuine communicative practice that is
typically unavailable to them in the environment outside of the immersion
classroom or in a tightly controlled teacher-centered classroom.

The third pedagogical argument advanced by Long and Porter is that
*group work helps individualize instruction*. A classroom contains a variety
of personalities, attitudes, motivations, interests, cognitive and learning
styles, and cultural backgrounds. In addition, varying levels of second-language comprehension, fluency, and grammar skills add to these myriad
differences. Careful selection of groups and assignments can lead to lessons that are better suited to individual needs.

The fourth argument is that *group work promotes a positive affective climate*. For many students, being called upon is very stressful, especially when they must "perform" in a second language. Small groups provide a much less threatening environment, often allowing students to take more risks. The fifth and related argument is that *group work motivates learners*. This point assumes that an environment that is more tailored to individual differences is nonthreatening, provides a change of pace from the typical teacher-controlled format, and increases student motivation.

## Cooperative Learning

Cooperative learning provides a second example of activities that incorporate a communicative approach to teaching (also see Jacob & Mattson, 1990). This approach grew out of a concern that competitive classrooms do not promote access to learning for all students equally. To counteract the traditional classroom organizational structure, cooperative learning activities reconfigure the classroom, dividing the class "into small teams whose members are all positively interdependent" (Kagan, 1986, p. 241). In order to accomplish any assigned task, all members of the team have a designated role or responsibility. Groups are assigned a group grade, creating the interdependence among members that makes cooperative learning different from the more general group work activities described earlier.

Research on cooperative learning shows positive results on academic achievement, race relations, and the development of mutual concerns among students in a wide variety of settings, subject areas, and grade levels (Hawley, Rosenholtz, Goodstein, & Hasselbring, 1984). Cooperative learning also appears to be particularly effective with low-achieving students. However, Slavin (1983) noted that cooperative learning strategies only succeed to the extent that they are carefully and systematically implemented. He cited the following four necessary conditions for successful implementation:

(1) a high degree of structure;

(2) a regular schedule of learning activities and well-specified learning objectives;

(3) clear, individual accountability among team members; and

(4) a well-defined reward system, including rewards or recognition for successful groups.

Thus it appears that cooperative learning offers an important set of techniques and activities for any classroom. However, because our focus is on ways to create a more communicative immersion classroom, it is important to consider the additional benefits that cooperative learning provides for extended opportunities in second-language development. In addition to the more general academic and prosocial advantages that cooperative learning promotes, the methodology also holds tremendous potential for language development.

McGroarty (1989) noted several major benefits of cooperative learning for enhancing second-language learning in linguistically heterogeneous bilingual classroom situations. Five of her arguments can be applied with equal force to the foreign language setting of the immersion classroom:

(1) Cooperative learning, as exemplified in small group work, provides frequent opportunities for natural second-language practice and oral negotiation of meaning.

(2) Cooperative learning provides an additional way to incorporate content-area and language instruction.

(3) Cooperative learning requires a variety of materials, including texts and nonverbal, visual, and manipulative strategies to support instruction. This array creates a favorable context for instruction.

(4) Cooperative learning models redefine the role of the teacher in ways that allow them to expand their professional skills to deal with meaning as well as form.

(5) Cooperative learning encourages students to take an active role in the acquisition of language skills and to encourage each other as they work on problems of mutual interest.

In sum, cooperative learning techniques offer an exciting new challenge to immersion teachers through their well-documented contributions to learning in general and through the great potential they offer for extended opportunities in second-language practice.


## SOME REMAINING ISSUES


There are a number of other issues that may be unique to immersion teaching that a prospective teacher should be aware of. These are discussed in the final section.

(1) *Student selection.* Although immersion teachers may not be responsible for making decisions about student selection, their feedback is critical in formulating and reformulating guidelines for the screening of students. Few restrictions generally apply on admittance to immersion programs. Research has shown, for example, that special education students do as well in immersion as they would in monolingual programs (Bruck, 1978). Some immersion teachers have strong opinions about the kinds of children that should *not* participate in immersion programs; others feel equally strongly about open access for as many types of children as possible. It is important that experienced teachers have a say in the decision-making process so that policy is based on actual classroom experiences and not on general notions of who belongs in immersion and who does not.

(2) *Dealing with parents.* Immersion parents are frequently very active advocates of the immersion program. Initially, they raise a lot of questions and concerns. The immersion teacher must be well versed on the why's and how's of immersion in order to satisfy concerned parents. Second, immersion teachers must become skillful in channeling parental interest to form a positive and constructive component of the program. Third, immersion teachers must learn to deal with many practical issues, such as how parents can help their children at home in a language with which they are unfamiliar or how to train parents to be effective classroom volunteers.

(3) *Maintaining good staff relations.* Because most immersion programs are programs within a total school, immersion teachers usually must work with nonimmersion teachers at the same school site. Unfortunately, instances of divisiveness among the two staffs have been documented, for example, when one group feels that a particular program is receiving too much attention or more than its share of resources. Immersion teachers and administrators should be aware of the potential for this kind of conflict and of the need to develop strategies for creating positive relationships among the faculty.

(4) *Articulating immersion programs from kindergarten to twelfth grade.* Another important lesson we have learned from the past is that it is *never* too soon to plan for the continuation of the immersion program in the junior (or middle) and senior high schools. Long-range planning indicates a district's commitment to students and parents and thereby aids in the elementary school recruitment process. It also creates the needed time for program planning, curriculum and materials development, and teacher selection. Well-articulated junior and senior high school programs can

offer immersion students the extended opportunity to build on the foundation established in elementary school and to prepare them for future academic and professional pursuits. The investment in elementary immersion is too great to allow the progress made to slip in the upper grades. All immersion teachers must share the commitment to a well-articulated program from elementary school through high school.

(5) *Student assessment.* On what basis should promotion decisions be made in immersion? Should teachers base these decisions on students' standardized English test results or on their proficiency in the second language (which is rarely assessed formally due to lack of suitable instruments)? These are important questions that immersion teachers need to work out with school administrators to formulate a sound evaluation policy.

(6) *Teacher evaluation.* How can an immersion administrator, who typically does not speak the immersion language, fairly or effectively evaluate teachers who, particularly at the lower elementary levels, conduct their classes exclusively in the second language? Guidelines for teacher evaluation must be established that incorporate input from immersion teachers.

(7) *Coordinating goals.* In addition to the immersion program, many schools offer other educational programs such as Instrumental Music, Gifted and Talented Education (GATE), and Artists in Residence, which, of course, are typically conducted in English. Students may participate in these programs several times a week, losing exposure to the second language and increasing their exposure to English. Many teachers are concerned about how these possibly conflicting objectives can be reconciled. A need exists for close coordination of these various educational goals and objectives.

(8) *Formal second-language instruction.* Those interested in immersion education, from theorists to teachers, have debated the question of the role of formal language instruction in immersion programs. The original thinking, in keeping with the belief that second-language acquisition processes parallel first-language learning, was that there was no need to teach the formal rules of the second language. Through the years, however, more and more immersion teachers, noting persistent grammatical errors, have begun on their own to incorporate formal grammar teaching into their language arts curricula. In fact, most of the immersion teachers surveyed reported that they teach the formal rules of the immersion language as part of the curriculum. There is a range of opinion on when formal grammar teaching should commence, although the general consensus is that is should begin in the lower elementary grades. It is critical that, when

taught, grammar rules should be presented *in context* (or within the language arts or writing activities). This topic remains in need of further research; however, it is an excellent example of an area where teachers have recognized a need and developed materials to address it.

Other needs in immersion methodology require attention but are beyond the scope of this chapter. Certainly there is still a great need to develop appropriate, challenging materials in the many immersion languages. A second need area is treatment of instructional issues such as team teaching and strategies for teaching multigrade classrooms (a common immersion phenomenon). Experienced immersion teachers and researchers should tackle these and other topics. In keeping with the spirit of innovation that sparked the first immersion program, it is important to continue the search for effective methodology for teaching second languages via the immersion model.

## REFERENCES

Bruck, M. (1978). The suitability of early French immersion programs for the language disabled child. *Canadian Modern Language Review, 34,* 884–887.

Cummins, J. (1986). Empowering minority students: A framework for intervention. *Harvard Educational Review, 56*(1), 18–36.

*Early French immersion: Administrator's resource book.* (1981). Vancouver, British Columbia: Ministry of Education.

*Early French immersion: Teacher's resource book.* (1981). Vancouver, British Columbia: Ministry of Education.

Enright, D. S., & McCloskey, M. (1985). Yes, talking! Organizing the classroom to promote second language acquisition. *TESOL Quarterly, 19*(3), 431–453.

Hawley, W., Rosenholtz, S., Goodstein, H., & Hasselbring, T. (1984). Effective teaching. *Peabody Journal of Education, 61*(4), 15–52.

Jacob, E., & Mattson, B. (1990). Cooperative learning: Instructing limited-English-proficient students. In A. M. Padilla, H. H. Fairchild, & C. M. Valadez (Eds.), *Bilingual education: Issues and strategies.* Newbury Park, CA: Sage.

Kagan, S. (1986). Cooperative learning and sociocultural factors in schooling. In California State Department of Education, *Beyond language: Social and cultural factors in schooling language minority students* (pp. 231–298). Sacramento: California State Department of Education.

Krashen, S. D. (1984). Immersion: Why it works and what it has taught us. *Language and Society, 12,* 61–64.

Lapkin, S., & Cummins, J. (1984). Canadian French immersion education: Current administrative and instructional practices. In *Studies on immersion education: A collection for*

*United States educators* (pp. 87–112). Sacramento: California State Department of Education.

Long, M., & Porter, P. (1985). Group work, interlanguage talk, and second language acquisition. *TESOL Quarterly, 19*(2), 207–228.

McGroarty, M. (1989). The benefits of cooperative learning arrangements in second language instruction. *NABE Journal, 13*, 127–143.

Slavin, R. E. (1983). *Cooperative learning.* New York: Longman.

Swain, M., & Lapkin, S. (1986). Immersion French in secondary schools: "The goods" and the "The bads." *Contact, 5*(3), 2–9.

Wilton, F., Obadia, A., Roy, R., Saunders, A., & Tafler, R. (1984). *National study of French immersion teacher training and professional development.* Ottawa, Canada: Canadian Association of Immersion Teachers.

# 11

# Spanish Language Attrition of Immersion Graduates

## MARGUERITE ANN SNOW

Language attrition research is a small but growing field of inquiry. At the heart of the research agenda is the goal of identifying the patterns of, and influences on, attrition (the loss of an acquired language), whether as a first, second, or foreign language (see Weltens, de Bot, & van Els, 1986). Research efforts thus far have been motivated by the broad questions: "What does attrition look like?" "What are the appropriate methods for finding out what it looks like?"

Much work, however, remains to be done in a number of areas. For example, researchers need to determine the linguistic features to be specified in attrition studies. Predictive models must be developed that can account for both features lost in the attrition process and those that are retained. Once these features are specified and theoretically justified, diagnostic tests must be developed to gather useful information about patterns of language loss within and across languages. The identification of predictor variables such as individual or situational characteristics of lan guage attrition is another important problem requiring study.

The relationship between acquisition and attrition rate is not yet understood. For example, how do years of instruction, proficiency level, or type/method of instruction figure into retention or attrition? Moreover, characteristics of the period of attrition appear to affect language loss.

Such factors as the amount of postcourse exposure to the second/foreign language and culture, and the length of nonuse, need to be thoroughly investigated as factors influencing the rate of attrition over time. Other areas to be explored include examination of differential loss within linguistic skill areas, the effects of attrition on the learning of related foreign languages, and the more practical pedagogical implications for relearning a language.

Research efforts in the above areas have been constrained by a lack of theoretical models and methodological know-how, which is, of course, typical of any developing field of research. This chapter examines the processes that underlie language attrition and identifies several methodological issues within the immersion model of foreign language education.

## METHODOLOGICAL ISSUES IN
## THE IMMERSION CONTEXT

In addition to the general methodological considerations discussed above, a number of challenges confront researchers conducting attrition research. These issues are presented within the context of a study of attrition within a Spanish Immersion Program in Culver City, California.

### The Setting

The Culver City Spanish Immersion Program (SIP) was established in 1971 to provide an intensive foreign language experience for English-speaking children. Modeled after a French immersion program in Montreal, Canada (Lambert & Tucker, 1972), children in the immersion program receive the first three years of elementary school instruction in their second language (Spanish). English is introduced into the curriculum at grade three and an approximate 60/40 ratio of Spanish-English instruction is achieved by grade five, at which time the children can opt to continue in a partial immersion program at the middle school level. In the middle school, immersion students take two periods of Spanish (approximately 100 minutes) a day. There is no high school immersion program in the district; students choosing to continue in Spanish typically enroll in third-year Spanish courses that are designed for students who have had two years of high school language study.

## Baseline Data

Returning to our consideration of methodological issues in attrition research in the immersion setting, a first question is this: What should constitute the baseline data in attrition studies of immersion students? Or, more specifically, *when* should baseline data be collected?

Until recently, students attended the total immersion program through grade six, thus benefiting from a seventh year of intensive instruction in Spanish. Reorganization of the school district to deal with declining enrollment, however, necessitated placing the sixth-grade students in the middle school. Because middle school classes are departmentalized—that is, students move from class to class throughout the day—it was a major accommodation to continue the immersion program for a two-period block.

The most obvious point for baseline data collection is at the transition from the middle school to the high school when the majority of the students discontinue Spanish. However, because the middle school program is not as intensive as the elementary program, one could argue that attrition begins to set in after grade five and thus the transition from elementary to middle school would constitute the most appropriate baseline point. Furthermore, the middle school program has more of a traditional language arts focus. Thus grammar and writing skills are emphasized while reading and listening skills receive less attention in the curriculum.

A case may even be made that appropriate baseline data may be collected as early as third or fourth grade. Studies have consistently revealed that immersion students demonstrate subject matter achievement that is at or above that of students schooled in monolingual settings and that they have nativelike command of the receptive skills of reading and listening (Swain & Lapkin, 1984). However, their speaking and writing skills are generally not nativelike, with their grammar or written "accent" giving them away as second-language learners.

Genesee (1987) raises an interesting point that relates to the baseline issue. While acknowledging that immersion students in the upper elementary grades demonstrate progress in language development on standardized tests, he speculates that, in fact, "grade 6 students may simply be demonstrating that they are able to apply linguistic skills they have acquired earlier in new ways or in the service of new tasks" (Genesee, 1987, p. 60). Thus what has been considered as language development may not be linguistic growth at all but a plateau that remains until sustained opportunities to use the language for new communicative or cognitive purposes are present. Although attrition is not necessarily occurring, it does complicate the issue of appropriate baseline points when working with immersion students.

## Subject Selection

A second issue in the American immersion setting is subject selection. Generally, very limited samples of immersion graduates are available for study. In the original research plan, students who had continued in the middle school program were to be compared with dropouts. However, there were few dropouts in the transition between elementary and middle school; those few students who did drop out were—unfortunately, but not surprisingly—the weakest students in Spanish.

Two other variables are also problematic when working with immersion students. From the above description of the various options immersion students have for continuing their foreign language study, it is clear that some of the immersion students do continue to study Spanish. Therefore, the "incubation period" (see Gardner, 1982) is not free from foreign language input. Moreover, even for the immersion students who discontinue Spanish in school, informal exposure to Spanish is likely in the Southern California environment.

## Advantages

Clearly, numerous methodological difficulties must be overcome in conducting attrition research in the immersion setting. However, the immersion research site offers a number of important advantages. Compared with other types of foreign language programs in the United States, immersion produces the best results (Campbell, Gray, Rhodes, & Snow, 1985). Hence, if the objective is to study children who have achieved high levels of a foreign language, the immersion model offers a promising setting.

Moreover, the stability and longevity of immersion programs provide a chance to examine attrition over a much longer period of time than is typically possible. Obviously, there is a methodological trade-off in conducting research in the immersion setting. The trade-off may be worthwhile in the long run as longitudinal studies have the potential to reveal much more about patterns of attrition than results from short-term experiments with incubation periods of only a few months or more.

The final benefit of conducting attrition research in the immersion setting is the opportunity to contribute a new dimension to the large body of existing immersion research. Since 1965, there has been a plethora of research in first- and second-language development, academic achievement, and attitudinal and motivational correlates of learning in the United States and Canada; but, to date, little research has been published on what happens to the second-language skills of immersion students. Furthermore, from a pedagogical point of view, it is important to see what happens to language skills that have been acquired "naturally" in the elementary immersion classroom when the language teaching methodology in the middle and high schools changes to emphasize grammar-based language study. The differential effect on the skill areas may reveal interesting findings.

## FOLLOW-UP OF SPANISH IMMERSION GRADUATES

In a study of the graduates of the Culver City Spanish Immersion Program, the following research questions were addressed: (a) What are the linguistic consequences of attrition? (b) What attitudinal factors predict second-language retention/attrition? (c) What are the students' patterns of formal and informal Spanish language use?

### Methodology

Subjects for the study are three groups of students included in the follow-up study. Group 1 exited the program in 1985; Group 2, in 1984; and Group 3, in 1983.

A test battery was designed to collect data on Spanish language skills, language use, attitudes and motivation, and language aptitude. The battery consisted of the following instruments: (a) the Modern Language Aptitude Test (MLAT); (b) the Modern Language Association (MLA) Cooperative Test of Spanish, Form LA—Reading and Listening subtests; and (c) the Attitude/Motivation Questionnaire—modeled after the *Attitude and Motivation Test Battery* (Gardner, Clement, Smythe, & Smythe, 1979) and used in several previous studies with Spanish immersion students (see Snow, 1985; Snow, Padilla, & Campbell, 1988).

A fourth measure was a Spanish oral interview developed for these purposes. The interview agenda included a variety of topics including questions about trips students have taken outside of the United States, their favorite childhood activities, plans for their future careers, and scenarios in which the subjects have to give directions, state preferences, apologize, and make suggestions. They are also asked to respond to a hypothetical situation by describing, for example, who they would choose to be if they could be any other person besides themselves. The final section of the interview is a picture description task.

The three groups of subjects were tested upon exiting the elementary school Spanish immersion program. For purposes of the longitudinal study, students were tested at the end of each school year in their Spanish classes at Culver City Middle School and Culver City High School. The Spanish interview was conducted by a native Spanish speaker with individual students in a small private room adjacent to the classrooms. The interviews were transcribed after each data collection period by a native Spanish speaker and reviewed for accuracy by a second native Spanish speaker.

## Preliminary Findings

*MLA test scores.* The MLA Listening and Reading subtests were administered at the end of the second year of the project for the 36 Spanish immersion graduates who had persisted in studying Spanish in middle or high school. Mean listening scores indicated a slight increase from the baseline scores for groups 1 (from 35.6 to 37.5) and 2 (38.3 to 41.3) and a statistically significant increase for group 3 (from 31.8 to 38.2). On the reading subtest, group 1 scores again increased only slightly (31.9 to 33.2), whereas groups 2 (29.6 to 36.0) and 3 (25.8 to 37.1) made much more substantial (and statistically significant) gains in reading scores from the baseline year.

The MLA Listening and Reading scores were next analyzed using the statistical technique of Rasch Modeling. The objective was to detect patterns in the data beyond those discussed above in the descriptive statistics. Rasch Modeling is commonly used in the development of educational tests to determine, for example, whether or not individual items within a test fit the patterns of all the items within the test.

The goal in test development is to ensure that a particular item measures the same thing (e.g., listening comprehension) as the other items with which it is grouped. Rasch Modeling, applied in the context of language attrition research, offers a promising statistical alternative to regression analysis when sample sizes are small (see Chen & Henning, 1985). Rasch Modeling analysis converts each test item to a scale based on probability, which in the case of the MLA test scores is the amount of fit between ability (in Spanish) and difficulty of the test item. The Rasch analysis of the baseline scores of the listening subtest revealed that there were many items that, given the subjects' current ability levels, were easy for the students. In other words, there was a mismatch in item difficulty and student ability in Spanish. The results reinforce the descriptive statistics and group comparisons, revealing that the persisters' current abilities in Spanish listening and reading, in Rasch Modeling terms, are sufficiently high, rendering the majority of the MLA items easy.

Rasch analysis of the reading results generally provided the same picture as the listening data, indicating that at this point there were not enough challenging items for the students' current skill levels in listening and reading.

### Spanish Oral Interview

Excerpts of the oral interviews of two subjects are presented below. These excerpts were taken from the picture description task and provided the most directly comparable data because the cartoon confined the subjects to a particular sequence of events. Two students were interviewed at the end of grade six and then again at the end of grade seven. The first excerpt is taken from an interview with Nina, a persister in the immersion program. Nina was selected for the follow-up interview because her MLA test scores were the highest in her group and it was of interest to see what kind of oral language skills accompanied such high levels of proficiency in the receptive skills of listening and reading.

*Nina (persister): Grade Six*

I: *Muy bien. Ahora te voy a mostrar esta caricatura. Describe lo que ves.*

S: *Un señor está servido en su cama y estaba como casi durmiendo y cayó en y durmió para unas horas y cuando (uhm) woke up como se dice, fue a su sala y su (uhm) su la mujer tenía amigas in la casa y vió en en sus pajamas.*

I: *¿Y son pajamas esas?*

S: *No es su (uhm) en su traje se baño de ella y ella está la mujer da el una chaqueta para poner porque ella estaba embarrassed.*

*Grade Seven*

S: *(laugh) (uhm) el señor está (uhm) en la cama y esta (uhm)*
   *quiere dormier y está dormiendo y unas horas despues el está*
   *levantando y caminando en tu casa pero cuando (uhm) cuando*
   *estaba en (uhm) en la en la (uhm) en la . . . ¿Es sala?*

I: *Sí.*

S: *¿Cuando está en la sala (uhm) su esposa tiene (uhm) tiene unas*
   *mujeres para (uhm) para té y café para (uhm uhm) para*
   *lonche? ¿Y cuando ella ve a su esposo, el tiene solamente (uhm)*
   *su no no tiene ropa y ella está corriendo para poner su (uhm)*
   *para poner su jaqueta a el porque el no sabía que ella tenía*
   *(uhm) tenía companía?*

\* \* \*

*John (program drop out): Grade Six*

I: *John, te voy a mostrar esta caricatura, dime lo que ves.*

S: *Están dizzy! (laugh) (uhm) número uno están están sleepy ellos*
   *y va a dormir, no están muy no están son ready to go to sleep...*
   *dormir (uhm) el I guess (uhm) el (uhm) el niño esta pará te for*
   *dos niñas y el niño están comi...comiendo el niño con un co...*

*Grade Seven*

S: *Este niño están muy...dizzy y están...muy tired y...están en el*
   *bed y...y...(yawns) y...tam...(long pause) y...y (uhm) walk down*
   *el stairs y open el door y...y es mamá (uhm)...runs y están put*
   *on un coat.*

Examination of the excerpt reveals that Nina shifted in tense usage from the first to the second interview. In the grade-six interview, her narration of events was mainly accomplished using the past tense while the story line in the grade-seven interview was described mainly in the present. There are two possible explanations for this shift in tense usage. In the elementary immersion program, students had much more opportunity to use the language productively. The elementary program was more intensive and the classroom activities more conducive to oral language use. In contrast, as mentioned, the middle school program is set up more in the manner of a traditional foreign language class. The students receive instruction in formal grammar (e.g., irregular past tense forms), but they have little opportunity to use the language spontaneously in an open-ended format such as the interview required. The second possible explanation is that Nina chose a different mode of narration in the grade-seven interview. In English, it is possible to use the present tense to describe events in a sequence. Perhaps her use of the present tense in Spanish was an alternative way to provide the information requested in the picture description task.

There was also a shift in strategy for vocabulary usage between the two interviews. In the first interview, Nina resorted to English for words she could not recall or did not know (e.g., *woke up, embarrassed*) whereas in the second interview she avoided the use of English and instead used a false cognate for the word she was uncertain of (i.e., *compania*).

The second excerpt is taken from interviews with John, a program dropout after grade six. In contrast to Nina, John had the lowest MLA scores of his group. It is clear from the excerpt that his baseline Spanish is very weak; he had a great deal of trouble describing the cartoon in both grades, but with the exception of one phrase of English (ready to go to sleep), he at least attempted the task in Spanish in grade six. In the grade seven interview, he used the Spanish *y* ("and") to connect the action verbs provided in English. A year after dropping out of the program, John is basically incapable of describing the cartoon.


DISCUSSION AND CONCLUSION


The results of the MLA Listening and Reading subtests provide a continuous record of the receptive language skills of the immersion students being examined in this study. Because the students are still exposed to Spanish in the partial immersion program, it is not surprising that their test scores improved. However, because their exposure is more limited in the middle school and the focus of instruction is on formal aspects of the second language, it is somewhat surprising that the groups exhibited increases in receptive skills. Certainly, one explanation is that the students are learning more Spanish. Another possibility is that a kind of "residual" learning is taking place. This residual learning may be a manifestation of continued cognitive development and expanding competence in the first language, which produces a positive effect on Spanish language growth quite independent of the formal instruction they are currently receiving in Spanish.

The research plan calls for administering the MLA to the three groups of students at the end of each school year, although it is difficult to predict what patterns of retention and attrition should occur when the students' exposure to Spanish is severely reduced or when they leave the immersion program altogether. Two recent studies have also employed objective tests, although with mixed results. Gardner, Lalonde, Moorcraft, and Evers (1987) found no significant differences on an objective battery, which included measures of work production, composition writing, and listening comprehension, between students who continued the study of French after grade twelve and those who had dropped out. Similar to the interim findings reported here, Weltens and van Els (1986) found an increase in the cloze test scores of students who had dropped out of French for two years and no significant differences on a French grammar test. They attributed the increase on the cloze test to several possible sources: general cognitive growth, increasing test wiseness, or retroactive transfer to French of skills learned in other foreign languages.

The results from the Rasch Modeling analysis provide useful information about the listening and reading skills of the immersion persisters, especially because the results of the descriptive statistics may be difficult to interpret. Over time, the patterns of the preliminary results are expected to change as the students discontinue Spanish in the later grades. As their abilities in the receptive skills decline, the model predicts that the students will begin to have trouble with the items that currently present little or no difficulty and, therefore, that there will not be such a large differential between ability and difficulty.

The results also confirm earlier findings regarding the durability of the receptive skills of the immersion students. In a previous study with immersion graduates, Snow, Padilla, and Campbell (1988) found that their receptive skills did not show signs of erosion until high school, whereas their productive skills evidenced decline shortly after the students completed the elementary immersion program. There is some evidence from the oral interviews of a loss of productive skills when exposure to the foreign language is reduced.

The student interviews promise a rich source of data for examining the students' oral skills in more detail. The difficulty in distinguishing between "failure to acquire" and actual attrition, raised by Andersen (1982), is illustrated in some of the oral interview data. Nevertheless, those data provide a great deal of information about students' speaking abilities as they progress through high school. Future analyses of the oral interviews will yield detailed quantitative information on the type, frequency, and function of content words in both Spanish and English as well as isolation of the particular semantic and syntactic contexts of language usage. Current plans call for adding a retrospective task to the test battery. Retrospective techniques have been used by a number of researchers in second-language acquisition research (see Cohen, 1983, 1987; Faerch & Kasper, 1987; Kasper, 1988) and show promise as a useful data collection procedure in language attrition research.

In sessions immediately after taking the MLA subtests, students will be asked to tell an interviewer which items gave them trouble and speculate as to the causes of difficulty. These retrospective data will provide qualitative data to complement the MLA test scores and may reveal the compensatory strategies that learners invoke when their language skills decline. In addition, over the period of project funding, a variety of types of statistical techniques, such as Rasch Modeling, will be utilized in hopes of finding promising ways of detecting changes in the subjects' Spanish language skills over time.

The objective of this chapter has been to focus on methodological considerations in undertaking attrition research in the context of the immersion foreign language setting. It is believed that, notwithstanding several important methodological constraints, the immersion setting provides a rich environment for investigating issues in foreign language attrition, which should contribute to this growing field of inquiry.

## REFERENCES

Andersen, R. (1982). Determining the linguistic attributes of language attrition. In R. Lambert & B. Freed (Eds.), *The loss of language skills* (pp. 83–118). Rowley, MA: Newbury House.

Campbell, R. N., Gray, T. C., Rhodes, N. C., & Snow, M. A. (1985). Foreign language learning in the elementary schools: A comparison of three language programs. *Modern Language Journal, 69*, 44–54.

Chen, Z., & Henning, G. (1985). Linguistic and cultural bias in language proficiency tests. *Language Testing, 2*, 155–163.

Cohen, A. (1983). Introspecting about second language learning. *Studia Anglica Posnaniensia, 15*, 149–156.

Cohen, A. (1987). Using verbal reports in research on language learning. In C. Faerch & G. Kasper (Eds.), *Introspection in second language research* (pp. 82–95). Clevedon, England: Multilingual Matters.

Faerch, C., & Kasper, G. (1987). *Introspection in second language research*. Clevedon, England: Multilingual Matters.

Gardner, R. C. (1982). Social factors in language retention. In R. D. Lambert & B. Freed (Eds.), *The loss of language skills* (pp. 24–43). Rowley, MA: Newbury House.

Gardner, R. C., Clement, R., Smythe, P. C., & Smythe, C. L. (1979). *Attitudes and motivation test battery—revised manual*. London, Ontario: University of Western Ontario.

Gardner, R. C., Lalonde, R. N., Moorcroft, R., & Evers, F. (1987). Second language attrition: The role of motivation and use. *Journal of Language and Social Psychology, 6*(1), 29–47.

Genesee, F. (1987). *Learning through two languages: Studies of immersion and bilingual education*. Cambridge, MA: Newbury House.

Kasper, G. (1988). *Transfer of culture-specific concepts*. Paper presented at the 8th Second Language Research Forum, Honolulu, HI.

Lambert, W. E., & Tucker, G. R. (1972). *Bilingual education of children: The St. Lambert experiment*. Rowley, MA: Newbury House.

Snow, M. A. (1985). *A descriptive comparison of four Spanish immersion programs*. Unpublished doctoral dissertation, University of California, Los Angeles.

Snow, M. A., Padilla, A. M., & Campbell, R. N. (1988). Factors influencing language retention of graduates of a Spanish immersion program. *Applied Linguistics, 9*, 182 197.

Swain, M., & Lapkin, S. (1984). *Evaluating bilingual education: A Canadian case study*. Clevedon, England: Multilingual Matters.

Weltens, B. (1987). The attrition of foreign language skills: A literature review. *Applied Linguistics, 8*, 22–38.

Weltens, B., de Bot, K., & van Els, T. (Eds.). (1986). *Language attrition in progress*. Dordrecht, Holland (Providence, USA): Foris.

Weltens, B., & van Els, T. (1986). The attrition of French as a foreign language: Interim results. In B. Weltens, K. de Bot, & T. van Els (Eds.), *Language attrition in progress*. Dordrecht, Holland (Providence, USA): Foris.

# PART IV

# Content-Based Instruction and Foreign Language Education

*In Part IV, JoAnn Crandall and G. Richard Tucker, in "Content-Based Instruction in Second and Foreign Languages" (Chapter 12), define content-based instruction and describe techniques, strategies, and suggestions for program implementation. In addition, they cover areas of needed research and development.*

Crandall and Tucker identify the benefits of content-based instruction for both language minority and language majority students. In exploring a variety of models of content-based instruction, Crandall and Tucker provide specific suggestions for developing instructional objectives, content-compatible language, curricular materials, and hands-on learning experiences. They conclude with a call for future work in teacher education, student assessment, program evaluation, materials development, and research into the process of content-based instruction.

Helena A. Curtain and Linda S. Martínez, in "Elementary School, Content-Based Foreign Language Instruction" (Chapter 13), review the background and rationales for content-based instruction and note that students both gain a general education and acquire a foreign language. Curtain and Martínez note that using the foreign language to teach traditional content areas makes the learning of the language *purposeful*, thereby enhancing acquisition.

Curtain and Martínez provide a number of specific guidelines for integrating language and content, including suggestions for planning the curriculum, instructional coordination among language teachers and content teachers, identifying materials, planning lessons, and evaluation. They note that instructors must be wary of providing a "watered down" curriculum and emphasize that the simplification of language should not connote the simplification of concepts. The first appendix provides six sample lesson plans drawn from math, science, and social studies. The second appendix provides further readings.

Sheila M. Shannon, in "Spanish for Spanish Speakers: A Translation Skills Curriculum" (Chapter 14), reveals the unique foreign language learning needs of native speakers of the target language. These students, when mainstreamed with native English speakers, often meander in classes geared to develop only a minimal language proficiency. Shannon, therefore, describes a unique program of teaching Spanish to native Spanish speakers. The program involves using the students as translators and interpreters, thus contextualizing their language learning in a real-world type of application.

Shannon's description of the program is as one that "empowers" students (see Cummins, 1986). She reports the compromises made between the intended curriculum, the implemented curriculum, and the experienced curriculum, and notes that students and teachers had to overcome some initial resistance to their empowerment.

Halford H. Fairchild and Amado Padilla, in "Innovations in Foreign Language Education: Contributions from Bilingual Education" (Chapter 15), provide synthesis of the volume. In describing contributions to foreign language education from ESL and bilingual education, Fairchild and Padilla review the contents of the companion volume to this one (Padilla, Fairchild, & Valadez, 1990). The authors, and the volume, conclude with a call for continued innovations in language education and for making education as transformative as possible for individuals and the broader society.

## REFERENCES

Cummins, J. (1986). Empowering minority students: A framework for intervention. *Harvard Educational Review, 56* 18–36.

Padilla, A. M., Fairchild, H. H., & Valadez, C. M. (Eds.). (1990). *Bilingual education: Issues and strategies.* Newbury Park, CA: Sage.

# 12

# Content-Based Instruction in Second and Foreign Languages

JOANN CRANDALL
G. RICHARD TUCKER

Content-based instruction is an approach to language instruction that integrates the presentation of topics or tasks from subject matter classes (e.g., math, social studies) within the context of teaching a second or foreign language. This chapter discusses the intent and design of content-based instructional programs, describes some of the techniques and strategies in content-based instruction, suggests mechanisms of program implementation, and illuminates needed areas of research and development.

## THE BENEFITS OF LANGUAGE/CONTENT INTEGRATION

Educators are increasingly using academic subject matter as a means of improving language instruction and tailoring instruction to the specific language needs of individual students. The dramatic increase in the size of the language minority population in the United States, and the increased recognition of the importance of foreign language communicative proficiency on the part of all Americans, underscore the importance of improving the practice of second-language pedagogy.

By integrating language and content, students' proficiency in the foreign language is enhanced while they are also being provided with content instruction necessary for success in scholastic environments. Moreover, this model of instruction is beneficial for both language minority and language majority individuals.

Integrated language and content instructional programs provide students with the opportunity to acquire the more formal, "decontextualized" (Snow, 1987), cognitively complex academic language used in problem solving and in the oral and written communication of ideas (see Cummins, 1981). As such, these programs promote the achievement of language proficiency beyond the mere development of social language skills, which is more commonly addressed in traditional language classrooms (Cantoni-Harvey, 1987; Curtain & Pesola, 1988; Mohan, 1986).

Thus the integration of language and content instruction is of major interest to both foreign language educators and educators of English as a second language. For second-language educators, the need is acute. For teachers of ESL, the dramatic increase in the number of language minority individuals in the United States mandates a similar concern with their mastery of both English and traditional academic content.

## THE ESL STUDENT

Due to recent demographic trends, many metropolitan school districts have a majority of their school-age population coming from homes in which a language other than English is spoken. By the year 2000, the majority of children in major metropolitan area schools will most likely be language minority students (Crandall & Tucker, in press).

Although some of these students enter school with a demonstrated proficiency in English, their proficiency is usually inadequate for the complex cognitive tasks, in English, that school demands. For those with limited or no English proficiency, the challenges are even greater. Although bilingual education programs enable students to continue cognitive and academic growth in their mother tongue, these programs are relatively scarce for the more common, and virtually nonexistent for the less common, non-English languages (i.e., languages other than Spanish, French, and German).

Language minority youth, as a result, are more commonly assigned to transitional programs in which students are provided with English as a second language instruction for an hour or so daily, usually for one to three years, during which time they are expected to acquire enough English to make the transition into regular, English-only classes with native English-speaking peers.

Unfortunately, although these students may acquire social skills in English—to talk informally with other children and with their teachers—they are frequently not able to perform the more cognitively complex academic language tasks that are required in math, science, or social studies classes.

This learning impediment has been traced to the lack of "cognitive academic language proficiency" (Cummins, 1981; Dawe, 1984) or the inability to deal with increasingly decontextualized language (Snow, 1987), the kind of language needed to understand math, science, and social studies. Almost immediately after graduation from ESL programs and "mainstreaming" into English-medium classes, these students frequently experience academic difficulty and fall progressively behind their English-speaking peers (Collier, 1987).

This problem is particularly acute for Hispanic students, who constitute the largest language minority group in North America. Approximately half of these students leave school prior to high school graduation. An even more grim statistic is the following: If a student in the United States is a male Hispanic, born outside of the United States, who entered school with little or no English proficiency, and lives in a family at or below the poverty line, his chances of graduating from high school are nearly zero (Cardenas, Robledo, & Waggoner, 1988).

Whereas the lack of proper role models (i.e., models with a strong educational background), problems in cross-cultural communication, low socioeconomic status, and other factors play a role, a significant factor in the achievement failures of these students is the burden that English language medium instruction places on them, especially in math and science (Crandall, Dale, Rhodes, & Spanos, 1986; Cuevas, 1984).

## THE FOREIGN LANGUAGE STUDENT

For language majority students, the need for curricular innovation is also great. Relatively few American students study a foreign language for more than two years, and even those with formal foreign language instruction seldom attain sufficient communicative proficiency to gain access to more than the most basic texts written in that language. Moreover, they are typically unable to carry on discussions of a complex nature or otherwise interact or negotiate effectively in that language (Crandall & Tucker, 1989).

If students are not presented with complex cognitive texts and tasks, with opportunities to develop advanced oral and written language skills in their foreign language classes, then it is not surprising that they exit from these programs with limited proficiency. Foreign language educators, therefore, are looking toward content-enriched or content-based language instruction to help expand the proficiency of language majority students by presenting portions of their traditional academic curriculum through the medium of a foreign language (Curtain & Pesola, 1988; Schinke-Llano, 1985).

## SOME PROGRAM MODELS

The integration of academic content and language instruction is not new to the teaching of English as a second language. It has been used in tertiary programs (such as "English for Specific Purposes") as well as secondary programs (such as "English for Academic Purposes"). Similarly, language/content integration is not new to adult programs that teach vocational English while teaching job-related skills.

The origins of language/content instructional programs may be traced to efforts to teach writing across the curriculum or reading skills in various content areas (see Crandall, 1987, for a fuller discussion). However, the scope of language/content integration programs has increased dramatically in recent years, with instruction provided by language teachers, content teachers, or both.

Foreign language teachers have implemented content-based language instructional models in a number of disparate programs. These include partial or total immersion programs, where part of the child's academic instruction is received through the medium of a foreign language (also see Lindholm, 1990, in this connection, for a treatment of immersion programs for language minority youngsters). It has also been incorporated into the teaching of a traditional academic course (often history or social studies) through the foreign language. Finally, two-way interlocking or bilingual immersion programs in which students of two or more ethnolinguistic backgrounds are brought together, have also beneficially adopted the integration of language and content (Campbell, Gray, Rhodes, & Snow, 1985; Tucker & Crandall, 1985, 1989).

The integration of language and content may be found in all grade levels, from elementary through college level. These programs may be within the domain of the language teacher, the content teacher, or both, depending upon specific circumstances. In a content-based language program, the language teacher (usually with collegial assistance from a teacher who teaches another content area) develops a special language class that adopts the concepts, tasks, and curricular materials from the content area. For example, the class could be a math/ESL course in which English language skills are taught as a mechanism for instruction in mathematical problem solving. As another example, a history course might be taught in a foreign language such as Spanish, French, German, or Russian.

Language/content integration enables students to acquire academic language skills in that language, although the extent to which the teacher is responsible for actual subject matter instruction varies from providing the necessary language skills for the content class to actually teaching the subject matter of the content class (see Crandall, Spanos, Christian, Simich-Dudgeon, & Willetts, 1987; Short, Crandall, & Christian, 1989).

Conversely, subject matter teachers (frequently with the assistance of the language specialist) may adapt their instruction to accommodate different levels of language proficiency in their classes. These classes, known as sheltered English, or language-sensitive content, classes, are increasingly available in schools where language minority students constitute a large proportion of the entire student body. Here, the language teacher acts as a resource for other teachers and, ideally, helps those other teachers to increase the mastery of academic concepts and skills on the part of linguistic minority students.

These techniques might focus on the use of demonstrations, visuals, or other objects in order to establish meaning. In a similar vein, the use of interaction and communication activities in the classroom enables students to effectively communicate in the terminology of the subject matter. And, in some instances, they might involve the use of adapted or simplified texts and materials (Crandall, Spanos, Christian, Simich-Dudgeon, & Willetts, 1987; Short, Crandall, & Christian, 1989).

Some programs—especially at the tertiary level—have parallel instructional designs, also referred to as paired or adjunct courses (Snow & Brinton, 1988). In these designs, students receive instruction from two teachers, a language teacher, who may focus on the reading or writing skills required for a history or psychology course, and the history or psychology professor, who focuses on concept development while promoting students' writing skills in collaboration with the language instructor.

An example of a program that used all three approaches, with integrated instruction offered by the language teacher, the content teacher, and in parallel courses, is a program provided by the Center for Applied Linguistics (CAL) to Honduran students in Tegucigalpa preparing for university study in the United States. In that program, bilingual instructors taught the math and science classes by progressively integrating more English language in their instruction during the three trimesters. The first semester is marked by the use of Spanish-medium textbooks and instruction. The second is characterized by instruction in English at a level appropriate to the level of the students in a "sheltered" setting. The third uses English as the medium for texts and instruction. Simultaneously, English teachers introduce progressively more content into their language arts instruction, using both content-based and parallel instructional techniques.

At the elementary level, a two-way bilingual or interlocking immersion model may be employed. According to this model, students from two different language and ethnic groups are taught in one language in one class and are then shifted to another class and language for other curricular content. In these programs, all instruction must be sheltered or integrated with language development, because at any time at least some of the students in the class are not proficient in the language of instruction (see Tucker & Crandall, 1989).

## FEATURES OF A CONTENT-BASED
## INSTRUCTIONAL PROGRAM

Effective implementation of a content-based instructional program must give attention to the following eight characteristics (for a fuller discussion, see Cuevas, 1984; Short, Crandall, & Christian, 1989; Snow, Met, & Genesee, in press).

### Deriving Instructional Objectives

Instructional objectives are typically drawn from the intersection of language, academic content, and thinking or study skills. A language instructor might, for example, focus on the ways that addition is signalled in mathematics or algebraic word problems (e.g., *the sum of, and, increased by,* or *in addition to*) and help students to use this language as individuals or in groups. The math teacher, in contrast, might include strategies for setting up and solving these problems, while noting the special language in which these problems are embedded. Both would directly or indirectly involve the thinking skills of analysis and classification (see Spanos, Rhodes, Dale, & Crandall, 1988, for a discussion of the special language features of mathematics and algebra that pose difficulty to both linguistically different and English-speaking students).

## Developing Background Knowledge

Schema or background knowledge must be developed in the language. This is typically accomplished through oral language activities that precede extensive reading and writing activities. Using top-down processing, general knowledge is developed before details are addressed.

## Content-Compatible Language

Both content-compatible and content-obligatory language can be included (see Snow, Met, & Genesee, in press). Thus, while the teaching of magnetism necessarily includes terms such as *to attract, to repel, magnetic properties, magnetic fields,* and classification language and skills, it also provides an opportunity for developing vocabulary on a variety of items that can be evaluated as to their magnetic properties. Other content-compatible language may include descriptive language and rhetorical skills concerning, for example, the patterns iron filings make when a magnet is used.

## Social Language

Paired and small group interaction techniques are used to develop and demonstrate proficiency in the academic language. Cooperative learning strategies (see Jacob & Mattson, 1990) and peer tutoring may also be employed. Activities should be specifically developed to encourage student interaction with the content material and with their deliberate "negotiation of meaning" with each other. When feasible (class size and conditions permitting), the teacher's role may shift to one of being a facilitator of learning rather than the didactic presenter of information or lecturer. Although didactic instruction is still necessary in certain contexts, teachers find it beneficial to interact with small groups of students when redirection, clarification, or other explanations are needed.

## Materials

A wide range of materials are used in the classroom. In the past, language classes focused on two kinds of texts: extended discourse, such as that found in textbooks or novels, and dialogues, such as those found in plays or in other language textbooks. However, among the practical outcomes of language/content integration, students must be able to interact with and produce a variety of texts: maps, charts, graphs, tables, lists, diagrams, lab reports, time lines, and the like.

Authentic materials from the content area can be used, although it is often necessary to adapt the information to make it maximally accessible to students with limited proficiency in the language of instruction. This does not imply that the material is "watered down" or less conceptually rich. It does, however, require that the information be restructured so that relationships among ideas become clearer and the new vocabulary is sufficiently contextualized in the early presentations.

Ironically, the restructuring of large amounts of connected discourse often results in the presentation of that information in other kinds of texts, such as tables or flowcharts, that are particularly amenable to assimilation on the part of the students. For example, in a lesson dealing with the branches of government, it may be more effective to use a chart presentation that reflects the specific responsibilities of each branch. In this manner, the necessary terminology within the language is developed while the concepts necessary to the topic are being clarified.

## Multiple Media

A variety of media and presentation techniques should be used to reduce the overreliance on spoken or written language as the sole means of conveying information or demonstrating meaning. Thus content-based language programs typically utilize demonstrations, a wide variety of audio-video aides, authentic materials, objects, and even guest speakers. As an example, an elementary science class on the classification of animals might benefit from a guest lecture by a veterinarian or zookeeper who brings animals and illustrates their differences and similarities. Such an exercise allows students close observation and the real-life experience that concretizes their understanding of the classification system. Although oral and written language are employed, they are supported by sources of information that use other media.

## Hands-on Learning Experiences

Experiential, discovery, and "hands-on" learning are also used to encourage students to develop concepts and to promote social interaction. These experiences place the language learning into relevant, meaningful contexts. Conducting of experiments or other research projects is especially appropriate, as are games and role-playing situations. Moreover, cooperative learning experiences (see Jacob & Mattson, 1990) promote the acquisition of social and academic language simultaneously.

## Writing

Writing is included both as a means of thinking and learning and as a mechanism for allowing students to demonstrate their level of content mastery. Developing story sequences that reflect the students' activities is a useful way of reinforcing the curriculum. Even drawings and diagrams, with appropriate labels, can be helpful. Of special value is having students write their own mathematics word problems, because this promotes the mastery of the special language of word problems as well as students' understanding of the underlying mathematical and/or scientific principles involved. Writing activities also serve as models for the kind of writing styles that are required in the content area (e.g., lab reports, essays, and research papers).

Sample lesson plans, incorporating the above strategies, are provided in Short, Crandall, and Christian (1989), Cantoni-Harvey (1987), and Mohan (1986).

## IMPLEMENTING A CONTENT-BASED INSTRUCTIONAL PROGRAM

In some cases, schools may decide to integrate the teaching of language—especially reading and writing—across the curriculum. Thus teams of language teachers and other subject matter teachers necessarily work together to develop a more integrated program. In other instances, a school district may decide to develop integrated curricula so that instructors, as individuals, seek integration between language and content.

Programs are typically implemented because of interested teachers who seek to learn from each other through classroom observation, informal interviews, and a collaborative analysis of texts and other curricular materials. To accomplish the shared discussion and collaboration, administrators must grant adequate planning time, both before the academic year and during the year. Time is needed to plan the curriculum, to develop lesson plans, to coordinate evaluations, and to revise these as they are being implemented.

A critical factor in the successful implementation of language/content programs is the support of an administrator (such as a school principal) who provides resources for planning, preservice and in-service training, and curriculum development. It is also critical for administrators to ensure that collaborating teachers have the same students in their classes. Although this is obvious, more than one content-based language program has experienced difficulty because this kind of planning had not taken place (see Crandall & Tucker, 1989).

## FUTURE DEVELOPMENTS

Because of the recency of the content-based instructional approach, a number of areas remain in which additional work is needed. These include teacher education, student assessment, program evaluation, and the preparation of textbooks and other curricular materials. Additional research into the academic language and specific linguistic requirements of mathematics, science, and other content areas is also vitally needed.

Unfortunately, current language teacher preservice and in-service education does not specifically address ways of integrating language and content instruction. Even more problematic is the inadequate instruction for teachers to perform needs assessments or to analyze curricular materials for their language and cognitive requirements. As a result, language teachers may feel inadequately prepared to structure and teach a content-based course.

To help provide needed education and training, a number of educational programs have been developed for elementary-, secondary-, and tertiary-level instructors at local, state, and national levels. For example, a number of summer institutes for elementary foreign language immersion teachers are available as are institutes for college and university professors seeking to integrate language and content. But these are in short supply and are often only at isolated educational sites. It is rare, indeed, to provide peer observation and feedback, or sustained coaching, to assist teachers in implementing this curricular innovation.

What is needed is a comprehensive educational program, inserting appropriate course work into preservice education and then providing an ongoing program of in-service education. This in-service education must involve observation, discussion, demonstration, and coaching for teachers attempting to implement this challenging approach. Ideally, master teachers should be identified and trained to function as trainers in their institutions, providing observation, feedback, and collaborative learning.

Another critical challenge is in the area of student assessment and evaluation. What should be assessed? How should it be assessed?

If a program is truly integrated, then both academic concepts and language should be tested, but we are aware of few instruments that are truly appropriate (but see Rhodes & Thompson, Chapter 5, this volume). Instead, teachers typically use a battery of language proficiency tests, achievement tests, and other information measures.

What is needed is a series of measures that evaluate how well a student has mastered academic language and academic content (in the target language) as well as tests that sufficiently separate these components to identify students' strengths and weaknesses.

Some initial attempts in both second- and foreign language programs have been made by testing language within a content framework. In addition, a series of sample assessment items in mathematics have been developed that teachers use to measure student progress in understanding math and language concepts.

Another area for continued work is in program evaluation. It is not too surprising that no longitudinal evaluations of content-based instructional programs have been published, perhaps due to the notoriously complex and difficult methods required to assess the efficacy of different language teaching methods. In addition, because these programs are relatively new, they are difficult to characterize in a way that makes them amenable to quantitative or qualitative evaluations. Nevertheless, such evaluations are necessary if we are to be fully convinced of the effectiveness of the content-based approach and if we are to untangle the specific process variables that contribute to achievement outcomes.

Most important, however, is the pressing need for adequate materials upon which to base these programs. Currently, materials are developed idiosyncratically (or not at all), resulting in inordinate amounts of time and inefficiencies. Because the development of integrated curricula and materials is very complex and demanding, an orchestrated effort is needed among teachers, researchers, and publishers to redress this void.

For example, identifying grade-appropriate objectives from various subject areas, and then combining these with second-language and language arts objectives (as well as objectives for the development of critical thinking and problem-solving skills), is enormously challenging. Still, such materials are needed if we are to successfully encourage teachers to increase the academic and cognitive load in their language teaching.

Foreign language teachers have a right to expect relevant texts on geography, history, government, business, and culture to be available in the languages they teach, and even to set aside a part of the current curriculum to be taught in another language, as is done in some innovative language programs that enroll elementary immersion program graduates.

Finally, a great deal more research is needed to describe the ways in which language is used in content courses, and to identify the specific lexical and semantic, syntactic, and discourse features associated with, for example, math and science (see Spanos, Rhodes, Dale, & Crandall, 1988).

The number of innovative programs of integrated language and content instruction is increasing in both second and foreign languages, at elementary, secondary, and tertiary levels. Additional research, teacher education, materials and test development, and program evaluation can only serve to strengthen what has emerged as an exciting instructional approach.

## REFERENCES

Campbell, R. N., Gray, T. C., Rhodes, N. C., & Snow, M. A. (1985). Foreign language learning in the elementary schools: A comparison of three language programs. *Modern Language Journal, 69*, 44–54.

Cantoni-Harvey, G. (1987). *Content-area language instruction: Approaches and strategies.* Reading, MA: Addison-Wesley.

Cardenas, J. A., Robledo, M., & Waggoner, D. (1988). *The undereducation of American youth.* San Antonio, TX: Intercultural Development Research Association.

Chamot, A. U., & O'Malley, J. M. (1987). The cognitive academic learning approach. *TESOL Quarterly, 21*(2), 227–247.

Collier, V. P. (1987). Age and rate of acquisition of second language for academic purposes. *TESOL Quarterly, 21*(4), 617–641.

Crandall, J. A. (Ed.). (1987). *ESL through content-area instruction.* Englewood Cliffs, NJ: Prentice-Hall-Regents/Center for Applied Linguistics.

Crandall, J. A., Dale, T. C., Rhodes, N. C., & Spanos, G. A. (1986). *The language of mathematics: The English barrier.* In J. Lantolf (Ed.), *Proceedings of the Delaware Symposium on Language Studies, VII.* Newark, DE: University of Delaware Press.

Crandall, J. A., Spanos, G., Christian, D., Simich-Dudgeon, C., & Willetts, K. (1987). *Integrating language and content instruction for language minority students* (Teacher Resource Guide Number 4). Wheaton, MD: National Clearinghouse for Bilingual Education.

Crandall, J. A., & Tucker, G. R. (in press). Content-based language instruction in second and foreign languages. In *Proceedings of the 1989 Regional Language Conference.* Singapore: SEAMEO Regional Language Center.

Cuevas, G. (1984). Mathematics learning in English as a second language. *Journal for Research in Mathematics Education, 15,* 134–144.

Cummins, J. (1981). Four misconceptions about language proficiency in bilingual education. *NABE Journal, 5*(3), 31–45.

Curtain, H. A., & Pesola, C.A. (1988). *Languages and children: Making the match.* Reading, MA: Addison-Wesley.

Dawe, L. (1984, August 24–30). *A theoretical framework for the study of the effects of bilingualism on mathematics teaching and learning.* Paper presented at the Fifth International Congress on Mathematical Education, Adelaide, Australia.

Jacob, E., & Mattson, B. (1990). Cooperative learning: Instructing limited-English-proficient students. In A. M. Padilla, H. H. Fairchild, & C. M. Valadez (Eds.), *Bilingual education: Issues and strategies.* Newbury Park, CA: Sage.

Lindholm, K. J. (1987). *Directory of bilingual immersion programs: Two-way bilingual education for language minority and majority students* (Educational Report No. 8). Los Angeles: University of California, Center for Language Education and Research.

Lindholm, K. J. (1990). Bilingual immersion education: Criteria for program development. In A. M. Padilla, H. H. Fairchild, & C. M. Valadez (Eds.), *Bilingual education: Issues and strategies.* Newbury Park, CA: Sage.

Mohan, B. A. (1986). *Language and content.* Reading, MA: Addison-Wesley.

Rhodes, N. C., & Oxford, R. (1988). Foreign language in elementary and secondary schools: Results of a national survey. *Foreign Language Annals, 21,* 51–69.

Schinke-Llano, L. (1985). *Foreign language in the elementary school: State of the art.* Orlando, FL: Harcourt Brace Jovanovich.

Short, D. J., Crandall, J. A., & Christian, D. (1989). *How to integrate language and content instruction: A training manual* (Educational Report No. 15). Los Angeles: University of California, Center for Language Education and Research.

Snow, M. A. (1986). *Innovative second language education: Bilingual immersion programs* (Educational Report No. 1). Los Angeles: University of California, Center for Language Education and Research.

Snow, C. E. (1987). Beyond conversation: Second language learners' acquisition of description and explanation. In J. P. Lantolf & A. Labarca (Eds.), *Research in second language learning: Focus on the classroom.* Norwood, NJ: Ablex.

Snow, M. A., & Brinton, D. M. (1988). Content-based language instruction: Investigating the effectiveness of the adjunct model. *TESOL Quarterly, 22,* 553–574.

Snow, M. A., Met, M., & Genesee, F. (in press). A conceptual framework for the integration of language and content in second/foreign language instruction. *TESOL Quarterly*.

Spanos, G. A. Rhodes, N. C., Dale, T. C., & Crandall, J. A. (1988). Linguistic features of mathematical problem solving: Insights and applications. In R. R. Cocking & J. P. Mestre (Eds.), *Linguistic and cultural influences on learning mathematics* (pp. 221–240). Hillsdale, NJ: Lawrence Erlbaum.

Tucker, G. R. (1986). Implications of Canadian research for promoting a language competent society. In J. A. Fishman (Ed.), *Festschrift for Charles A. Ferguson*. The Hague: Mouton.

Tucker, G. R., & Crandall, J. A. (1985). Innovative foreign language teaching in elementary schools. In P. H. Nelde (Ed.), *Methods in contact linguistic research*. Bonn: Dummler.

Tucker, G. R., & Crandall, J. A. (1989, March 10). *The integration of language and content instruction for language minority and language majority students*. Paper delivered at the Georgetown University Round Table on Languages and Linguistics, Washington, DC.

Willetts, K. (1986). *Integrating language and content instruction* (Educational Report No. 5). Los Angeles: University of California, Center for Language Education and Research.

# 13

# Elementary School, Content-Based Foreign Language Instruction

HELENA A. CURTAIN
LINDA S. MARTÍNEZ

## BACKGROUND AND RATIONALE

Content-based instruction is a method of foreign language instruction in which the main topics being taught come from the regular curriculum or content areas (i.e., mathematics, social studies, science). The primary purpose of content-based instruction in elementary school foreign language programs is to integrate language development with content learning. This is accomplished by providing activities in which the learner's experiences are a vehicle for both language learning and content learning. Content-based activities can also provide a framework for developing higher-level cognitive skills.

This chapter is divided into three sections. The first gives the background and rationale for content-based instruction. The second section provides planning guidelines for teachers wishing to implement content-based instruction in the classrooms. The third section lists a number of concerns that FLES teachers should be alert to in planning their instructional activities. Appendix A provides sample lesson plans in mathematics, science, and social studies for both the primary and the intermediate grades. Appendix B provides suggestions for further reading.

Bernard Mohan (1986, p. 8) provides a convincing rationale for content-based instruction:

> Language is not just a medium of communication but a medium of learning across the curriculum. The goal of integration is both language learning and content learning. Content-based classrooms are not merely places where a student learns a second language; they are places where a student gains an education.

Researchers and practitioners have identified the importance of using language in meaningful contexts. Language practitioners know that, in order for meaningful communication to take place in a second-language classroom, there must be an "information gap" or an "opinion gap." That is, some type of real information must be exchanged or real opinions shared. The communicative classroom must move beyond the empty manipulation of language found in situations where the teacher holds up an object, such as a pen, and asks, "What is this?" Of course, the answer is obvious because students do not have to think about the response beyond providing a label for the item in the target language. Questions found in content-based foreign language classrooms ask students to provide answers that are not known in advance, such as "Which is heavier, the glove or the ball?" "How does a rabbit move?" When content-based instruction is incorporated into a foreign language in the elementary school (FLES) program, language practice has a purpose other than the isolated manipulation of language features such as plurals or negatives or object pronouns.

Content-based instruction is holistic. It encompasses the rich texture of the curriculum and provides opportunities to call critical thinking skills into play. In addition to talking about the language itself and learning how to communicate, students also talk about things such as odd and even numbers, animal habitats, or latitude and longitude. They may engage in activities such as comparing the length of classroom objects, using a pan and pointer scale, or graphing numbers of family pets. Research by Dulay, Burt, and Krashen (1982) indicated that time spent in content-based instruction provided more effective second-language instruction than in a language class alone.

Content-based instruction also helps to provide a solution to the frequent complaint that, in order to make a place for elementary school foreign language instruction in the curriculum, something else must be taken out. Integrating aspects of the regular curriculum into the FLES program demonstrates that the program is not a frill but a central part of the regular academic program. Nothing needs to be removed from the curriculum in order to implement such a program. Incorporating content-based instruction into the FLES class shows the students that the foreign language can be used in different settings and for different purposes.

Examples of content-based instruction can be found in bilingual education programs in which students are placed in "sheltered" content and English classes. In those classes, students receive instruction through strategies especially adapted to their level of language proficiency. Other examples of content-based instruction can be found in elementary school foreign language immersion programs. In immersion programs, the usual curriculum activities are conducted in the second language. This means that the second language is the medium as well as the object of instruction. Students learn both the second language and content through the second language. Immersion programs, and "sheltered" content classes in bilingual education programs, demonstrate the successful results of content-based instruction (see Lindholm & Fairchild, 1990; Snow, Chapter 7, this volume). Some of these activities can be accomplished even though the language skills of students in FLES programs are much more limited than those of students in immersion and bilingual programs.

## Content-Based Instruction in Various Subject Areas

Many areas of the curriculum are suitable for content-based FLES instruction. The following paragraphs present examples in mathematics, science, social studies, art, music, and physical education.

*Mathematics.* In elementary school mathematics, activity-oriented instruction and the use of manipulatives provide an appropriate vehicle for content instruction combined with language instruction. Computations and problem solving provide the concrete contexts necessary for the meaningful exchange of information. The vocabulary of mathematics, especially at the lower elementary level, is simple and results in a low vocabulary load in the foreign language class.

*Science.* In elementary school science lessons, students are encouraged to develop skills in problem solving such as observing, comparing, classifying, and predicting. Concrete contexts can be provided by hands-on activities and experimental activities. These activities are well suited to teaching both language and content at the same time and well suited to furthering development of higher-order thinking skills. Some science topics require a high number of vocabulary items. In these cases, science vocabulary must be carefully chosen when planning lessons. Often, the high number of vocabulary items is offset by the fact that many of these words are closely related to English and are thus easily recognizable to the students.

*Social studies.* The elementary school social studies curriculum begins with the immediate environment. Children learn about themselves, the family, the school, and the neighborhood. Students map and graph items in their classroom and in their neighborhood. Especially in the early grades, the social studies curriculum is experiential and activity oriented and provides the necessary meaningful context for language instruction.

The elementary school social studies curriculum deals with many of the same concepts that are often taught in the FLES curriculum. Whereas in the primary grades the level of vocabulary in social studies classes is manageable, in the intermediate and upper elementary grades, the vocabulary load can be extremely high. In the intermediate and upper grades, therefore, concepts taught through the second language must be very carefully chosen.

*Art, music, and physical education.* Because art, music, and physical education are activity oriented, little background language is required for meaningful participation in them. These subject areas also lend themselves to practice in following directions, a skill that is essential for beginning foreign language students.


PLANNING FOR CONTENT-BASED INSTRUCTION


In planning for content-based instruction, teachers must keep three things in mind: (a) the language skills needed by the students, (b) the content skills that will correlate with the language skills, and (c) the cognitive skills that are necessary to complete the lesson.

The following guidelines are addressed to teachers who are planning content-based FLES classes. They have been organized according to five major areas: identifying curriculum, coordinating with classroom content teachers, identifying instructional materials, planning the lesson, and evaluating the lesson.

## Identifying Curriculum

(1) Become familiar with the curriculum outside of the language strand. Look at the school's curriculum guides, textbooks, and other instructional materials as well as the charts of competencies in basic skills that are used in the school district.

(2) Compare the regular curriculum with the language curriculum currently in place. Determine whether any areas of overlap already exist. Consider the vocabulary and language functions the students need in the various subject areas.

(3) Select the appropriate curriculum concept(s)—the ones that lend themselves to activity-oriented approaches—and incorporate them into the FLES curriculum.

(4) Include culture as part of the content. Identify cultural information and concepts that can be integrated with the subject area. For example, nutrition units would have a cultural content if foods from the target culture were compared with American foods.

(5) Incorporate global education concepts where possible. For example, rather than focusing on just one country where the language is spoken, it would be appropriate to teach about *all* the countries where the target language is spoken, or at least as many as possible depending on the age of the students.

## Coordinating with Content-Classroom Teachers

(6) Communicate with the content-classroom teachers and inform them of the areas in the basic curriculum that will be reinforced in the FLES class. In this way, both strands can be coordinated. Specialist teachers who do not have their own classroom, as is the case with many elementary foreign language teachers, may coordinate their teaching with the curriculum set for the school and use that as the focal point. It is important to reinforce the regular curriculum, either by introducing certain content lessons in the FLES class on which the content-classroom teacher would subsequently elaborate or vice versa. Reinforcing the regular curriculum

in the elementary school foreign language class may help to provide the repetition that some students need in order to master concepts.

## Identifying Instructional Materials

(7) Identify the instructional materials to be used. If necessary, simplify the instructional materials if the print involved is too difficult, or amplify them if they do not provide enough concrete context for foreign language students. Translate materials as needed.

(8) Ensure that the materials needed to teach the particular lessons are readily available (and that they are portable, in the case of traveling teachers who do not have their own classrooms).

(9) Examine English as a second language (ESL) and bilingual education curricula as sources for lessons. They can provide good models.

(10) Use authentic materials when possible. Simplify them for the students by extracting the main ideas. Ask students to look for global concepts rather than to focus on a lot of detail. Beginning-level target language textbooks and workbooks used in the country where the target language is spoken are a good source of authentic content-based materials.

## Planning the Lesson

(11) Identify the language needed. Include both specialized content vocabulary for the particular subject area and for the rest of the lesson. Decide how much content vocabulary can reasonably be taught in the second language.

(12) Plan active hands-on strategies for helping students understand the concepts. These strategies should not demand heavy verbal involvement of the students but should focus on receptive language. Surround the activity with language. Use visuals, demonstrations, and vocabulary the students already know to explain the new content vocabulary. Make sure the components of the lesson are observable and manipulable.

(13) Incorporate methodologies that stress the importance of meaningful communication over grammar, and that also stress the importance of concrete context. Total Physical Response (see Asher, 1986) and Natural Approach (see Krashen & Terrell, 1983) activities can help to provide the meaningful context necessary in content-based classes.

(14) Focus on the main point or overall objective of the lesson. For example, in a lesson on vertebrates and invertebrates, the FLES teacher

would focus only on a list of animals that fall into each category; but in the science classroom, the teacher would extend the lesson to include body coverings (fur, scales, feathers, and skin), habitat, number and type of body parts, types of insects, animals with lungs versus those with gills, and so forth.

In another example, a lesson on magnets, the FLES teacher would introduce the concept that magnets attract metals but not wood, rocks, plastic, or paper. The content-classroom teacher would extend the lesson to teach that magnets attract only those metals that contain iron, steel, nickel, or cobalt.

(15) Present concepts in a way that challenges the students' thinking skills. For example, instead of simply naming animals, children can be asked to classify them as vertebrates and invertebrates; instead of simply labeling food items, children can be asked to plan menus that meet a variety of criteria.

(16) Incorporate reading and writing skills into every lesson, especially for older students. Reading and writing activities should be developed directly from the content lessons. For example, if a graph were developed in a mathematics lesson, the students could read and/or write sentences based on the graph. For a lesson on magnets, the students could make a booklet based on that lesson. Integrating classroom activities with reading and writing activities is an important component of the whole language approach. (See "Appendix B: Further Reading.")

*Evaluating the Lesson*

(17) Evaluation is an important component of each lesson. In addition to evaluating the content-based FLES lesson itself, it is important to communicate with classroom teachers about successful strategies and to rethink those that may need improvement.

## AREAS OF CONCERN IN CONTENT-BASED INSTRUCTION

There are several areas of concern that must be considered when planning for content-based instruction.

(1) Providing a watered down curriculum is a danger to be avoided. The content-based foreign language curriculum should not be seen as a

substitute for the regular curriculum but as a means of reinforcing the regular curriculum.

(2) Because of the amount of vocabulary involved, and the complexity of the subject matter, implementing content-based instruction is more difficult at the intermediate and upper elementary levels than at the primary levels.

(3) Simplifying the vocabulary used is one of the procedures for incorporating content-based instruction in FLES classes. This language simplification should not result in concept simplification. The development of higher-order thinking skills and concepts must be a central concern.

(4) Progress in the productive skills of speaking and writing is much slower than in the receptive skills of listening and reading. Much of the content-based activity should focus on the receptive skills.

(5) Due to time limitations, the FLES teacher may not have enough time to deal with an entire content unit but may be able to deal only with selected concepts from that unit.

(6) It may be difficult for the traveling teacher to obtain appropriate materials. Because most science activities stress the discovery approach, a large number of different items are needed. For example, a lesson on sound may require a tuning fork and other examples of materials that produce sound by vibration.


CONCLUSION


The concept of combining language and content instruction in FLES classes is relatively new, and additional insights are being gained every day. Teachers need to keep up to date with developments in the field. New and appropriate commercial materials may become available at any time. However, at present, the integration of language and content instruction must be planned and carried out mainly through the leadership of the elementary school foreign language teacher. (See "Appendix B: Further Reading.")

Planning content-based instruction is a challenging undertaking, but it can result in better language teaching and learning. Content-based language programs are not planned in isolation but within the framework of the entire curriculum. Incorporating content-based instruction into the FLES classroom is a way of providing a meaningful context for language instruction while at the same time providing a vehicle for increasing academic skills.

# APPENDIX A:
# Sample Content-based Lessons in Mathematics, Science, and Social Studies for Primary and Intermediate Grades

The following lesson plans are examples of methodologies appropriate for content-based FLES instruction and indicate the components and steps involved in a successful content-based lesson. An additional list of lesson topics at the end is intended to suggest other possibilities for content-based lessons. Finally, although the lessons in this section are presented in English, they are designed to be carried out *entirely in the target language*.

The lessons are planned around the following parameters. (Note that some of these criteria may not apply in every school district.)

- They are designed for use in a program that has a minimum of 30 minutes per day of instruction (90 hours per year).
- They are beginning lessons for primary (K, grades 1, 2, and 3) and intermediate (grades 4, 5, and 6) students.
  - They have been developed to reinforce the regular elementary school curriculum.
- They are portable and not dependent on elaborate setups that are not feasible for the itinerant FLES teacher.
- They can be used with whole group instruction.
- They provide a concrete context.
- Lesson components are observable and manipulable.
- Needed materials are low cost or readily available.

- Critical thinking skills are emphasized as much as possible.
- In instances where vocabulary development is necessary, Total Physical Response (Asher, 1986) methodology has been suggested. A combination of other methodologies or approaches could also be successfully used.


## 1. MATHEMATICS

*Title:* Comparing the Length of Classroom Objects
*Grade Level:* Primary
*Second-Language Objectives:*

- When directed by the teacher in the second language, the students will measure different classroom objects by using a paper clip as the unit of measurement.
- The students will identify the length of different classroom objects in the second language.
- The students will record the lengths on a chart and interpret the chart in the second language.

*Content Objectives:*

- The students will measure and compare lengths of different objects using a nonstandard unit of measurement.

*Second-Language Vocabulary:*

- *Receptive Language:* Measure, length, paper clip, longer, shorter, longest, shortest, equal, point, touch, put
  - "Give me the _____." "Is this a _____?"
- *Productive Language:* pencil, crayon, pen, chalk, chalkboard eraser, scissors, numbers from 0 to 20
  - "Yes, it is a _____."

*Materials Needed:*

- a small table for demonstrating the classroom objects
- a marking pen (permanent or water color)
- one each of the following: pencil, crayon, chalkboard, eraser, pair of scissors, pen, piece of chalk
- 10–20 paper clips
- a set of number flash cards from 0 to 20
- a small beanbag

- 6 rolls of gummed paper (assorted colors) cut into one-inch squares
- a pictograph (to show the number of paper clips each object measured) made from Kraft or chart paper. You can draw the classroom objects or cut pictures from magazines or school supply catalogs, or you can glue the actual item to the chart.

*Procedure:*

(1) If students do not know the vocabulary for the classroom objects, use the actual objects and Total Physical Response (TPR) activities to introduce the vocabulary. Use different commands, such as "Point to the crayon." "Touch the eraser." "Put the pencil on the table."

(2) Have the students practice the numbers 0 to 20 by counting various objects in the room or items on picture cards or by playing a circle game with the number flash cards. Gather the class in a circle on the floor. Have the students pass a beanbag around the circle until you give a signal to stop. The student with the beanbag must identify the number on the flash card that you show to him or her.

(3) Begin by demonstrating how to measure the classroom objects by lining paper clips end to end along the length of an object. Use the scissors to demonstrate the procedure. Place the scissors on a table or desktop where the students can easily observe the measurement.

(4) Say, "How long do you think the scissors are? Let's use a paper clip to measure the scissors. How many paper clips will we need?" After measuring the scissors, lead the class in counting the number of paper clips. Record this number on the pictograph that is displayed behind you. Refer to the key on the pictograph, which states that one square equals one paper clip. Stick the correct number of gummed paper squares (sticky tape) next to the picture of the scissors on the graph.

(5) Call on volunteers to come to the table and help measure and record the remaining classroom objects. As each item is about to be measured, say to the volunteer, "Point to the pencil. Give me the pencil." Show the object to the class and say, "Is this a pencil?" The class should respond with "Yes, it is a pencil." Repeat this procedure with the remaining objects. Record the length of each object with the gummed paper squares.

*Evaluation:* After all of the items have been measured and recorded on the chart, check the students' comprehension of the lesson by asking the following questions. Point to the chart and say, "Which is longer, the pencil or the pen? Which object is the shortest? Which object is the longest? Which two are equal in length?"

## 2. MATHEMATICS

*Title:* Finding the Perimeter and Area in Centimeters
*Grade Level:* Intermediate
*Second-Language Objectives:*

- When directed by the teacher in the second language, the students will measure different classroom objects.
- The students will give the length, width, perimeter, and area of different classroom objects in the second language.

*Content Objectives:*

- The students will use a metric ruler and a meter stick to measure objects in centimeters.

*Second-Language Vocabulary:*

- *Receptive Language:* measure, length, width, perimeter, area, metric ruler, meter stick, long, wide, add, multiply
  - "How long is _____?" "How wide is _____?"
- *Productive Language:* pupil desk, teacher desk, map, chalkboard, door, bulletin board, projection screen, table, book, centimeters, numbers 0 to 1,000
  - "It is _____ centimeters." "It is _____ meters."

*Materials Needed:*

- 2 metric rulers and 2 meter sticks for each small group
- 1 copy (8 x 11) of the perimeter and area chart for each small group
- pencils for recording measurements
- large perimeter and area chart made from Kraft or chart paper. You can list the classroom objects on the chart or use drawings or pictures cut from magazines or supply catalogs.
- number flash cards (use an assortment of numbers in the 0–1,000 range but concentrating on the higher numbers)

*Procedure:*

(1) If the students do not know the vocabulary for classroom objects, use the actual objects or pictures of the objects and TPR activities to introduce the vocabulary. Use different commands, such as "Point to the map." "Touch the chalkboard." "Walk to the door."

(2) Practice the numbers 0 to 1,000 by using the number flash cards. Place the cards face down and ask the students to pick a card and say the number in the second language. Send two students to the chalkboard and

give a number in the second language, the first to correctly write the number wins. The practice should concentrate on the higher numbers, which will be needed for the measuring of the classroom objects.

(3) Demonstrate how to measure the classroom objects for their length, width, perimeter, and area. Teach the procedure by measuring a book. The students will only be measuring flat surfaces. Display the large perimeter and area chart behind the teacher. Hold up the book and say, "How long is this book? Let's measure the book with the ruler." Give the answer using centimeters. Say, "The book is _____ centimeters long." Write the number of centimeters under the length column on the large chart. Next measure the width. Say, "How wide is the book? The book is _____ centimeters wide." Write the number of centimeters under the width column. Next demonstrate how to add the length and width and then multiply the answer by two to get the perimeter. Write the answer under the appropriate column. Do the same for the area (which is the length times the width), and then write the number under the appropriate column on the chart.

(4) Demonstrate how to use the meter stick by measuring a tabletop in the classroom. Follow the same procedure as stated above.

(5) Divide the class into small groups. Give each group 2 meter sticks, 2 metric rulers, a copy of the perimeter and area chart, and pencils for recording the measurements. Assign each group 2 or 3 classroom objects from the chart to measure. Give the students 8–10 minutes to complete their measurements.

*Evaluation:* Summarize the activity by having the pupils return to their desks after they have completed their tasks. Check the students' comprehension of the lesson by asking individuals to answer the following questions. Say, "What is the area of the map?" or "What is the perimeter of the pupil's desk?" The students should say, "It is _____ (square) centimeters," or "It is _____ (square) meters."

## 3. SCIENCE

*Title:* How Animals Move and Where They Live
*Grade Level:* Primary
*Second-Language Objectives:*

- When shown a picture of an animal, the students will be able to name the animal in the second language.

- When directed by the teacher in the second language, the students will perform the movement of the animal named.
- When directed by the teacher in the second language, the students will classify the animal picture cards according to how they move and where they live.

## Content Objectives:

- The students will observe and describe animal differences and classify these differences according to how the animal moves and where it lives.

## Second-Language Vocabulary:

- *Receptive Language:* flies, swims, hops, follow, point, classify
  - "What is this?" "It lives here."
- *Productive Language:* rabbit, frog, turtle, fish, robin, owl
  - "It is _____."

## Materials Needed:

- pictures of the following animals: rabbit, frog, turtle, fish, robin, owl
- pictures of the following habitats: water, land, sky
- three shoe boxes (decorate the boxes with construction paper; glue one of the following pictures on each of the boxes: an airplane, a swimmer, a pogo stick; pictures can be found in magazines or catalogs)
- cassette of instrumental background music
- a roll of masking tape

## Procedure:

(1) If the students do not know the animal names, use the animal pictures and TPR to introduce the vocabulary. Use different commands, such as "Point to the frog." "Touch the turtle." "Give the owl to a classmate."

(2) Provide additional practice for naming the animals in the second language by having the students classify them according to habitat. Tape the pictures of the following habitats on the chalkboard: land, water, and sky. Show the pictures of the fish to the class. Say, "What is this?" The class should respond: "It lives here." Call on volunteers to name the remaining animal pictures and to place them under the correct habitat.

(3) Next, play the cassette of background instrumental music. The music should evoke an image of the animal habitat. For example, the sounds of a babbling brook could represent water, or sounds of animals in the woods (e.g., squirrels chattering) could represent land. As the music

plays, show the class an animal picture and have them perform the movement of that animal to the music. Show a picture and say, "The fish swims." Then do the movement. Continue to do this for all of the animal pictures.

*Evaluation:* Check the students on their ability to name and classify the animals introduced in this lesson. End the activity by having the children sit on the floor. Place the three boxes in front of them. Direct their attention to the pictures on the boxes. Review the vocabulary from the animal movements (hops, swims, flies) by giving TPR commands. Say, "Hop five times." "Fly to the chair." "Swim to the chalkboard." Show the students an animal picture and say, "What is this?" They answer: "It is a _____." Demonstrate how they should classify the animal pictures according to movement. Show the picture of the rabbit and, after the student names the animal, place it in the box decorated with the pogo stick (because it hops). Call on volunteers to name and classify the remaining animal pictures.

## 4. SCIENCE

*Title:* Using a Pan and Pointer Scale
*Grade Level:* Intermediate
*Second-Language Objectives:*

- Using a pan and pointer scale, the students will weigh different objects and describe the weight in the second language.
- Using a pan and pointer scale, the students will weigh different objects, record the weights on a graph, and interpret the graph in the second language.

*Content Objectives:*

- The students will use a scale to measure and collect data.
- The students will record and interpret data from a graph.

*Second-Language Vocabulary:*

- *Receptive Language:* weighs, lighter, heavier, most, least, scale, thing, toy car, rubber ball, rock, book, stapler, object
- *Productive Language:* weighs, ounces, numbers from 0 to 50

*Materials Needed:*

- a pan and pointer scale
- objects for weighing: toy car, small rubber ball, rock, book, stapler

- a marking pen (permanent or water color)
- a large bar graph made from Kraft or chart paper. Drawings or pictures cut from magazines can be used to illustrate the items on the chart
- number flash cards 0 to 50

*Procedure:*

(1) If the students do not know the vocabulary for the objects to be weighed, use TPR to introduce the vocabulary. Use different commands, such as "Touch the rock." "Give me the car." "Point to the ball."

(2) Practice the numbers 0 to 50 by using number flash cards. Place the cards face down and ask the students to pick a card and say the number in the second language. Provide additional practice with the numbers by playing a relay game. Call on two volunteers. Say a number from 0 to 50 in the second language. The first student who writes the correct number on the chalkboard and returns to his or her seat is the winner.

(3) Place the scale on a table where the students can see it clearly. Display the bar graph behind the teacher. Demonstrate how each object will be weighed and recorded on the graph. Use the toy car to teach the procedure. Pick up the car and say, "How much does the car weigh?" Place the car on the scale and read the ounces aloud to the class. Say, "It weighs _____ ounces." Record the number of ounces on the graph.

(4) Call on volunteers to come to the table and help weigh and record the remaining objects. As each item is about to be weighed, say to the volunteer, "Point to the ball. Put the ball on the scale. How many ounces does it weigh?" The student should respond with, "It weighs _____ ounces." Have the student record the weight on the graph.

*Evaluation:* Check the students' ability to interpret the graph in the second language by asking volunteers to make weight comparisons by reading the graph. Ask, "Which object weighs the most?" "Which object weighs the least?" "Which is heavier, the car or the ball?" and so forth. If the students cannot name the object in the second language then have them point to the item on the graph when making the comparisons. Use hand gestures to help the students comprehend the terms *heavier, lighter, most,* and so on.


5. SOCIAL STUDIES

*Title:* Our Favorite Pets
*Grade Level:* Primary

*Second-Language Objectives:*

- The students will identify the animals on the picture cards in the second language.
- When directed by the teacher in the second language, the students will record the kind of pet or pets they have on the pictograph.
- The students will interpret the data on the pictograph in the second language.

*Content Objectives:*

- The students will use a pictograph to compare and record data.
- The students will interpret the data on the pictograph.

*Second-Language Vocabulary:*

- *Receptive Language:* more, less, owners
  - "Who has a dog?" "How many children have a fish?" "What is this?"
- *Productive Language:* dog, cat, goldfish, bird, hamster, and so on; numbers 0 to 20
  - "It is a _____."

*Materials Needed:*

- pictures of a dog, a cat, a bird, a goldfish, a hamster
- 20–25 picture cutouts of children (can also be stick drawings)
- a photograph of the teacher and his or her pet (can be teacher's own pet or borrowed)
- a large pictograph to show number of pet owners, made from Kraft or chart paper.

*Procedure:*

(1) If the students do not know the vocabulary for the animal names, use TPR to introduce the vocabulary. Use different commands, such as "Touch the hamster." "Point to the cat." "Give the bird to a classmate."

(2) Show the photograph of the teacher and his or her pet. Tell the class that this is the teacher's pet. Say, "This is my dog. His name is _____."

(3) Show the animal pictures. Ask: "What is this?" The student should respond: "It is a _____." Then ask: "Who has a cat?" and so forth. The students should respond by raising their hands to indicate if they have that kind of a family pet. Count the raised hands and record the number of students who have that kind of pet on the pictograph. Do this by gluing the same number of cutout pictures of children as the number of raised hands.

(4) Display the pictograph to the class. While pointing to the different animals on the graph, motion to the students to raise their hands if they have that kind of a pet. Count the raised hands. Demonstrate that the same number of cutout pictures of children as the number of raised hands will be glued onto the pictograph. Call on volunteers to help glue the cutouts for the remaining animals.

*Evaluation:* Check the students' ability to interpret the graph by answering the following questions. Say, "How many children had dogs? How many children had fish?" and so forth. Ask, "Which animal had more owners? Which animal had fewer owners?"

## 6. SOCIAL STUDIES

*Title:* Exploring Merged Relief Maps
*Grade Level:* Intermediate
*Second-Language Objectives:*

- Using a merged relief map, the students will identify the color used to represent various altitudes in the second language.
- Using a merged relief map, the students will give the altitude of different states in the second language.
- Using a merged relief map, the students will locate the national and state capitals when directed by the teacher in the second language.

*Content Objectives:*

- The students will use a map to gather geographic data.

*Second-Language Vocabulary:*

- *Receptive Vocabulary:* merged relief map, legend, represents, altitude, national capital, state capitals, touch
- *Productive Language:* the following color words: green, yellow, brown, orange, red, numbers 500 to 10,000 feet

*Materials Needed:*

- a merged relief map
- colored chalk
- large colored circle (12 inches diameter)

*Procedure:*

(1) Using colored circles, practice the color words by doing different TPR activities. For example, say, "Put the red circle on your desk. Put the green circle on the chair. Go to the board and draw a blue circle." and so forth.

(2) To check the students' productive language with the color words, hold up a colored circle and say, "Is this an orange circle?" The students should respond, "Yes, it is orange." Do this with all of the color words.

(3) To practice the numbers 500 to 10,000, call on two students to go to the board. Say a number in the second language; the first to write down the number correctly is the winner. Before the student can return to his or her desk, the student must say the number in the second language.

(4) Display the map to the students. Bring their attention to the legend. Ask the following, "What color represents 0–500 feet?" Demonstrate the answer by saying, "Green is 0–500 feet." Call on volunteers to give the colors and altitudes listed on the legend.

*Evaluation:* Check the students' ability to read a merged relief map by asking them to locate the national and state capitals and by giving the average altitude found in different states. Call on individuals and say, "What is the altitude of Louisiana, Colorado, or Wisconsin?" The students should respond with the altitude in the second language. Point out the symbols for the national and state capitals given on the legend. Say, "Where is the capital of the United States?" Next touch Washington, D.C., on the map. Call on volunteers to touch and say the capitals of the states you give them. Give a TPR command such as, "Go to the map and touch the capital of Georgia."

ADDITIONAL ACTIVITIES

*Mathematics*

- Identify basic shapes
- Identify sphere, cube, cone, cylinder
- Identify congruent figures
- Measure liquids, quart, gallon, pint
- Use symbols
- Use a number line for simple addition and subtraction
- Measure with a measuring tape (body parts, classroom objects)
- Sort by size, shape, thickness (attribute blocks)

- Use fractions ¼,½, ⅓, and so on to see which is larger or smaller
- Use a 2-pan balance to compare weights of objects
- Give the correct amount of change after a purchase of $1.00 or less
- Measure capacity and volume of various containers

## Science

- Chart weight, height, eye or hair color
- Investigate teeth
- Investigate the five senses
- Investigate the four basic food groups
- Classify living and nonliving objects
- Identify body coverings for animals
- Chart the weather (rainfall, snowfall)
- Use a thermometer
- Investigate magnets
- Identify sounds as high, low, loud, or soft
- Classify objects that sink and float

## Social Studies

- Identify countries that speak Spanish (or another language)
- Locate highest/lowest elevations on a merged relief map
- Study family relationships (mother, father, sister, brother, aunt, uncle, and so on)
- Use a map scale to measure distance between cities
- Use compass rose to locate different cities on a map
- Use a grid system to identify and locate states on U.S. map
- Use a bar graph to record family size, family pets, birthdays, and so on
- Classify vehicles according to modes of travel: air, land, sea
- Use a map key for interpreting items on a map
- Classify communities as city, suburban, or rural
- Locate cities and countries by latitude and longitude
- Recognize political borders of countries
- Identify the seven continents and five oceans

# APPENDIX B:
# Further Reading

Andrade, C., Pesola, C. A., & Christian, D. (1986). *Strategies for integrating language and content instruction: Art, music and physical education.* Washington, DC: Center for Language Education and Research (CLEAR), Center for Applied Linguistics.

Cantoni-Harvey, G. (1987). *Content-area language instruction: Approaches and strategies.* Reading, MA: Addison-Wesley.

Costa, A. L. (Ed.). (1985). *Developing minds: A resource book for teaching thinking.* Alexandria, VA: Association for Supervision and Curriculum Development [Reference work for thinking skills].

Crandall, J. (Ed.). (1987). *ESL through content-area instruction: Math, science, social studies.* Englewood Cliffs, NJ: Prentice-Hall [Focus is at the secondary level, but concepts presented can be applied at any level].

Curtain, H. A., & Pesola, C. A. (1988). *Languages and children: Making the match.* Reading, MA: Addison-Wesley [See especially chap. 7, "Drawing on the whole curriculum: Content based instruction"].

Enright, S. D., & McCloskey, M. L. (1988). *Integrating English.* Reading, MA: Addison Wesley [Useful for practical ideas on how to integrate language and content instruction; although the focus is on English as a second language, the concepts can readily be adapted to FLES classes].

Goodman, K. (1986). *What's whole about whole language?* Portsmouth, NH: Heinemann Educational [Explains the whole language movement, and the importance of integrating different parts of the curriculum].

Met, M. (1989). Learning language through content: Learning context through language. In K. E. Müller (Ed.), *Language in elementary schools.* New York: The American Forum.

Snow, M. A. (1987). *The Immersion Teacher Handbook* (Educational Report No. 10). Los Angeles: University of California, Center for Language Education and Research (CLEAR) [Contains a list of strategies that would be useful in any content-based lesson].

Willetts, K. F. (Ed.). (1986). *Integrating language and content instruction.* Los Angeles: University of California, Center for Language Education and Research (CLEAR).

Winocur, S. L. (1985). Developing lesson plans with cognitive objectives. In A. S. Costa (Ed.), *Developing minds: A resource book for teaching thinking.* Alexandria, VA: Association for Supervision and Curriculum Development.

## REFERENCES

Asher, J. J. (1986). *Learning another language through actions: The complete teacher's guidebook* (3rd ed.). Los Gatos, CA: Sky Oaks.

Dulay, H., Burt, M., & Krashen, S. (1982). *Language two.* New York: Oxford University Press.

Krashen, S. M., & Terrell, T. (1983). *The natural approach: Language acquisition in the classroom.* Oxford: Pergamon.

Lindholm, K. J., & Fairchild, H. H. (1990). Evaluation of an elementary school bilingual immersion program. In A. M. Padilla, H. H. Fairchild, & C. M. Valadez (Eds.), *Bilingual education: Issues and strategies.* Newbury Park, CA: Sage.

Mohan, B. (1986). *Language and content.* Reading, MA: Addison Wesley.

# 14

# Spanish for Spanish Speakers
## A Translation Skills Curriculum

### SHEILA M. SHANNON

Knowledge of more than one language involves some level of interaction between and among the languages. This interaction can include interference, translation, interpretation, and transfer and can present problems or solutions to the bilingual or multilingual person (Faerch & Kasper, 1983; Weinreich, 1953). Interference is where two languages conflict, and transfer represents the area where the languages are on common ground and interactions can be facilitated. Translation, generally referring to transposing written text from one language to another, and interpretation, that which is transposed orally, are areas where bilinguals can creatively use their two languages by capitalizing on transfer between two languages and holding interference in check (Nida, 1976).

Second- and foreign-language educators have paid attention to the problematic and constructive ways that languages interact for the learner.

AUTHOR'S NOTE: The work presented here comes from ethnographic data collected by the author over the 1987–1988 academic year, and made possible by CLEAR and the Hakuta project at Yale. I would like to acknowledge the administrators and teachers of the New Haven Public Schools, particularly those with the Foreign Language and Bilingual Programs, for their cooperation. A special thanks goes to José Delgado and the students of his second-period Spanish class.

223

Translation exercises, for example, were once a mainstay of the foreign language curriculum; however, in recent years language educators have virtually banned them (Cordero, 1982). They have advised that translation be avoided so as not to promote what they considered bad habits in the language learner. Their concern was that a learner's indiscriminate mapping of foreign language structures onto those of the native language, and vice versa, encouraged problems associated with interference. Therefore, they argued that the two languages should be kept separate.

More recently, however, a handful of foreign language educators have again considered the place of translation in the foreign language curriculum (Friesen, 1975; Griffiths, 1985; Layton, 1985; Teuscher, 1975). This latest discussion, unfortunately void of any empirical support, has suggested that translation exercises are conceivably appropriate for advanced language learners, who are capable of keeping their languages separate, and who can productively use two languages in tandem through translation and interpretation activities.

Foreign language learners who would qualify as advanced learners in this country are easily found within the large language minority population in our schools. These students advance through school while acquiring English as their second language, and many live in homes and communities where their first language—a "foreign language"—continues to be used. By middle and high school levels, those students who have remained in school become bilingual, whether or not they experienced bilingual programs (and excluding those with special needs impairing first- or second-language learning ability).

We must recognize, however, that the bilingual label for language minority children is misleading, because their first or native language gradually but surely gives way to English, which becomes their dominant language; indeed, this is the precise goal of transitional bilingual education as broadly mandated in this country (Heath, 1984).

A period of bilingualism may, in fact, be a rather fleeting moment for language minorities on the road to English dominance. Rather than view this transition to English as an example of first-language attrition, or subtractive bilingualism, we suggest that the first language, or ethnic minority language, comes to lie in some degree of dormancy throughout their lives. This chapter explores a perspective of additive bilingualism by examining an innovative foreign language curriculum based on translation skills for Latino students for whom their native language, Spanish, is dormant to some extent.

When language minority students reach middle school, they may elect or are required to study a foreign language. Latino students often find that their own first language, Spanish, is among their choices. How appropriate is it to allow or require language minority students to study their first language in classrooms alongside students for whom that language is truly foreign? What message do language minority students receive when they find themselves in a classroom where the foreign language they study is the one they may have acquired as a first language and one that they speak with adults and younger siblings in the home? How do foreign language teachers cope when faced with classes comprising students with very heterogeneous language backgrounds? To address these questions, this chapter describes an alternative curricular approach to Spanish language instruction for students with a Spanish language background.

The Spanish-speaking population is the largest language minority group in this country. Moore and Pachon (1985) reported that 11.5 million people indicated on the 1980 Census that they spoke Spanish at home. This group, then, represents an appreciable pool from which to draw students who could benefit from a language curriculum that recognizes their rich language backgrounds. Additionally, as members of a minority group who have suffered a history of educational discrimination and failure, they stand to gain from curricular approaches that seek to enhance their educational experiences (Orfield, 1986).

The goals for appropriateness, enrichment, and professionalism, in a curriculum designed specifically for language minority students, match the elements of the framework that Cummins (1986) suggested for the "empowerment" of minority students. This chapter explores how reaching those goals came about in a Spanish class based on a curriculum that employed empowering features. In addition, it is recognized that a curriculum or any educational program is rarely carried out precisely as planned, and that original goals often are not accomplished. Thornton (1988) showed how we can discern three critical aspects to the implementation of curriculum: the intended curriculum is that which the teacher plans or is expected to teach; the operationalized curriculum is that which the teacher actually teaches; and the experienced curriculum involves the students' response. The three elements interact toward what Thornton calls "curriculum consonance." The approach we take in this chapter is to embed Thornton's threefold view of curriculum implementation in a larger view of translation in the foreign language classroom as a means of empowering language minority students.

## THE INTENDED CURRICULUM

Mr. José Delgado was the Spanish language teacher who subsequently held the reins of the original experimental curriculum. He taught seventh- and eighth-grade Spanish in a New Haven, Connecticut, middle school. The school was situated in a predominantly Black and Puerto Rican community lying on the fringes of the downtown area. Many of Delgado's students in his Spanish classes were from Spanish-speaking backgrounds. It was not surprising that he was eager to participate when asked to be involved with an innovative program dealing with translation in the Spanish classroom. The program was designed for students who were more or less fluent in Spanish. He was delighted with the idea of having a homogeneous group of students because his two years of teaching Spanish to classes of mixed proficiencies "had proved to be a poor formula for success."

Delgado became a part of a team charged with developing a translation curriculum. The team included students and associates of Kenji Hakuta, a psycholinguist at Yale, and another middle school Spanish teacher. They developed a curriculum titled "Multilingual Skills Development." Delgado's view of the team's rationale behind the curriculum was that they shared an assumption that the Puerto Rican students often acted as translators and interpreters in their everyday lives (see Hakuta & Malakoff, 1987; Shannon, 1987). The curriculum was to highlight the students' dual linguistic skills that they brought from their homes to the classroom.

Another assumption upon which the curriculum was based was that the Spanish language ability of the students would not be as developed as their English skills. The teachers on the team emphasized that the Latino students they had encountered often lacked vocabulary and standard forms of the language. Therefore, the curriculum included translation and interpretation activities with an emphasis on filling the gaps in the students' Spanish language ability.

The curriculum was divided into 10 units based on activities in which translation or interpretation was required, some of which reflected the kinds of activities the students may have experienced in their own lives. Each unit targeted vocabulary, grammar, or sociolinguistic aspects of language use for discussion stemming from the translation activity. The units were designed to include enrichment activities from a spectrum of choices including role-playing, dictionary building on a word processor, community service projects, and development of a newsletter.

Delgado was successful in obtaining one class period of students with bilingual backgrounds with which to implement the curriculum for the 1987–1988 year. However, only nine eighth graders met the criteria to enroll in his innovative language class. In order to elect a foreign language in the school district at the middle school level, students had to have been at or above grade level in English reading. The nine students in Delgado's class were not only from Spanish-speaking backgrounds, they were top students. Three boys in the class were in the gifted and talented program and all nine students were regularly on the honor roll.

The original curriculum almost immediately began a transformation after Delgado had assessed the group of nine students. Delgado found the original curriculum problematic on three major points related to the somewhat erroneous assumptions about the students. He felt that the team had designed a curriculum for students whose "linguistic quality and extension was minimal" and that it resembled a standard foreign language curriculum. He also found that the group was not as homogeneous in Spanish language ability as originally assumed; whereas some students were not equally bilingual, some were as strong in oral and literate skills in Spanish as they were in English. Finally, he felt that the students did not need instruction about Spanish; rather, they needed instruction *in* Spanish.

The original curriculum was intended to help students develop a positive attitude toward both English and their native language, to introduce them to the fields of translating and interpreting, and to incorporate creative and novel techniques into comparative language teaching and learning. Delgado had no argument with those objectives; what he found problematic was the design for reaching those objectives that would not, in his estimation, challenge the linguistic and perhaps cognitive abilities of the students.

All nine students were born in the United States, and, with the exception of one student's mother, all of their parents were born in Puerto Rico. Spanish was the first language for six of the nine students; the other three students reported that Spanish was their second language. All students lived in the neighborhood surrounding the school; Spanish was the dominant language of adults and preschool children in all nine students' homes; and English was the language of school-age children. Three students described themselves as bilingual and felt equally comfortable speaking either language in most situations. Two students said they preferred English to Spanish in all instances and felt their Spanish was quite limited although they understood far more than they could produce. The remaining four students were English dominant but were fairly comfortable in Spanish. Thus the assumption about their bilingualism was false, and, in fact, their Spanish ability was quite variable. The nine students were, however, homogeneous in English reading, writing, and speaking ability as well as sharing overall high academic achievement throughout their schooling.

Delgado realized that these students' pressing needs were quite different from those presented in the curriculum. On one hand, he did not find the original curriculum challenging; and on the other, he discovered that the students' Spanish language skills were quite variable. Delgado was nagged by his intuition that the original plan did not match the backgrounds and needs of the nine students in his group. Thus he encountered the dilemma that foreign language educators face when they try to deal appropriately with language minority students in their classes.

## THE OPERATIONALIZED CURRICULUM

Delgado admitted that his knowledge—that the original curriculum, while an innovative approach, failed to be appropriate for the nine students in his eighth-grade Spanish class—was based on intuition. A decade ago, Valdés-Fallis (1978) warned the field of foreign language education in this country that ethnic minority students required a very different experience if they were in foreign language classes that taught their minority language. She prescribed a curricular approach that recognized their special needs and bilingual backgrounds. She criticized the normative approach to foreign language teaching for ethnic minorities as one based on an assumption that teaching the standard dialect was like teaching a foreign language. Valdés-Fallis (1978, p. 106) called her alternative approach a comprehensive language development program that was "based on the fundamental premise that language varieties will be best learned when they serve as media of instruction." Recently, Teschner (1985), who had earlier coauthored several pieces with Valdés-Fallis on the comprehensive program, has reiterated the same concerns. Delgado's concerns and recommendations are fundamentally similar to those that Valdés-Fallis and Teschner voiced concerning their curriculum. While the objectives for the Multilingual Skills Development curriculum were innovative, and its features were empowering, the teacher implementing the curriculum found the methods for reaching those goals inappropriate.

Because Delgado abandoned the original curriculum almost immediately, and because he felt that neither it nor any quasi-foreign language approach would be adequate, he created his own approach. In his new approach, Delgado used Spanish literature as the vehicle for translation activities that he felt would provide the students with challenging material and expose the students to genres of Spanish with which they had had little experience. Literary texts became the sources for translations or the bases for discussions about translation and interpretive uses of language. The curriculum was expanded from that literary core into three general areas: lexical and syntactic development of Spanish, controversial language issues, and the science and profession of translation. The following is an overview of the operationalized curriculum.

Literary pieces representing genres from various Spanish-speaking countries included poetry by Martí of Cuba, Palos Matos of Puerto Rico, and García Lorca of Spain. Prose included Cervantes's *Don Quixote*, the Spanish epic *Lazarillo de Tormes*, and children's classics in Spanish and English. Delgado explained that classic and contemporary Spanish literature might engender a sense of value, beyond a narrowly linguistic appreciation, for the students' cultural heritage. He also felt that the rhythm and tones of expertly crafted language might help the students in their translation efforts, particularly where interpretation was concerned.

Delgado closed and reinforced the gaps he found in his students' Spanish first by identifying them through work with literature. For development of vocabulary and grammar, Delgado chose a textbook by Rubén Pfeiffer, *Cuentos Simpáticos*. He also used cloze exercises he developed through an activity favored by the students called "Mad Libs." This activity involved a short story with items in the sentences missing. The blanks were completed by supplying the missing part of speech. The Mad Libs were commercially available in English, so Delgado had the students translate the short stories and then complete the stories by supplying the items in Spanish. In addition to these activities, most discussions around the reading and translation of the literary texts included talk about vocabulary and grammar.

Delgado also included in this aspect of the curriculum lessons around the differences between spoken and written Spanish. While some of the students had received bilingual education—and, therefore, formal instruction with Spanish as the medium and the goal of instruction—most had had little or no experience with literary or literate forms of Spanish. He emphasized the correct use of the written accent and how dialectical pronunciation could lead to orthographic errors.

Topics for discussion in the class included controversial issues about and involving language. Delgado used current media consistently throughout the class whenever relevant issues arose. Newscasts involving translators were scrutinized, an article about Spanish in the United States was argued about, and the history of English from an article in the *New York Times* was the basis for discussion. Students were encouraged to bring up their own topics for discussion about language use and attitudes. The science and profession of translation was a component of the curriculum. The students were introduced to translation from a theoretical perspective including the different levels of translation from literal to interpretative. They discovered where certain levels were appropriate and with what the debate in the professional field of translation was concerned. A professional translator presented a lecture to the students, and information from training institutes was read and discussed. Relative to the experiences the students may have had themselves in their own lives, the rights and responsibilities of the translator, and those requiring their services, were included in the material. The students videotaped improvisational and rehearsed situations of themselves in the roles of monolinguals and translators. They viewed, discussed, and analyzed the tapes based on the knowledge of translating that they had gained in the class.

## THE EXPERIENCED CURRICULUM

The nine students in Delgado's class responded variably to the class in general and showed preferences for certain kinds of activities. Generally, they found the new approach challenging, although they sometimes found the challenge disagreeable as part of a typical response to school along with an initial frustration with the constant provocation of their Spanish language ability.

Overall, the students felt that being in a "Spanish for Spanish speakers'" class was preferable to being in a Spanish class with English monolinguals. All of the students had had that experience the previous year with Delgado as their teacher. One student recalled that "it was boring because it was easy." Some students thought having the mixed class was better because it was easy and fun to witness the others learn Spanish, although they agreed that they did not learn much themselves. By midyear a seventh-grade student in a mixed Spanish class asked Delgado if he could join the eighth graders in the Spanish speakers' class; as a Spanish speaker he said "he was climbing the walls" in the other class. Perhaps as a succinct way of expressing how the students perceived themselves as Spanish speakers and their Spanish class, a student pointed out during one class discussion, "This ain't no foreign language, this is Spanish!" The students reacted most negatively to the literature component of Delgado's curriculum. Initially it was thought that their reaction was a reflection of their resistance to using Spanish extensively in the classroom, an unprecedented or long-forgotten activity. Analysis revealed that their response may have been more of a preference for nontraditional classroom activities that were also available in the class, and resistance to Spanish continued to be an element.

While the students complained about studying literature and translating literary texts, they produced the greatest quantity and quality of work in that component. For example, the time they spent on the translation tasks was greater than with other tasks, the tasks were challenging without being frustrating, students completed assignments, and they did cooperative group work. In one activity, Delgado had the class translate an English translation of a poem by Nicanor Parra that the poet had originally written in Spanish. When the students compared their translations to Parra's original, they not only argued about the professional translator's product but also about their own. Consider the following examples:

Translator: *A speaker you can't trust*

Parra: *Un interlocutor de mal carácter*

Students: *Un hablador que no puedes confiar*

Translator: *a mirror that doesn't lie*

Parra: *un espejo que dice la verdad*

Students: *un espejo que no miente*

Translator: *an armchair revolutionary*

Parra: *un revolucionario de bolsillo*

Students: *un revolucionario del sillón*

If the reader cannot read Spanish, suffice it to say that in each of these examples the students collectively translated the lines literally—how the phrase would be directly transposed into Spanish; while the translator, on the other hand, translated the lines freely (or interpretively)—re-creating the phrase in a way it might be expressed in Spanish (Catford, 1965). When the students compared their translations, they became furious at times, and one student angrily exclaimed, "What's bolsillo [pocket] got to do with armchair?" with the last example above. Delgado gave a detailed description of the metaphor used in the line and how the two phrases expressed the same meaning. The students did not include strategies in this translation task that would take them to the level of free translation. Consider, however, the following translation:

Translator: *and is mean just for the hell of it*

Parra: *deliberadamente miserable*

Students: *es malo porque quiere*

At a level of free translation in this example, the students insisted on avoiding the vulgar expression "for the hell of it" and any possible one that might produce an equally vulgar expression in Spanish. Their free translation demonstrated their ability to move away from the source text and explore alternative ways of getting the sense of the line across in Spanish.

For all translating and interpreting tasks, whether oral or written, most students preferred translating from Spanish into English rather than in the other direction. Their preference can be predicted from their English dominance; production is more taxing than comprehension and, therefore, translating in the direction of English would be easier for the students (Thiery, 1978). Students also preferred to translate as a group rather than individually. One student explained that "when it's by yourself, it's only your view and if it's the whole class, you have other ways; other people might know different words and that way you can learn."

Students most enjoyed games and improvisations. However, creating role-playing situations for the improvisation of translation situations posed logistical problems due to the variability of the students' Spanish. For example, few students felt comfortable being the person who took the role of the monolingual Spanish speaker in production tasks. One student was usually targeted as the monolingual Spanish speaker and was accused of being the class's "walking Spanish dictionary." Another dilemma was that the roles of the monolinguals were played by actual bilinguals, at least at the receptive level. Everyone in the situation understood what was being communicated, which shifted the focus to how well the interpreter was handling his or her job because everyone monitored performance.

All the students who role-played demonstrated the following: They could facilitate communication as the interpreter; they carried out interpretation with ease, however flawed; and they possessed remarkable linguistic and sociolinguistic knowledge as interpreters and as clients. These observations suggest to some extent that the students had had experience at some level in acting as interpreters and that being bilingual carries with it a flexibility for moving between two languages and cultures.

Oral and spontaneous interpreting liberated the students to get on with communication rather than being restricted by a source text as they were with written texts. For example, in an improvised activity, a student translated "turning" as "curveando," a false cognate, rather than "volteando," but he produced the Spanish spontaneously and freely. The false cognate appeared within an otherwise well-formed sentence, and communication was successful.

The students responded indirectly to the promotion of translation and interpretation skills as a way of empowerment, through their exposure to a marketable and prestigious profession that utilized their bilingualism. Their comments below show how they did not speak of themselves as translating professionally, rather, translation was something they did within the community as an informal service.

An advantage that bilingualism offers is helping the community, among friends and even family. So this is how I feel and I couldn't be happier. Someone who comes from another country to stay probably would need more help than a tourist. The immigrants might need help until they can settle down and continue living a normal life. Some ways that a translator can help this person is by helping them apply for a job or for special services, getting a home, or talking to an owner of a house so that the person can get an apartment, ordering service for utilities such as a telephone, electricity, cable, gas, or oil if the house takes it.

I just do translating as a favor and because I am available. Availability is the key.

One example of a disadvantage to being bilingual is suddenly finding yourself doing favors around the clock. You try helping a person one time and you end up always in the same place.

The students' sentiments must be read critically. If we are aiming to transform curriculum in a way that empowers minority students, we must hear that they do not view their bilingual skills in the same way that linguists, educators, and international politicians and businesspersons do. It is one thing to recognize skills, to incorporate them into curriculum, and to develop them in the classroom; it is yet another to understand how real-life situations and idealized ones do not match up.

One of Delgado's goals for this class was to provoke whatever Spanish was dormant within the students. The students admitted that they had been reluctant to speak Spanish in the class in the early part of the year. Toward the end of the year, the students often spoke Spanish spontaneously among themselves and participated fully in discussions in Spanish. The students' actual abilities in Spanish were surprising, something Delgado was not able to observe while the same students had been in a mixed-proficiency Spanish class the previous year. Students' Spanish was not only awakened, but it virtually blossomed over the year. One student, who had insisted at the beginning of the year that she did not speak Spanish very well, could come up with a phrase or word in Spanish as quickly as others. For a written assignment toward the end of the school year, Delgado asked the students to critically review a television program—in writing and in Spanish. The following is that student's review:

> *Lethal Weapon* Es una película de dos policías que tratan de capturar a una organización que mata a la gente con "mercury switches" y distribuye heroína. Aparentemente parecía verdadera porque un personaje tenía una familia normal, y el otro vive solo con el perro. La historia parecía real porque la gente se moría y se caían. Corrían, no como otras películas que le disparan a la gente y nunca mueren. El vestuario de los policías era perfecto. Uno siempre estaba con traje y el otro vestía siempre bummy. La ropa pegaba a los personajes.

## CONCLUSION

The problem presented in this chapter was not the assessment and evaluation of one teacher's change to a curriculum. Neither was the concern with whether or not the teacher's reasons for changing the original curriculum were, by some measure, "correct." Rather, we presented what was learned from what emerged in this one eighth-grade Spanish class for Spanish speakers.

What did emerge? Resistance best describes what the innovative approach brought out in the teacher and his students. By challenging the original or intended curriculum—expanding its limits and exploring areas of his own preference and expertise with the Spanish language—the teacher resisted the students' lack of ambition to recognize and develop their linguistic heritage. In turn, the students resisted their teacher provoking their dormant Spanish. Both the teacher and his group of students found it difficult to ascribe to the original premise of a translation skills curriculum because of their basic resistances. Mr. Delgado felt the students could not translate and interpret without a developed Spanish language repertoire, and the students were not only reluctant to translate into Spanish, they were unprepared to allow that much space for the language in the classroom.

Regardless of this resistance, the students did engage in a variety of activities that promoted their Spanish. Once the Spanish language was part of the classroom discourse, it became tangible, that is, "stuff" to recognize, experience, work with, and develop—and potentially add to the students' repertoires. Only then could translating and interpreting between the two languages take place—only after one of the languages, Spanish, was sufficiently awakened.

Delgado's view was that societal pressures make it such that *el español se convierte en una idioma de las trincheras. Y una vez que salen de la comunidad ellos no ven ningún tipo de necesidad en utilizarlo y esto hasta con ellos mismos* [Spanish becomes the language of the trenches. Once they leave the community they see no need to use the language—even among themselves]. The experimental curriculum brought Spanish out of the trenches and into the classroom where the students least expected to find it. The students' resistance to the notion that the Spanish language could possess an academic nature equivalent to their experience with English was challenged by their exposure in this class. After all, if the intention is to use both languages in the class for translation and interpretation, the students' proficiencies need not be equal, but the student must at least possess something more than a minimal knowledge of both languages in order to translate or interpret.

Students from Spanish and other non-English language home backgrounds are bombarded by messages from teachers and school administrators that English is to be valued and learned while other languages are denigrated. These messages are very important to school-age children who are very impressionable and who wish to do the "right" thing. Accordingly, it is not surprising, then, that the students in Delgado's class initially resisted when he expected them to express themselves in English *and* Spanish. Resistance to empowerment is a result of the way in which linguistic minority children have had to adapt to a school environment that views their bilingualism negatively. Overcoming such resistance takes time and patience, as demonstrated by Delgado. However, the investment in time pays off when we see how well students can use their two languages when challenged.

We recommend that an innovative curriculum for the Spanish foreign language classroom should include two basic components. One, that students with a Spanish language background be offered the course apart from those for whom the language is truly foreign. Two, that a basic component involve, if not the promotion of Spanish and bilingualism, a serious discussion of the nature of those issues in this country. A goal of bilingualism in our society is clearly not the message students receive, therefore, any "foreign" language teaching approach involving an ethnic minority language and language minority students should address that issue in a fundamental way.

## REFERENCES

Catford, J. C. (1965). *A linguistic theory of translation.* London: Oxford University Press.

Cordero, A. D. (1982, December). *The role of translation in second language acquisition.* Paper presented at the Annual Convention of the Modern Language Association of America, Los Angeles.

Cummins, J. (1986). Empowering minority students: A framework for intervention. *Harvard Educational Review, 56* 18–36.

Faerch, C., & Kasper, G. (1983). *Strategies in interlanguage communication.* New York: Longman.

Friesen, A. (1975). Why teach translation and how? In M. S. Batts (Ed.), *Translation and interpretation the multi-cultural context: A symposium.* Vancouver: Benwell Atkins.

Griffiths, B. T. (1985, January). The ear has its reasons—interpreting and the modern languages curriculum. In G. Doble & B. T. Griffiths (Eds.), *Oral skills in the modern languages degree: Proceedings of a conference* (at the University of Bradford). Bradford, England. (ERIC Document Reproduction Service No. ED 277 265)

Hakuta, K., & Malakoff, M. (1987, April). *Translation skills in bilingual children.* Paper presented at the meeting of the Society for Research in Child Development, Baltimore.

Heath, S. B. (1984). Language policies: Patterns of retention and maintenance. In *Mexican-Americans in comparative perspective.* Washington, DC: Urban Institute.

Layton, A. B. (1985). Interpreting and the communicative approach. In G. Doble & B. T. Griffiths (Eds.), *Oral skills in the modern languages degree: Proceedings of a conference* (at the University of Bradford). Bradford, England. (ERIC Document Reproduction Service No. ED 277 265)

Moore, J., & Pachon, H. (1985). *Hispanics in the United States*. Englewood Cliffs, NJ: Prentice-Hall.

Nida, E. (1976). A framework for the analysis and evaluation of theories of translation. In R. Brislin (Ed.), *Translation*. New York: Gardner.

Orfield, G. (1986). Hispanic education: Challenges, research, and policies. *American Journal of Education, 95*, 1–25.

Pfeiffer, R. (1986). *Cuentos simpáticos*. Lincolnwood, IL: National Textbook.

Shannon, S. M. (1987). *English in el barrio: A sociolinguistic study of second language contact.* Unpublished doctoral dissertation, Stanford University.

Teschner, R. V. (1985). Improving language learning for the non-English-language native speaker. *Theory into Practice, 26*, 267–275.

Teuscher, G. (1975). Some remarks about the implications of translation as a subject for teaching. In M. S. Batts (Ed.), *Translation and interpretation the multi-cultural context: A symposium*. Vancouver: Benwell Atkins.

Thiery, C. (1978). True bilingualism and second-language learning. In D. Gerver & H. W. Sinaiko (Eds.), *Language interpretation and communication*. New York: Plenum.

Thornton, S. (1988). Curriculum consonance in United States history classrooms. *Journal of Curriculum and Supervision, 3*, 82–100.

Valdés-Fallis, G. (1978). A comprehensive approach to the teaching of Spanish to bilingual Spanish-speaking students. *Modern Language Journal, 62*, 102–110.

Weinreich, U. (1953). *Languages in contact: Findings and problems* (Publications of the Linguistic Circle of New York, No. 1). New York: Mouton.

# 15

# Innovations in
# Foreign Language Education
## Contributions from Bilingual Education

HALFORD H. FAIRCHILD
AMADO M. PADILLA

The chapters that compose this volume present an overview to a number of new developments in immersion and foreign language education. After nearly 100 years of formal foreign language instruction in the United States, we now recognize that the way in which foreign languages were taught has been seriously flawed. In particular, the emphasis on language as subject matter, rather than as a means of acquiring information, has resulted in a general lack of second-language proficiency on the part of English-speaking students.

We now know that earlier models of teaching vocabulary and formal rules of grammar were ineffective. Although a majority of English-speaking Americans have had some educational exposure to a foreign language, the percentage of native English-speaking Americans who are proficient in a second language is exceedingly small. Those who do possess bilingual proficiency typically acquired that proficiency from direct experience in a country of the target language rather than from formal instruction in schools.

This dismal picture, however, is changing. With new models of foreign language education that emphasize communicative competence and the meaningful use of the second language to teach and acquire basic subject matter, students are developing some true proficiency in a language other than English. Part of this evolution comes from advances in bilingual education and the education of linguistic minorities.

## CONTRIBUTIONS FROM BILINGUAL EDUCATION

Bilingual education is part of an ongoing revolution in American education. The pursuit of equal opportunity in the provision of educational resources has resulted in programs that are geared to the specific needs of individuals and groups. In particular, beginning with the 1968 Bilingual Education Act, educational programming was prescribed to meet the unique needs of non-English-speaking students (see Leibowitz, 1980; Malakoff & Hakuta, 1990; Padilla, 1990).

Bilingual education programs, however, are marked by tremendous public misunderstanding and scientific controversy. On one hand, the public is polarized because bilingual education is perceived by many to create social barriers and cultural separation (Hakuta & Gould, 1987; "When Children Speak," 1986). And from an instructional perspective, debates continue about what constitutes the best ways to deliver bilingual instruction and the general effectiveness of bilingual education for linguistic minority students (Garcia & Flores, 1986; Hakuta & Gould, 1987; Troike, 1981).

The following pages present the chapter summaries of the companion volume on bilingual education (see Padilla, Fairchild, & Valadez, 1990). That volume covers issues and perspectives, research contributions, program design and evaluation, and suggestions for classroom practice.

### *Issues and Perspectives*

Bilingual education has undergone a number of dramatic changes in the past two decades. Its history, and concomitant political issues, are reviewed in Part I, "Issues and Perspectives," of Padilla, Fairchild, and Valadez (1990).

Amado Padilla (1990), in "Bilingual Education: Issues and Perspectives," reviews the policy, research, and programmatic debates surrounding bilingual education. Noting the strong opposition to bilingual educa-

tion by former Secretary of Education William Bennett, Padilla emphasizes the need for bilingual education proponents to develop both a "paradigm" and a "mission."

By "paradigm," Padilla underscores the need for developing a "coher-
ent tradition" in the development of bilingual education programs, teaching strategies, and research approaches. He notes, for example, that the
majority of studies on bilingual education consist "of a loosely connected
mosaic of 'facts.'" It is not surprising, then, that evaluations of the effectiveness of bilingual education are inconsistent.

In terms of a "mission," Padilla calls for the joining together of people,
organizations, and institutions to establish a goal of a "language-competent society." Here, he prescribes the development of a commitment to
bilingualism on the part of all Americans. In this respect, Padilla joins
with foreign language educators who see language and bilingualism as
personal and national resources (see Tucker, Chapter 1, this volume).
Padilla reviews the research controversies concerning bilingual education,
particularly with respect to the lively debate between Baker and de Kanter
(1981, 1983) and Willig (1985, 1987). He also notes the relationship between the need for bilingual education and the demographic projections
pointing to increasing linguistic diversity in the United States over the
next four decades.

Marguerite Malakoff and Kenji Hakuta (1990), in "History of Language Minority Education in the United States," provide a comprehensive
review of the public policy debates, and legislative actions, concerning
bilingual education. Malakoff and Hakuta identify the changing dynamics
of American attitudes toward bilingual education beginning in the eighteenth and nineteenth centuries. For example, although bilingual education
was common for a number of northern and western European groups in
the United States in the eighteenth century (i.e., the Spanish, French, Nor-
wegians, Lithuanians, Dutch, and so on), in the late nineteenth century,
the "new immigration" from southern and eastern Europe stimulated eth-
nocentric, racist, and "English-only" sentiments among the "old immigrants."

Malakoff and Hakuta focus their review on contemporary models of
bilingual education, particularly since the 1968 passage of the Bilingual
Education Act and the legislative consequences of the ruling in *Lau v.
Nichols* in 1970. They identify various models of programs, including
transitional, maintenance, English as a second language, submersion
("sink or swim"), and bilingual immersion programs. According to their
analysis, most of these programs are "subtractive" in the sense that they

seek to replace individuals' native language with English and fail to foster bilingual proficiency.

In reviewing research on the effectiveness of bilingual education programs, Malakoff and Hakuta define myriad methodological difficulties in conducting effectiveness research and call instead for research on the *process* of implementing innovative teaching strategies and curricula.

In sum, Part I provides an overview of the history of bilingual education, the changing nature of public sentiment and legislative actions, and the context for evaluating research findings and supporting the development of new pedagogical models.

## Research Perspectives

Part II, "Research Perspectives in Bilingual Education," provides a generally nontechnical review of the major issues involved in conducting research on language education. These issues range from the basic research questions of the relationship between language, bilingualism, and cognition to the more focused topics of native language instruction and African American dialects and the learning process.

Kenji Hakuta (1990), in "Language and Cognition in Bilingual Education," reveals the social-cultural context of research in bilingual education by debunking the traditional assumptions that bilingualism is a cognitive handicap and that bilingual individuals are intellectually inferior. He shows how the more recent research tradition in bilingualism shows a number of cognitive and/or intellectual benefits: enhanced cognitive flexibility and the early development of "metalinguistic" skills (i.e., the ability to think in the abstract about the nature of language). In addition, bilingual proficiency is associated with enhanced nonverbal IQ and better than average academic achievement scores. Hakuta's conclusion calls for an emphasis on native language instruction and calls for the "holistic development" of the linguistic minority child's language and education.

Catherine E. Snow (1990), in "Rationales for Native Language Instruction: Evidence from Research," reviews the pros and cons of using language minority children's native language in initial education and literacy training. According to Snow, four arguments are articulated against the use of native language instruction: (a) the history argument points to the success of certain European immigrant groups in the absence of federally sponsored bilingual education; (b) the "ghettoization" of linguistic minority children results in segregation, stigma, and the maintenance of intergroup schisms; (c) the amount of "time on task" is reduced by bilingual education; and (d) the inevitable attrition of native languages makes for a "hopeless cause" in bilingual education.

In contrast, Snow identifies three arguments in favor of native language instruction: (a) to enhance the cultural-social identity of linguistic minority children (i.e., increasing the match between the culture of the teacher/school and the culture of the student/home); (b) to take advantage of the cognitive and social benefits of bilingualism; and (c) to enhance the development of early literacy skills (which occurs most readily in young children's first language). She concludes by strongly supporting the use of native language instruction in order to maximize achievement in both the children's native language and in English.

Fairchild and Edwards-Evans (1990), in "African American Dialects and Schooling: A Review," present an overview of the research and teaching issues pertinent to the topic of "African American dialects." Fairchild and Edwards-Evans note that research on African American dialects has been embedded in an ideological climate of White racism, and, as a result, the early research tended to degrade these dialects as inferior or deficient in much the same way as bilingualism has been viewed.

Focusing on the attitudes and behaviors of teachers, Fairchild and Edwards-Evans review the literature on teacher effects and offer a number of general principles for pedagogical practice. They conclude that a more fundamental revolution in American education is needed if the problems of academic underachievement on the part of African Americans are to be addressed.

As a group, the three chapters that compose Part II cover a variety of issues in language education: the relationship between language and thinking; the role of children's native language in their early education; and the issues pertinent to dialect minorities (e.g., speakers of African American dialects).

### Program Design and Evaluation

Part III, "Program Design and Evaluation," includes three chapters that (a) offer suggestions for the development of bilingual immersion programs, (b) trace the development of a bilingual education "master plan" in a metropolitan school district, and (c) report the results of an evaluation of a two-way bilingual immersion program.

Kathryn Lindholm (1990), in "Bilingual Immersion Education: Criteria for Program Development," recalls many of the demographic projections of earlier chapters and emphasizes the increasing need to address linguistic diversity in American schools. She notes that the current thrust is to simultaneously meet the language education needs of linguistic minority and majority students by the use of bilingual immersion programs. Bilingual immersion programs, particularly when designed for "two-way" or "interlocking" teaching strategies, use two languages for the purposes of content instruction. For example, native Spanish-speaking and native English-speaking students receive instruction in math, science, social studies, and so on in both English and Spanish. In this way, students from the two groups serve as linguistic role models for each other.

Lindholm notes four critical features of bilingual immersion: dual language immersion (both languages used for instruction); language isolation (the two languages are used in distinctly different periods and the proportion of one language or the other may vary over the grade levels); student mixing (language minority and language majority students mixed in roughly equal proportions); and the integration of language arts curriculum with the traditional academic content areas (using a second language to teach math, science, or social studies).

Lindholm concludes by showing that bilingual immersion requires the same pedagogical features that are related to positive educational outcomes generally: high-quality staff, strong administrative support, positive school atmosphere, frequent opportunities to demonstrate mastery of language and content, positive rewards, and home-school collaboration.

Concepción Valadez and Clementina Gregoire (1990), in "Development of a Bilingual Education Plan," present a detailed description of a school district's response to its changing student population. Their focus includes a brief demographic history of the ABC Unified School District in Southern California, how the district responded to legislation concerning language education, and how the district implemented its comprehensive "master plan" for bilingual education. Valadez and Gregoire include a discussion of staff development, training, contributions from abroad, and staff morale. Their chapter illustrates an exemplary response of a metropolitan school district to the changing demography, and language education needs, of its students. They conclude that strong and unequivocal leadership is the most important factor in the success of the district's language education programming.

Kathryn Lindholm and Halford H. Fairchild (1990), in "Evaluation of an Elementary School Bilingual Immersion Program," describe the implementation of a model program in Santa Monica, California, and report the results of a preliminary evaluation. According to Lindholm and Fairchild, the goals of the Edison School Program were to produce normal to superior academic achievement in both English and Spanish, age-appropriate bilingual oral proficiency and literacy, enhanced feelings of self-competence on the part of the children, and positive cross-cultural attitudes and relationships.

They compared 112 kindergarten and first-grade students with students enrolled in regular classrooms. Lindholm and Fairchild report that the bilingual immersion students demonstrated significant achievement gains and had higher scores than the comparison group on every measure (although only the math scores were statistically significant). Self-competence scores for the bilingual immersion students were comparable to those reported for a middle-class sample. The authors conclude that the interaction of the language groups was beneficial to both groups and that bilingual immersion programs produce average to better than average achievement levels.

As a whole, the chapters in Part III compose a collection that covers curriculum development for classrooms, schools, and school districts. Implementation and evaluation strategies are highlighted.

### *Theory into Practice: Strategies for the Classroom*

Part IV, "Theory into Practice: Strategies for the Classroom," provides coverage on specific guidelines for how teachers can accomplish many of the goals outlined in earlier chapters, with an emphasis specifically on the teaching of content and language simultaneously. The integration of language and content is accomplished by purposely using the second language to teach the traditional academic content of math, social studies, science, art, and the humanities.

Donna Christian and her colleagues (1990), in "Combining Language and Content for Second-Language Students," provide the broad parameters of language-content integration. The authors provide specific examples of classrooms using integrative approaches and show teachers how to develop content-language lesson plans and activities. This hands-on chapter is very useful to educators who wonder how language instruction can be introduced into subject matter instruction. Appendixes to the chapter provide sample lesson plans and suggestions for further reading.

Marguerite Ann Snow and Donna M. Brinton (1990), in "Innovative Second-Language Instruction at the University," discuss how a language-content integration model can be implemented even in a university setting. The University of California, Los Angeles, Freshman Summer Program (FSP) is described, with a focus on the program's strengths and limitations. Their evaluation indicated positive outcomes for the limited-English-proficient freshmen participating in the program. The point is that language-content instruction can be implemented at any educational level where there is a need. Language educators have only begun to be creative in how and where they have sought to integrate language and content instruction.

Joy Kreeft Peyton provides two related chapters: "Dialogue Journal Writing: Effective Student-Teacher Communication" (1990b) and "Beginning at the Beginning: First-Grade ESL Students Learn to Write" (1990a). The first chapter provides a detailed description of a form of written communication between teacher and student that allows for the building of a meaningful interpersonal relationship. Although the dialogue journal model is intentionally nonevaluative, students acquire writing skills because of the activity's meaningful context and interaction with a positive adult writing model (i.e., the teacher). The second chapter elaborates on the dialogue journal approach and presents findings from a case study using dialogue journals in an early elementary classroom.

Taken together, Peyton's chapters provide teachers with sufficient details to implement a dialogue journal in their own classrooms. The importance of the approach to literacy development advocated by Peyton is that students can learn to write in a nonthreatening manner, in union with a teacher, using a form that is personalized and that is receptive rather than judgmental. This approach appears especially valuable with linguistic minority students in the early phase of literacy development in English.

Evelyn Jacob and Beverly Mattson (1990), in "Cooperative Learning: Instructing Limited-English-Proficient Students," discuss the utility of cooperative learning strategies with diverse linguistic groups. The purposes of cooperative learning include language and content mastery and positive intercultural relations. They review varieties of cooperative learning techniques, describe learning outcomes, and suggest steps for classroom implementation. It is clear that cooperative learning environments have become increasingly important in education in this past decade. We fully expect to see more emphasis on cooperative learning in the decade to come. This chapter provides the reader with some useful suggestions when working with diverse linguistic groups.

Karen Willetts and Donna Christian (1990), in "Material Needed for Bilingual Immersion Programs," offer guidelines for appropriate and effective materials and curricula. They note that the programs discussed require a wide variety of materials that must provide instruction in two languages and that must be suitable for at least two groups of students with very different language proficiencies. Moreover, Willetts and Christian strongly urge the adoption of bilingual materials for the teaching of the traditional academic content areas. The authors discuss the availability of materials and the preparation of lesson plans, and they provide appendixes with clearinghouse addresses and a listing of sample materials.

Finally, Halford H. Fairchild and Amado M. Padilla (1990), in "Innovations in Bilingual Education: Contributions from Foreign Language Education," provide a summary of the volume and integrate contributions from the closely allied field of foreign language education in the context of the current volume. The chapter, and the volume, conclude with some speculations about the future of bilingual education in the United States.

## SYNTHESIS AND CONCLUSION

Learning a second language is no longer a luxury for the middle class. With increasing international interdependence, our ability to communicate with other cultural and linguistic groups is a requirement for living and working in the modern world. Particularly in the United States, where immigration from Europe, Asia, Africa, and Latin America continues to increase, we should capitalize on the rich linguistic diversity available and seek to promote a language-competent society that includes proficiency in more than just English.

Both foreign language education and bilingual education have benefited from each other's developments. The development of language immersion models, for example, now includes two-way bilingual immersion in which language minority and language majority children study and learn together. For language minority students, the experience provides them with the opportunity to maintain their native language while acquiring proficiency in English. For native English-speaking students, immersion programs offer an intensive and heretofore unavailable opportunity to acquire true communicative competence in a foreign language. For both groups of students, the immersion model offers a number of social and cultural benefits as well: greater interpersonal understanding, positive intergroup attitudes, and more awareness of the cultural diversity of the world in which we live.

Both foreign language education and bilingual education recognize that language is a means to an end, not an end in itself. In this respect, the content-based approaches offer students an opportunity to acquire a second language in a way that is more incidental to the acquisition of subject matter mastery. This approach offers a *purposefulness* in foreign language acquisition that enhances bilingual competencies. This is a considerable advance over the more traditional approach that taught a foreign language as subject matter and that emphasized translation rather than oral proficiency.

Even more important, recent analyses suggest a more "transformative" role of education generally and of language education more specifically (Graman, 1988). According to this view, the purpose of language education should be to empower students to use language to solve personal and social problems. As such, language education, and education more generally, must target its activities to addressing the variety of contemporary problems that confront our society. This is particularly true for historically disenfranchised groups such as language or dialect minorities.

One strategy for obtaining this kind of meaningfulness in language education is to allow students to communicate their issues and concerns as part of the instructional processes. Peyton's (1990a, 1990b) description of the "dialogue journal" is an excellent step in this direction. Here, students and teachers dialogue in an informal, nonevaluative framework in which individual concerns are raised and students and teachers can develop a meaningful human relationship while literacy skills are simultaneously being acquired. Another possibility lies in using educational media to present models of language diversity in a way that promotes intercultural understanding and the reinforcement of peaceful resolutions to conflict (see Fairchild, 1988).

Even more fundamental, students should be challenged, within the context of foreign language education, to grapple with the pressing problems of our planet. How can varying cultural and linguistic groups overcome territorial, economic, and racial rivalries that plague contemporary international relations? How can individuals affect the need for a shifting of priorities from conflict and warfare to peace and full human development?

The future of language education is uncertain. The current political climates suggest some retrenchment on the part of policymakers and the general public in terms of the priority given to bilingual education and bilingualism. "English-only" movements, in particular, are especially threatening to both foreign language education and bilingual education because they support a very restricted policy on what the role of languages should be in a diverse society such as the United States.

We can paint an optimistic future scenario for language education only after the public at large recognizes the tremendous urgency in equipping our citizenry with the vital resources of human commerce: language. Doubling the language capacities of individuals doubles the language resources of our society. We urge the adoption of a national agenda that will bring this result to fruition.

## REFERENCES

Baker, K., & de Kanter, A. A. (1981). *Effectiveness of bilingual education: A review of literature*. Washington, DC: Office of Planning, Budget and Education, U.S. Department of Education.

Baker, K., & de Kanter, A. A. (Eds.). (1983). *Bilingual education: A reappraisal of federal policy*. Lexington, MA: Lexington.

Christian, D., Spanos, G., Crandall, J., Simich-Dudgeon, C., & Willetts, K. (1990). Combining language and content for second language students. In A. M. Padilla, H. H. Fairchild, & C. M. Valadez (Eds.), *Bilingual education: Issues and strategies*. Newbury Park, CA: Sage.

Fairchild, H. H. (1988). Creating positive television images. In S. Oskamp (Ed.), *Applied social psychology annual: Vol. 8. Television as a social issue* (pp. 270–279). Newbury Park, CA: Sage.

Fairchild, H. H., & Edwards-Evans, S. (1990). African American dialects and schooling: A review. In A. M. Padilla, H. H. Fairchild, & C. M. Valadez (Eds.), *Bilingual education: Issues and strategies*. Newbury Park, CA: Sage.

Fairchild, H. H., & Padilla, A. M. (1990). Innovations in bilingual language education: Contributions from foreign language education. In A. M. Padilla, H. H. Fairchild, & C. M. Valadez (Eds.), *Bilingual education: Issues and strategies*. Newbury Park, CA: Sage.

Garcia, E. E., & Flores, B. (Eds.). (1986). *Language and literacy research in bilingual education*. Tempe: Arizona State University, Center for Bilingual Education.

Graman, T. (1988). Education for humanization: Applying Paulo Freire's pedagogy to learning a second language. *Harvard Educational Review, 58*(4), 433–448.

Hakuta, K. (1990). Language and cognition in bilingual education. In A. M. Padilla, H. H. Fairchild, & C. M. Valadez (Eds.), *Bilingual education: Issues and strategies*. Newbury Park, CA: Sage.

Hakuta, K., & Gould, L. J. (1987, March). Synthesis of research on bilingual education. *Educational Leadership*, pp. 38–45.

Jacob, E., & Mattson, B. (1990). Cooperative learning: Instructing limited-English-proficient students. In A. M. Padilla, H. H. Fairchild, & C. M. Valadez (Eds.), *Bilingual education: Issues and strategies*. Newbury Park, CA: Sage.

Leibowitz, A. H. (1980). *Bilingual education act: A legislative analysis*. Wheaton, MD: National Clearinghouse for Bilingual Education.

Lindholm, K. J. (1990). Bilingual immersion education: Criteria for program development. In A. M. Padilla, H. H. Fairchild, & C. M. Valadez (Eds.), *Bilingual education: Issues and strategies*. Newbury Park, CA: Sage.

Lindholm, K. J., & Fairchild, H. H. (1990). Evaluation of an elementary school bilingual immersion program. In A. M. Padilla, H. H. Fairchild, & C. M. Valadez (Eds.), *Bilingual education: Issues and strategies*. Newbury Park, CA: Sage.

Malakoff, M., & Hakuta, K. (1990). History of language minority education in the United States. In A. M. Padilla, H. H. Fairchild, & C. M. Valadez (Eds.), *Bilingual education: Issues and strategies*. Newbury Park, CA: Sage.

Padilla, A. M. (1990). Bilingual education: Issues and perspectives. In A. M. Padilla, H. H. Fairchild, & C. M. Valadez (Eds.), *Bilingual education: Issues and strategies*. Newbury Park, CA: Sage.

Padilla, A. M., Fairchild, H. H., & Valadez, C. M. (Eds.). (1990). *Bilingual education: Issues and strategies*. Newbury Park, CA: Sage.

Peyton, J. K. (1990a). Beginning at the beginning: First-grade ESL students learn to write. In A. M. Padilla, H. H. Fairchild, & C. M. Valadez (Eds.), *Bilingual education: Issues and strategies*. Newbury Park, CA: Sage.

Peyton, J. K. (1990b). Dialogue journal writing: Effective student-teacher communication. In A. M. Padilla, H. H. Fairchild, & C. M. Valadez (Eds.), *Bilingual education: Issues and strategies*. Newbury Park, CA: Sage.

Rotberg, I. C. (1982). Some legal and research considerations in establishing federal policy in bilingual education. *Harvard Educational Review, 52*(6), 149–168.

Snow, C. E. (1990). Rationales for native language instruction: Evidence from research. In A. M. Padilla, H. H. Fairchild, & C. M. Valadez (Eds.), *Bilingual education: Issues and strategies*. Newbury Park, CA: Sage.

Snow, M. A., & Brinton, D. M. (1990). Innovative second-language instruction at the university. In A. M. Padilla, H. H. Fairchild, & C. M. Valadez (Eds.), *Bilingual education: Issues and strategies*. Newbury Park, CA: Sage.

Spanos, G., & Crandall, J. (1990). Language and problem solving: Some examples from math and science. In A. M. Padilla, H. H. Fairchild, & C. M. Valadez (Eds.), *Bilingual education: Issues and strategies*. Newbury Park, CA: Sage.

Troike, R. C. (1981). Synthesis of research on bilingual education. *Educational Leadership, 38*(6), 498–504.

Valadez, C. M., & Gregoire, C. P. (1990). Development of a bilingual education plan. In A. M. Padilla, H. H. Fairchild, & C. M. Valadez (Eds.), *Bilingual education: Issues and strategies*. Newbury Park, CA: Sage.

When children speak little English: How effective is bilingual education? (1986). *Harvard Education Letter, 2*(6), 1–4.

Willetts, K., & Christian, D. (1990). Material needed for bilingual immersion programs. In A. M. Padilla, H. H. Fairchild, & C. M. Valadez (Eds.), *Bilingual education: Issues and strategies*. Newbury Park, CA: Sage.

Willig, A. C. (1985). A meta-analysis of studies on the effectiveness of bilingual education. *Review of Educational Research, 55*(3), 269–317.

Willig, A. C. (1987). Examining bilingual education research through meta-analysis and narrative review: A response to Baker. *Review of Educational Research, 57*, 363–376.

# Index

# About the Contributors

DONNA CHRISTIAN  received her Ph.D. in sociolinguistics from Georgetown University in 1978. She is Director of the Research Division at the Center for Applied Linguistics in Washington, D.C. Her research concerns the role of language in education, including issues of second-language education and dialect diversity.

JOANN CRANDALL  received her Ph.D. in sociolinguistics from Georgetown University in 1982. She is Director of the International and Corporate Education Division at the Center for Applied Linguistics. Her primary interests are in teacher education and curriculum development, with a focus on the integration of academic content and culture into language education.

HELENA A. CURTAIN  is a Foreign Language Curriculum Specialist for the Milwaukee Public Schools, supervising foreign language programs for kindergarten through grade twelve. Her interests are second-language education for elementary school students and teacher preparation for elementary school second-language teachers.

HALFORD H. FAIRCHILD  received his Ph.D. in social psychology from the University of Michigan in 1977. He is a principal of Fairchild, Fairchild, and Associates, a Los Angeles-based planning, research, and development firm. His primary interests are in intergroup relations, educational opportunity, and mass media.

DORRY MANN KENYON  received his M.A. in teaching English as a foreign language from the American University in Cairo, Egypt, in 1984. He is a Test Development Specialist at the Center for Applied Linguistics and is working on a Ph.D. in Educational Measurement at the University of Maryland. He has published materials for teaching ESL and has presented frequently at TESOL and other conferences. He has worked extensively in the semidirect testing of oral proficiency in selected less commonly taught languages.

KATHRYN LINDHOLM  received her Ph.D. in developmental psychology from the University of California, Los Angeles, in 1981. She is now Assistant Professor of Education at San Jose State University. Her main areas of interest are bilingual and second-language development, cognitive development, factors associated with school achievement, and bilingual education.

**LINDA S. MARTÍNEZ** has a B.A. in education (1977) and an M.A. in curriculum and instruction (1983), both from the University of Wisconsin in Milwaukee. Currently, she is a Spanish FLES teacher, kindergarten through grade six, at Tonawanda School in Elm Grove, Wisconsin. Among her professional interests are training teachers in methods of FLES instruction, writing curricula for foreign language at the elementary level, and previewing materials to be used in elementary school classrooms.

**MARY MCGROARTY** received her Ph.D. in language education from Stanford University in 1982. She is currently Associate Professor at Northern Arizona University in the Applied Linguistics Program of the English Department. Her research deals with second-language learning and teaching in a variety of contexts, including bilingual and foreign language settings. Her work has appeared in such publications as *TESOL Quarterly, NABE Journal,* and *Canadian Modern Language Review.*

**REBECCA OXFORD** holds an M.Ed. and a Ph.D. in educational psychology (Boston University and the University of North Carolina) and is currently Associate Professor of Language Instructional Methodology and Russian at the University of Alabama. She has published widely on language learning styles and strategies, including a book titled *Language Learning Strategies: What Every Teacher Should Know.*

**AMADO M. PADILLA** received his Ph.D. in experimental psychology from the University of New Mexico in 1969. He is currently Professor of Education at Stanford University and has interests in language education, Hispanic issues in psychology, and interethnic relations.

**NANCY RHODES** received her M.S. in sociolinguistics in 1981 from Georgetown University. She is currently Research Associate at the Center for Applied Linguistics, specializing in foreign language teaching in the elementary school. Her main areas of interest include foreign language education, language attitudes, and ESL methodology.

**SHEILA M. SHANNON** is Assistant Professor in the School of Education at the University of Colorado at Denver. She received her Ph.D. from the School of Education at Stanford University in 1987, and completed a postdoctoral year at Yale University with Dr. Kenji Hakuta.

**MARGUERITE ANN SNOW** received her Ph.D. in applied linguistics from the University of California, Los Angeles, in 1985. She is currently Assistant Professor in the School of Education at California State University, Los Angeles. Her primary areas of interest are immersion language education, foreign language attrition, and TESL methodology.

**GEORGE SPANOS** received his Ph.D. in oriental studies from the University of Arizona in 1977. Currently he is Research Associate at the Center for Applied Linguistics in Washington, D.C. His interests include teacher training, curriculum development, math and science problem solving, and language-sensitive content instruction.

**CHARLES W. STANSFIELD** received his Ph.D. in foreign and second-language education from Florida State University in 1973. He is currently Director of the ERIC Clearinghouse on Languages and Linguistics and Director of the Division of Foreign Language Education and Testing at the Center for Applied Linguistics in Washington, D.C. His primary interest is second-language testing.

**HYEKYUNG SUNG** is a Ph.D student in the School of Education, Stanford University. She received her M.A. in Linguistics from Stanford University (1989) and in French from Seoul National University (1982). She taught French for two years at the Hankuk University of Foreign Studies in Seoul, Korea. Her interests are in foreign and second-language education.

**LYNN THOMPSON** received her M.A. in International Communication from American University in 1985. She received her M.S. in Applied Linguistics from Georgetown University in 1982 and a Bacc-es-Arts en Français from the Université Laval in 1980. She is currently a consultant in language teaching, training, and testing. Her areas of interest include foreign language education, teacher training, language learning, language attrition, and testing.

**G. RICHARD TUCKER** received his Ph.D. in psycholinguistics in 1967 from McGill University. He is currently President of the Center for Applied Linguistics and Associate Director of CLEAR. His professional interests include work in the areas of language policy, bilingualism and bilingual education, and second-language learning/teaching.